The Mirror of the World

Christopher Peacocke presents a philosophical theory of subjects of consciousness, together with a theory of the nature of first person representation of such a subject of consciousness. He develops a new treatment of subjects, distinct from previous theories under which subjects were regarded either as constructs from mental events, or fundamentally embodied, or Cartesian egos. Peacocke's theory of the first person integrates with the positive treatment of subjects. It contributes to the explanation of various distinctive first person phenomena in the theory of thought and knowledge. These are issues on which contributions have been made by some of the greatest philosophers, and Peacocke brings his points to bear on the writings of Hume, Kant, Frege, Wittgenstein, and Strawson. He also relates his position to the recent literature in the philosophy of mind, and then goes on to distinguish and characterize three varieties of self-consciousness. Perspectival self-consciousness involves the subject's capacity to appreciate that she is of the same kind as things given in a third personal way, and attributes the subject to a certain kind of objective thought about herself. Reflective self-consciousness involves awareness of the subject's own mental states, reached in a distinctive way. Interpersonal self-consciousness is awareness that one features, as a subject, in some other person's mental states. These varieties, and the relations and the forms of co-operation between them, are important in explaining features of our knowledge, our social relations, and our emotional lives. The theses of *The Mirror of the World* are of importance not only for philosophy, but also for psychology, the arts, and anywhere else that the self and self-representation loom large.

Context and Content

Series editor: François Recanati, Institut Nicod

Published in this series:
The Inessential Indexical
On the Philosophical Insignificance of Perspective and the First Person
Herman Cappelen and Josh Dever

The Mirror of the World
Subjects, Consciousness, and Self-Consciousness
Christopher Peacocke

Assessment Sensitivity
Relative Truth and its Applications
John MacFarlane

Context
Robert Stalnaker

Propositional Content
Peter Hanks

Fixing Reference
Imogen Dickie

The Mirror of the World

Subjects, Consciousness, and Self-Consciousness

Christopher Peacocke

OXFORD
UNIVERSITY PRESS

Great Clarendon Street, Oxford, OX2 6DP,
United Kingdom

Oxford University Press is a department of the University of Oxford.
It furthers the University's objective of excellence in research, scholarship,
and education by publishing worldwide. Oxford is a registered trade mark of
Oxford University Press in the UK and in certain other countries

Published in the United States of America by Oxford University Press
198 Madison Avenue, New York, NY 10016, United States of America

British Library Cataloguing in Publication Data
Data available

Library of Congress Cataloging in Publication Data
Data available

ISBN 978-0-19-969956-8 (Hbk.)
ISBN 978-0-19-877682-6 (Pbk.)

Preface

This book contains a revised version of the text from which I drew two sets of lectures, both given under the title 'Subjects, Consciousness, and Self-Consciousness'. The first set was given in the autumn of 2010 in the 'Context and Content' series directed by François Recanati at the Institut Jean Nicod, in the École Normale Supérieure in Paris. The second set was given a few months later in the Winter Quarter of 2011 as the Kohut Lectures at the Committee on Social Thought at the University of Chicago. I warmly thank François Recanati, Jonathan Lear, Robert Pippin, and the Committee on Social Thought for these invitations, and thank too all those involved in the stimulating exchanges that followed each of these lectures in Paris and Chicago. The present text results from revisions made in the light of those discussions, and of discussions at my seminars at Columbia University and University College London.

In the revised text I have tried to preserve the direct and concise style appropriate for a lecture. This is not a comprehensive critical survey of the literature to a certain date. Nor does the material touch upon all the topics with which issues about the self and self-consciousness have important internal connections. Rather, the material develops, cumulatively, a few basic ideas about subjects and the first person, and applies them to some classical and to some recent issues in the philosophy of mind, epistemology, metaphysics, and the theory of intentional content.

In the title of this book I borrow the image of the subject of consciousness as the mirror of the world from Schopenhauer, who employed it in connection with what he called the pure subject of cognition. Though pleasing in several respects, the image can also mislead. Mirrors do not usually reflect themselves, whereas the subject is part of the world to be reflected. If these lectures are correct, subjects do partially reflect themselves. Perhaps it is good to keep in mind an image that in its nature reminds us of the ever-present dangers of paradox, ungroundedness, and impossibility in this perennially fascinating topic.

The choice of cover illustration for this book posed a problem. While there is certainly no dearth of attempts to depict the self in Western art, I was looking for something that would also illustrate the varieties of self-consciousness discussed in the book, including those that I call the perspectival and the interpersonal. As I turned through the pages of collections of candidate illustrations, it hit me that Velázquez' incomparable *Las Meninas* had everything I could want. The scene is depicted from the viewpoint of the king. This is the world as mirrored by him. Velázquez himself, and the blonde infanta, are looking at, and are seen by, the king. They are each interpersonally self-conscious with respect to the king, in a sense I try to elucidate later in the book. The king and queen are reflected in a mirror. If the king notices that, it will be an illustration of what I call perspectival self-consciousness. Though several of the people depicted are interpersonally self-conscious with respect to the king, it is notable that no two of them are interpersonally self-conscious with respect to one another, a chilling effect of monarchy. Anyone who appreciates *Las Meninas* has some tacit understanding of the distinctions invoked in making these points about the painting. In this book, I try to say what those distinctions are.

Contents

Acknowledgements and Sources   ix

I Introduction   1

II Primitive Self-Representation   6
  1. The Basic Notion   6
  2. Self-Files   14
  3. Three Degrees of Self-Representation   30

III The Metaphysics of Conscious Subjects   40
  1. Consciousness and Conscious Subjects: An
    Interdependence   40
  2. A Response to Hume   44
  3. The Consequences of Interdependence   57
  4. Contemporary Differences: A Historical Affinity   68

IV The First Person Concept and its Nonconceptual Parent   80
  1. Some Background on Concepts   81
  2. Explaining Four Phenomena   86
  3. Issues of Acquaintance   99

V Explaining First Person Phenomena   106
  1. Explaining Immunity to Error through Misidentification   106
  2. Can We Dispense with First Person Notions
    and Concepts?   113

VI Descartes Defended   127
  1. The Soundness of the *Cogito*   128
  2. What Can the Perspective of Consciousness Supply?   139
  3. Entitlement, the Second *Cogito*, and Anscombe   146

VII Paralogisms and First Person Illusions   154
  1. The Issues   154
  2. Some Replies to Kant's Objections   159
  3. Strawson's Neo-Kantian Conception of Subjects   178

VIII Perspectival Self-Consciousness   188
    1. What is the Significance of the Mirror Test?   190
    2. A Wider Criterion for Perspectival Self-Consciousness   194
    3. The Reorientation Account and Other Minds   203

  IX Reflective Self-Consciousness   213
    1. Characterizing Reflective Self-Consciousness   213
    2. Metaphysics and Epistemology of Reflective
       Self-Consciousness   217
    3. First Person Theories of Understanding, and Empirical
       Phenomena   223
    4. Reflective and Perspectival Self-Consciousness:
       Their Significance for Inquiry   232
    5. Reflective Self-Consciousness and the Conception of
       Many Minds   234

   X Interpersonal Self-Consciousness   236
    1. Illustration and Delineation   237
    2. Some Roles of Interpersonal Self-Consciousness   243
    3. Is There an Irreducible Second Person Concept?   247
    4. Philosophical and Psychological Issues   250
    5. Self-Consciousness: The Relations of the Interpersonal to
       Other Varieties   260
    6. Concluding Remarks   263
    Appendix A   264
    Appendix B   266

  XI Open Conclusion: The Place of Metaphysics   267

References   269
Index   277

Acknowledgements and Sources

In the fall of 2007, Béatrice Longuenesse and I gave a joint seminar under the general title 'Kant and Contemporary Issues'. Eventually we came to the topic of Kant's treatment of 'rational psychology' in the Paralogisms. Reflecting on what is plausible, and what is not, in Kant's extraordinary discussion of these issues plunged me back into the question of what a positive theory of these matters should be. These meetings were certainly the initial impetus that set in motion the work reported in this book.

In the discussions following the presentation of this material at the Paris and Chicago lectures mentioned in the Preface, I learned especially from the comments of Daniel Andler, Jason Bridges, David Finkelstein, Rachel Goodman, Jonathan Lear, Robert Pippin, Joëlle Proust, François Recanati, and Georges Rey. At Columbia, Patricia Kitcher has been a valuable source of advice on Kantian matters. Once again, I have bene-fited from extended and intensive discussion with Tyler Burge in 2011 on the earlier sections of this work.

Chapter II, 'Primitive Self-Representation', and Chapter III, 'The Metaphysics of Conscious Subjects', started life as the material for a Special Lecture at the Faculty of Philosophy at Oxford University in June 2008, for a Colloquium at Syracuse University, and for a conference organized by Annalisa Coliva at the Institute of Philosophy in London the same summer. An earlier version of the material appears in the volume based on the proceedings of that conference, *The Self and Self-Knowledge* (Coliva 2012). It was also presented at a conference and lectures at Brown University and the University of Stockholm in 2009. I was helped on those occasions by the comments of Selim Berker, John Campbell, Katalin Farkas, Anil Gupta, John Hawthorne, André Gallois, Joe Levine, Paul Snowdon, Ralph Walker, David Wiggins, Åsa Wikforss, and Timothy Williamson, and more recently by discussions with Paul Boghossian.

Some parts of Chapter IV, 'The First Person Concept and Its Non-conceptual Parent', together with some of the points on Hume in Chapter III, were drawn upon in my presentation at the conference at the CUNY Graduate Center in September 2011 to honour the publication of Saul Kripke's *Philosophical Troubles Volume 1* (see especially Kripke 2011a).

Chapter V, 'Explaining *De Se* Phenomena', uses material I presented in the conference on Mental Files at the Institut Jean Nicod, Ecole Normale Supérieure in November 2010, and in one of my Kohut Lectures at the University of Chicago early in 2011. I thank Jonathan Lear, John Perry, François Recanati, and Georges Rey for valuable comments. An earlier version of this material appears in Peacocke (2012a); the material here corrects some creaky formulations of immunity to error through misidentification in that earlier version.

Chapter VI, 'Descartes Defended', was presented at a meeting in March 2012 jointly celebrating the long tradition of philosophical activity at Magdalen College, Oxford, and honouring Ralph Walker on the occasion of his retirement. An earlier version of this material appears in the Proceedings of the Joint Session of the Aristotelian Society and the Mind Association at Stirling University, July 2012. My co-symposiast at Stirling was John Campbell, and I learned much from reflecting on his contribution (Campbell 2012), both on the topics discussed here, and the wider issues he raised. At the discussions at Magdalen and at Stirling, I benefited also from the prepared comments of Ralph Wedgwood, and from the contributions to discussion from Jeremy Butterfield, John Hawthorne, and Jane Heal.

Chapter VII grapples with some aspects of Kant's discussions in the Paralogisms, attempting to apply the approach of the earlier chapters of this book in assessing both Kant's critique of 'rational psychology' and his own positive account. Here my debts to discussions with Béatrice Longuenesse, both at the 2007 seminar and subsequently, will be evident. A self-contained version of this material has appeared in *Philosophical Perspectives* (Peacocke 2012c).

Somewhat earlier versions of Chapter VIII, 'Perspectival Self-Consciousness', and Chapter IX, 'Reflective Self-Consciousness', were developed for my Evans Memorial Lecture at Oxford in March 2010, and appeared in the paper 'Self-Consciousness' (Peacocke 2010b). Here thanks are due a second time to Béatrice Longuenesse both for this commission, and for steering me towards the interesting task of considering the relations between my approach and those of various continental writers. There is certainly more to be done in this direction.

Chapter X, 'Interpersonal Self-Consciousness', originated in one of my summer seminars at University College London, and was further developed as a presentation for one of David Chalmers' Consciousness Project Meetings at NYU in the fall of 2011. I thank Ned Block and David Chalmers for comments on that occasion. A version was also presented to the Oberlin Philosophy Colloquium in May 2012, the fortieth in that now famous series. At Oberlin I learned from the exemplary, insightful prepared commentary of Michael Martin. His points have resulted in changes both in exposition and in substance. I was helped also by the comments from the late, and much liked, Fred Dretske at the same occasion. There is a plan for the proceedings of the Oberlin Colloquium to appear in an issue of *Philosophical Studies*. A more recent version of this material was also presented at the Workshop on the Self, organized by Natalie Sebanz and Hong Yu Wong, at the Central European University in Budapest in the summer of 2012. I suspect everyone came away from that intensive and well planned interdisciplinary meeting rethinking one or another aspect of his or her position. I particularly remember the contributions of my UCL colleague Paul Snowdon and of the developmental psychologist Philippe Rochat.

In the later stages of preparing the manuscript, I benefited greatly from discussions at three events whose participants read in advance some or all of the text, as it then was. At Princeton in the fall of 2012, the material was the target of two sessions of the Metaphysics Seminar run by Mark Johnston and Gideon Rosen. Mark was charged with preparing written comments, and his excellent critical discussion, and the exchanges with Gideon, have clarified some important points for me. Later in the fall, I participated in a Workshop 'Self-Consciousness and Kinds of Self' in Fribourg, Switzerland, and particularly remember the contributions of Thomas Jacobi, Martine Nida-Rümelin, and Gianfranco Soldati. In the spring of 2013, the material formed the focus of a discussion group at Harvard, to which I was summoned to explain myself at a meeting in May. Farid Masrour assembled a written list of important questions emerging from that group's several previous discussions. At the May meeting, I was helped and stimulated by the observations and comments from Matthew Boyle, Cheryl Chen, Farid Masrour, and Charles Parsons. I apologize to anyone I have overlooked, and thank everyone mentioned here, without whose contributions the text would certainly be different.

Peter Momtchiloff's constant and diplomatic support, advice, and encouragement have been as important to me in the production of this book as they were in my three previous books since he has been Philosophy Editor in Oxford at Oxford University Press. My debt is but a small part of what the wider philosophical community owes to him.

I

Introduction

'... not of skill, as in van Gogh or Bacon, that showed the self revealed for what it is'

> D. Walcott, *White Egrets* (London:
> Faber & Faber, 2010), p.51

'Das Ich, das Ich ist das tief Geheimnisvolle'

> L. Wittgenstein, *Notebooks* (Oxford: Blackwell,
> 1979), tr. Anscombe, entry for 5.8.16

'Mapping the self is equivalent to dying; to have totally grasped oneself is death, the detective thinks, sitting upright like a statue'

> J. Zeh, *Dark Matter* (London: Harvill Secker,
> 2010) tr. Christine Lo, p.138.

What is it to represent something as yourself? What is the nature of the thing that you refer to when you think or perceive 'I am thus-and-so', if indeed there is any such thing? And what are the ramifications of the correct answers to these two questions? Those questions set my agenda.

My aims in this material are to present an account of the nature of first person representation in general; to present an account of the nature of the subject referred to by a first person representation; to integrate these two accounts; and to apply the integrated account to some classical issues in the philosophy of mind, the philosophy of psychology, metaphysics, and epistemology that turn on the nature of the first person and the self. No extant approach to these issues is in my view entirely satisfactory, though many of them contain important insights. I will be offering a different approach. There are seeds of some parts of the approach in some earlier writers, notably in John Locke and Thomas Nagel; but I will end up in a different place from both of their distinguished contributions.

There are three dimensions in which we ought to reorient our philo-sophical thought about subjects of consciousness and the first person. First, we ought to recognize a wider range of theoretical options on what subjects of consciousness are. I will be arguing for a fourth option on what subjects of consciousness are, an option distinct from the three classical views that subjects are either Cartesian egos; or Strawsonian persons; or are constructed entities, built from various other mental and non-mental entities, in the spirit of Hume. I think subjects of conscious-ness are not fundamentally of any of these three classically recognized kinds. We can gain some illumination from pursuing an investigation into a distinctive ontology of subjects that treats them as elements of a fourth kind.

The second reorientation that I recommend is that we acknowledge that in this area, the metaphysics of the domain—in our case, the meta-physics of subjects and of consciousness—has in the philosophy of these matters an explanatory priority over epistemology, over the theory of thought, over much of the theory of intentional content, over theories of the first person in language, and over theories of personal-level mental representation. How such a priority is possible I hope will become clearer as we proceed; these lectures as a whole develop a case for the position. These first two reorientations also bring new challenges of their own, as defenders of any one of the three classical options will be quick to point out.

The third reorientation concerns the identification of the most primi-tive level at which a distinctive form of self-representation is to be found. I will be arguing that the most primitive level at which self-representa-tion is located is that of the nonconceptual content of states that operate below the level of reasons, judgement and justification. Many of the distinctive phenomena involving conceptual forms of the first person can, I will argue, be understood theoretically only by relating them ultimately to this more primitive nonconceptual level. There is already some limited agreement in the philosophical literature that there is a form of the first person at this more primitive level: José Bermúdez (1998) and Susan Hurley (1998) are clear examples. The nature and significance of such contents needs much further investigation.

Before getting down to work, I issue a caution and a couple of observations. The caution concerns the difficulty of the topic itself. Subjects of experience and first person representation have engaged the attention of the very greatest of philosophers, from Augustine, through Descartes, Hume, Kant, and Frege; the topics have drawn new contributions from some of the most original philosophers of the past century, including Wittgenstein, Strawson, and Shoemaker; and they continue to engage the attention of our best thinkers. The issues are deep, central, and treacherous. Those great philosophers have sometimes combined extraordinary insight and significant error in the very same paragraph. There is surely more to be done in this territory; but only those who bizarrely think of themselves as outside history could believe their own work is not subject to the same real dangers. So let us proceed carefully, and with the right kind of respect for the issues. I will try to relate some of the positions I propose to these great classical writings.

The first of the two observations I want to make in advance of detailed discussions is that subjecthood and the first person are topics on which major contributions have been made in both the analytical and the continental traditions. I am optimistic that this area is one of the most fruitful for each side of this unfortunate, and rapidly disappearing, historical divide to learn from the other's insights—and for each side to learn too from the other's missteps.

The other observation concerns the role of the history of philosophy when we work today on the self and self-representation. Our understanding of these topics is not so advanced that we can simply ignore the writings of the past philosophers I have already mentioned, nor those of many others. Those writings sometimes describe phenomena that have not yet been adequately explained. Sometimes they contain approaches or insights thoroughly worth considering. The positive positions I develop in the present work have applications both to those writers already mentioned, and also to many thinkers in the tradition of German idealism. While I will be devoting some attention to Descartes and to Kant, since their thought on the self and the first person has been so influential, it will rapidly become clear that this is not primarily a work in the history of philosophy. If, however, the ideas presented here are moving in a plausible direction, I hope others will be attracted to the project of investigating their historical relations.

Here is a brief overview of the structure of the book. Chapters II and III are foundational for the treatment, and are presupposed by all of the later material. Chapter II develops an account of what I call primitive self-representation, found in perception, action-awareness, and memory.

Chapter III develops an account of the metaphysics of the conscious subject, a metaphysics that integrates with the theory of Chapter II. Chapter IV then treats the first person concept, the concept that so exercised the great philosophers mentioned above, by drawing on the accounts of Chapters II and III. By using all of the preceding, I attempt in Chapter V some explanation of the various phenomena, particularly epistemic phenomena, displayed by the first person concept.

The remaining material divides into three branches. One of these branches, consisting of Chapters VI and VII, considers some of the contributions of Descartes and Kant. I use the material preceding these chapters to argue for the soundness and epistemic interest of Descartes' *Cogito*, and to reflect upon some of Kant's criticisms of Descartes in the Paralogisms section of *The Critique of Pure Reason*.

The second branch discusses what I call perspectival self-consciousness (the variety which psychologists and ethologists aim to detect in the mirror test), reflective self-consciousness, and their relations to one another. This is the branch that is formed by Chapters VIII and IX.

Chapter X forms the third branch, and considers interpersonal self-consciousness. On this last topic, even more than in the other chapters, I am aware that there is a great deal more to be said. But I hope a starting point chosen on the basis of the considerations of the earlier chapters will prove fruitful.

The final brief reflection on the place of metaphysics in relation to the theory of content presents the discussion of this book as an instance of a quite general position on that large-scale issue, a topic on which I aim to write more.

The structure of the main chapters of the book is given in this Dependence Diagram (Figure 1), in which the item at the head of an arrow is represented as presupposing the material at the tail of the arrow:

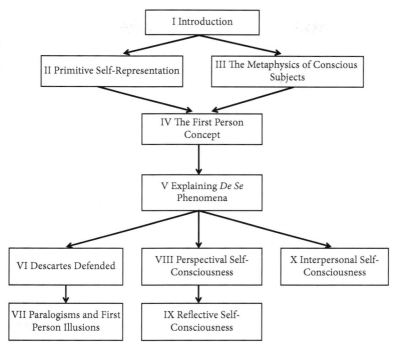

Figure 1 Dependence Diagram

II

Primitive Self-Representation

1. The Basic Notion

Self-representation is present in some of our most familiar, unsophisticated mental events.

A creature may see something as coming towards it. It may remember an encounter at a particular location. It may have an action-awareness of moving its head. All these conscious events involve self-representation. They each have an intentional content which it is natural to pick out using the first person: *that thing is coming towards me*; *I had such-and-such an encounter*; *I am moving my head*.

These contents have an intermediate status. Each content here is more than one which merely concerns the object that is in fact the subject who is seeing, is remembering, or who enjoying an action-awareness. You can see something that is in fact the subject who is seeing without seeing that thing as yourself. That occurs when you see someone who is in fact yourself in a mirror, without realizing that it is you, and perhaps without realizing that a mirror is there at all. Such an experience can occur without the seen object being in any way represented as you in the perceptual experience. Similarly, seeing something as coming towards you involves much more than merely reference to something that is in fact you. Seeing something as coming towards the person in the mirror is not necessarily seeing something as coming towards you. In all these three initial examples, the mental event has a content that represents something as you.

On the other hand, the contents in these examples involve something less than the full conceptual first person content. Seeing something as coming towards one is something that can occur in subjects who lack concepts. 'Concept' is a term of art, and a disputed one at that. But for those who do not just use 'concept' to cover all intentional content whatsoever, the following marks would be widely acknowledged as distinctive of concepts, even by theorists who disagree on much else. Concepts are constituents of the intentional contents of states that a subject can be in for reasons. Concepts are constituents of the contents of judgements. It is either in the nature of concepts, or at least a consequence of their nature, that they are constituents of the contents of states and events in which a subject displays a sensitivity to reasons. It seems that the perceptions, memories, and action-awarenesses involving self-representation in these initial examples can be present in creatures that have only a more primitive system of nonconceptual representations of the world, and who do not operate at the level of reasons at all. So a question arises. What is the nature of the self-representation in the content of these more primitive representational events and states?

It is in the very nature of the type of content in each of these events that their correctness conditions concern the subject who enjoys the event. A perception of an object as coming towards one has a correct content only if the object in question really is coming towards the subject of the experience. A subject has a correct memory of an encounter with a certain kind of animal at a certain location only if the subject enjoying the apparent memory really did have such an encounter. A subject's action-awareness of moving his head is correct only if the subject enjoying the action-awareness really is moving his head.

When I say that 'it is in the very nature of the type of content' that the correctness condition concerns the subject of the events, I mean at least this: that no further information about the reference of the way the object is given in the intentional content of these events is needed to settle whether or not the content refers to the subject of the event. The way in which the subject is given in the awareness entirely settles that it is the subject of the awareness that the content concerns. In this it differs from any perceptual mode of presentation that presents a person, and which just happens to refer to the subject who enjoys the perception. The fundamental reference rule for any instance of the perceptual-demonstrative type *that F* (such as *that man over there*), where the demonstrative is tied to an experience in which something is presented in a given way, is this: the demonstrative refers to the man that is perceived in that way. This fundamental reference condition makes clear that the reference of the perceptual demonstrative is not necessarily the subject who is enjoying the perceptual experience in question.

Actually, we need a stronger formulation of the point. In the conceptual case, we can conceive of a mixed descriptive-demonstrative content such as *the agent of this thinking,* or *the owner of this experience.* There is clearly a sense in which it is in the nature of the type of these contents too that they refer to the agent of the thinking and to the owner of the experience respectively. At the conceptual level, neither of these is equivalent to the first person concept. Although the referents of these complex descriptive-demonstrative concepts are guaranteed to be, respectively, the subject of the thinking and of the experience, the determination of this reference goes via a functor component *the agent of* and *the owner of* that features in the content itself. For the genuine first person, by contrast, the determination of the reference as the subject does not go via such a descriptive functional component in the content itself.

We should respect the distinction between complex descriptive-demonstrative notions and the genuine first person. The distinction is intuitive in itself, and it is needed for drawing real psychological distinctions. Consider, for instance, the phenomenology of ownership. Humans normally experience their sensations and their thoughts as their own. They also experience various body parts as their own, a different relation, but also one involving self-representation. In discussing the phenomenology of the ownership of experiences, Tim Bayne writes, 'I take the sense of ownership to be an experience whose representational content is roughly: this (target) experience is had by the subject of this (reflexive) experience' (2004: 231). It seems to me that this understates the sense of ownership. The sense of ownership is a sense that the experience in question is *mine,* and not merely something had by whoever may be the subject of this experience. We cannot properly capture the sense of ownership without mentioning a self-representing component as part of the nonconceptual content of the subject's consciousness. Any pathological syndrome in which someone experiences a pain but does not experience it as meeting the condition *This is mine* is a syndrome in which the subject lacks a sense of ownership of that particular pain, whatever else she may represent about whoever is the subject of the experience.[1]

So, in the requirement that it be in 'in the nature of the very type of content' of the event or state in question that it refer to the subject of the

---

[1] Bayne could certainly change his formulation in the way I recommend, consistently with, and arguably strengthening, the rest of the arguments in his paper, whose main points seem to me very well taken.

state or event possessing the content, this should be understood: that the determination of the subject as the reference does not proceed via satisfaction of some other condition that is involved in the nonconceptual content. It may help to point out that the distinction being invoked here is an analogue for these contents of Saul Kripke's distinction at the linguistic level between *de jure* and *de facto* rigid designation (1980: Introduction). The first person nonconceptual content of a mental event is of a type whose instances refer *de jure*, without any use of descriptive elements, to the subject of the mental event in question.[2]

These points are at the level of type of intentional content, rather than the particular intentional contents themselves. The fact that they are at the level of the type permits us to sidestep an objection. We can imagine an objector who believes in *de re* senses, senses that are constitutively of the object to which they refer, and (on some conceptions) contain the object as a constituent of the *de re* sense.[3] This objector might take a case like the one mentioned by Ernst Mach in which he sees a reflection—in fact of himself—in the window of a bus, and represents the object using the perceptual-demonstrative 'that shabby pedagogue' (1914: 4n). The believer in *de re* senses might develop his position in such a way that he insists both that: this particular *de re* content 'that shabby pedagogue', as employed in thought on this occasion, has Ernst Mach as its reference essentially and constitutively; and similarly that only Ernst Mach could be the subject who enjoys the particular token perceptual visual experience that makes the perceptual demonstrative available. We need not for present purposes enter discussion of the former (contentious) claim. My point is just that at the level of types of sense or mode of presentation, nothing analogous can be said of the perceptual-demonstrative type *that shabby pedagogue*. That is, it is not in general true that any intentional content of the perceptual demonstrative *type* 'that shabby pedagogue' will also refer to the subject who enjoys the relevant perception of the

---

[2] Tyler Burge has argued that the conceptual first person cannot be reduced to a complex descriptive-demonstrative concept in his paper 'Reason and the First Person' (1998). It would be a worthwhile exercise, for which I will not delay the argument here, to trace out the relations of the explanations of irreducibility noted by Burge to the irreducibility at the more primitive nonconceptual level.

[3] On *de re* or 'object-involving' senses, see Evans (1982) and McDowell (1984). On the relation between types and instances of types in the realm of the senses, see Peacocke (1981).

shabby pedagogue. By contrast, it is in the very nature of the first person type that any instance refers to the subject of the mental event whose content contains that instance. The points I am making about the first person type, whether conceptual or nonconceptual, are then orthogonal to the issue of whether or not there are *de re* senses or intentional contents.

De jure truths about the nonconceptual first person must have a source or explanation. What is the explanation or source of the *de jure* truth that any instance of the first person type refers to the subject of the mental state or event in whose content that instance features? One simple, natural answer is this:

> What *makes* a component of nonconceptual content something of the first person type is that the fundamental condition for an object x to be the reference of an instance of that type, when the instance occurs in the content of a mental event or state M, is that x be the subject of M (M's owner).

We can call this *the subject-constitutive hypothesis* about the nature of the nonconceptual first person. This hypothesis is an instance of the general position that an intentional content is individuated by its fundamental reference rule. That is the general Fregean-inspired position I developed for the case of conceptual content in *Truly Understood* (2008).

The subject-constitutive hypothesis does not imply that the nonconceptual first person is some disguised complex descriptive-demonstrative content. We must always distinguish the material involved in the reference rule for a concept (or nonconceptual content) from the concept (or content) itself. The conceptual content *now* is individuated by the rule that in any thinking, it refers to the time at which that thinking occurs. But concept *now* itself is not structured. It should not be identified with the complex descriptive-demonstrative *the time of this thinking*. Nor should the nonconceptual first person—i as I will label it—be regarded as identical with some complex content *the subject of this state*. The nonconceptual content i itself is unstructured.

There is a consequence of the fact that an instance of i refers *de jure* to the subject of any state in whose content it features. Suppose a particular conscious subject s is in a mental state with the nonconceptual first person content. My apologies for the use of the variable, but we need it to make the point sharply and in full generality. Then our subject s is in a mental state that, as a consequence of *de jure* conditions, represents something about *s*. Our subject is a self-representer.

Here we can use standard notation: λx[Fx] is the property of being F; λxλy[Rxy] is the relation R; and so forth. Then we formulate our conclusion about our subject *s* in the preceding paragraph by saying that *s* has the property

λy[y represents something about y].

Our subject *s* also has this property in virtue of the nature of the type of content of his mental state.

Elizabeth Anscombe famously argued that attempts to explain the first person are either inadequate, or simply presuppose grasp of the first person, leaving it unelucidated. She drew the radical conclusion that the first person does not refer at all (1975). Gareth Evans, in reply, noted that some of her arguments can be met by observing that the word 'I' is a device that each person knowingly and intentionally uses to refer to himself. That is, each person knowingly and intentionally has the property

λz[In using "I", z refers to z],

which is the property of being a self-referrer (Evans 1982: Appendix to Chapter 7). This condition distinguishes 'I' from any proper name, or, I would say, any other expression or concept other than the first person. Now we have just observed in the preceding paragraphs that our subject *s* in a state with a nonconceptual first person content has the property

λy[y represents something about y],

and does so as a result of the very nature of the content. This shows that a form of Evans's point applies equally at the nonconceptual level, at a level below that at which we can properly speak of the intentional and knowing use of either words or concepts. The immediate significance of this point is that Anscombe's arguments that attempts to explain the first person are either inadequate, or already presuppose the first person, can be answered at the nonconceptual level as well as at the conceptual level.

There is indeed a distinctive sense in which when someone sees something as coming to towards him, this occurrence of 'him' needs a distinctive explication. But, according to the subject-constitutive hypothesis, we can give that explication while doing justice to what is distinctive of *de se* content. The subject-constitutive hypothesis, as displayed above, does not presuppose, use, or leave unanalysed some use of the first person.

Whatever may be the explanation of the *de jure* truths about *i*, we can say that the (nonconceptual) content of the events and states in the intermediate cases in which we are interested is *intrinsically subject-referring*. It will be very convenient to have a label for this phenomenon. Suppose a particular subject *s* and one of its mental events *e* stand in the following relation, and do so as a result of the nature of the type of content *e* in the way we have been discussing:

$\lambda x \lambda y$[x is the subject of y & the content of y refers to x].

Then when that condition is met, I will say *e* stands in the relation of *subject-reflexivity* to the subject *s*. The same applies to states as well as to events. More briefly, I will often speak of the mental event *e having the property of subject-reflexivity* if there is some subject to which *e* stands in the relation of subject-reflexivity.

In the most recently displayed formula, within the square brackets the variable 'x' occurs twice in the characterization of subject-reflexivity. That is an initial identification of a respect in which these contents involve a kind of subject-reference in the subject's mental event. The property of being subject-reflexive in the sense characterized is a generic notion of an event or a state's having a *de se* content. It can apply both when an event or state's content is conceptual, and when it is nonconceptual built from notions, as I will call them.

A subject-reflexive state or event can have a content that refers to the subject of that state or event without the subject also being given at the same time in some other, further way—be it perceptually, or in some other demonstrative fashion made available by some conscious state. To be a subject-reflexive state or event, it suffices that the state or event's content be of a type whose instances refer *de jure* to its subject. Whether a subject enjoying mental states with *de se* contents also has to have other background capacities or representations of the world, or must conceive of the world as being of a certain kind, are major questions to which I will return in later chapters.

It is the subject-reflexivity of the state that we need to highlight if we are to characterize adequately what is distinctively required by the English locutions 'remembering being F', 'remembering doing so-and-so', as distinct from 'remembering my being F', 'remembering my doing so-and-so'. As James Higginbotham and Michael Martin have remarked to me, the latter pair of locutions can apply even when remembered from the third-person point of view, as for instance when you see oneself in the mirror or on closed circuit TV in the memory. The former pair, 'remembering being F' and 'remembering doing so-and-so', can be applied correctly only when the subject has a memory with the property of subject-reflexivity. You may remember your conducting the orchestra if you remember seeing the then-live video feed of your doing the conducting. But you remember conducting the orchestra only if you remember the conducting from the point of view of the conductor, with the orchestra in front of you. The utility of the linguistic form 'remembering ϕ-ing' is precisely that it allows us to pick out exclusively memories that are subject-reflexive in respect of the ϕ-ing in a way the locution 'remembering my ϕ-ing' does not.[4]

We could give an entirely parallel explication of the similar intermediate case of a present tense but nonconceptual analogue of *now*, one that features in the contents of apparent perceptions and action-awarenesses. For events with such an intermediate kind of present tense content, the following relation holds between the time *t* such an event *e* occurs, and the event *e* itself:

$$\lambda x \lambda y [x \text{ is the time of occurrence of y \& the content of y refers to x}].$$

Again, the relation holds as a result of the nature of the type of content, without reliance on further information about the case. This can equally, in the temporal case, be part of an initial identification of a respect in which these events can have a distinctively present-tense content without apparently requiring the subject to have a conceptual constituent *now*. We could similarly call the relation and property in question in this temporal case that of *time-reflexivity*.

Though the mental lives of a squirrel, an octopus, and a human must be very different, they may all be in mental states and events with such a

---

[4] The false claim that 'I remember being at the meeting' is equivalent to 'I remember that I was at the meeting' is implied in Prior (2003a: 225).

nonconceptual *now* content. What is common, even if the events occur at different times to members of these very different species, is that they all have a content whose correctness condition constitutively and fundamentally concerns the time of occurrence of that very event. The same applies to the *de se*. The difference between the mental lives of a squirrel, an octopus, and a human does not prevent them from sharing literally the same type of *de se* content. What is common across the contents of the mental events of those very different creatures, when those events each have a *de se* content, is that each such content has a correctness condition that constitutively and fundamentally concerns the subject of the event in question. There is no ambiguity of type as between your nonconceptual *de se* and that of the octopus. They are identical in type. The differences lie rather in what the various creatures represent as holding of themselves.

2. Self-Files

In central cases, when a subject has an experience of, say, having a pond to his left and also has an action-awareness of running straight ahead, the subject represents himself as instantiating the conjunction of these two properties. This raises a question. Under the characterization I have given, the fact that the subject is in a position to represent himself as having the conjunctive property does not immediately follow from his being in a subject-reflexive state that he has a pond to his left and is in a subject-reflexive state that he is running straight ahead. From the fact that someone is in a subject-reflexive state that concerns object x, and is at the same time in a subject-reflexive state that concerns y, where in fact $x = y$, it by no means follows that the subject is in a position to appreciate that it is one and the same thing that is in both states. Though a creature can be in a subject-reflexive state that represents it as F and also be in a subject-reflexive state that represents it as G, nothing in what I have said so far has explained how the subject is in a position to register that he is in a subject-reflexive state of being both F and G.

Now subjects must in fact be capable of integrating the contents of those of their conscious states that exhibit subject-reflexivity into such conjunctive representations. For a subject who possesses and exercises the first-person concept, it is unproblematic how this could be done. A perceptual experience which represents the subject as having a pond to his left entitles the subject, other things equal, to judge a conceptual content of the form *that pond is to the left of me.* This content contains the first-person concept, with 'me' as the accusative form of the English expression of the first person concept. The judged content *that pond is to the left of me* is then suitable for inferential integration with other first-person contents, such as *I am running quickly straight ahead.* A thinker who accepts these two conceptual contents will, as a result of an inference of conjunction-introduction, be in a position to self-ascribe the property of both having a pond to the left of him, and of running quickly straight ahead. This solution is evidently not available for subjects who do not have the first-person concept, yet who nevertheless succeed in integrating representations about themselves. It is quite implausible that the integration of the contents of such representational states is restricted to creatures who possess concepts (if we admit a conceptual/nonconceptual distinction at all). So we need a different explanation of this phenomenon.

When a subject has a perceptual experience of being *F* and, say, an action-awareness of being *G*, normally representations of those two properties each enter an object file on the subject. An object file is a store of mental representations whose contents are all taken, in one way or another, to apply to the same thing. The idea of an object-file has been used in the explanation of propositional-attitude phenomena by a series of writers including Paul Grice (1969), Michael Lockwood (1971), Peter Strawson (1974), Robin Jeshion (2002), and, most recently and most thoroughly, François Recanati (2012). Object-files have also been used in the explanation of perceptual phenomena by Daniel Kahneman, Anne Treisman, and Brian Gibbs (1992). In the propositional-attitude case, the taking to apply to the same thing is at the level of belief and judgement. In the perceptual case, it is a matter of the perceptual system representing to the subject one and the same thing as having several current properties, including relational properties. Some apparatus takes information from the subject's various sensory, perceptual, and action systems, and integrates that information by placing predicative materials drawn from various sources into the subject's file on itself. That will determine the subject's present-tense awareness, his experience of how things are with him now.

There is, however, a fundamental difference between the operation of a subject's file on itself and perceptual object files, even if we consider only the nonconceptual level. To articulate the difference, I consider first perceptual object files.

A file on a perceived object is indexed by where, egocentrically, the object is perceptually given. The file contains information about the object's currently perceived properties and relations. Human perceptual systems also have the ability to keep track of where the object has been recently, the location from which it has travelled to its current position. Humans can do this for several objects simultaneously, as Zenon Pylyshyn's well-known demonstrations show.[5] So as time passes from t_1 to t_2, in the case of perceptual object files the system has to accomplish two tasks. One task is to form new object files, with information about the current properties of the object at a given location at the new time t_2. The other task is to achieve representations of identities over time between the objects currently perceived at this later time t_2, and the objects as perceived as being at particular places at the earlier time t_1. Which of these identities hold is an entirely empirical and contingent matter. The object that is at a particular location at the later time might earlier have been at any one of many other locations.

By contrast, as time passes in the first person case, nothing of quite the same kind is required as is needed for the second task in the perceptual case. If a subject at t_1 has a nonconceptual representation of itself as f, by means of a file on itself, it suffices to update this at t_2 to a representation that at the earlier time, it was f. (I continue to use lower case italics for nonconceptual contents.) A past tense predicate capturing this can be combined with other present tense predicates in the subject's file on itself to yield representations to the effect that the subject was f and is g. In contrast to the perceptual case, here there is no empirical, contingent identity over time that needs further determination. If the earlier representation of itself as f was correct, then when the later representation is updated by the appropriate change of tense, so will the representation updated at t_2 also be correct. This holds unconditionally, and not merely in normal circumstances. It holds unconditionally because the later representation is a representation that is both by, and is about, the same subject as reference of the earlier *de se* representation. If you are tempted by the idea that when the earlier representation occurred, the truth-maker for *i am f* was present in consciousness in the good cases, this pure temporal updating mechanism will allow you to extend that conception to explain how it can be the case that in memory, one can be conscious at the later time of the truth-maker of the past tense *i was f*.

This is sharply distinguished from the effect of similarly pure temporal updating of the perceptual object files. Suppose a subject has this kind of perceptual object file at the earlier time t_1:

A file labeled 'the thing now at egocentrically identified location p'; with content including: 'is f now'.

The analogue of the kind of pure temporal updating we saw in the first person case would be that at a later time t_2, the subject has the following kind of perceptual object file:

A file labeled 'the thing now at egocentrically identified location p': with content including: 'was f a moment ago'.

Such updating will not usually preserve truth. It may be a different object at the location p at the later time t_2 than was there at the earlier time t_1. That different object may not at t_2 have been f a moment ago. That is why a tracking mechanism is needed in the perceptual case. It performs the second of the two tasks we mentioned earlier, a task for which there is no need in the case of first person representations.

In the case of perceptual object files, Pylyshyn has a theory of what he calls 'FINSTS', 'fingers of instantiation', subpersonal pointers that keep track of a perceived object over time.[6] When the same subpersonal finger of instantiation points to an object over time, it is experienced as the same object over time. On Pylyshyn's account, the explanation of our ability to keep track of an object over time involves these FINSTS. Perceptual object files must be supplemented with FINSTS if we are to explain our abilities to keep track of a particular object over time. My recent point has been that in the first person case, there is no need for an analogue of FINSTS. Pure temporal updating of the subject's file on himself suffices in a way in which it cannot suffice in the perceptual case.[7]

---

[6] For an overview of much previous work, see Pylyshyn (2007: Chapters 1, 2).

[7] I oversimplify, for the sake of making the structural point about the absence of any need for a tracking mechanism in the *de se* case. In fact the memory representation in the case of perceptual object files may not involve the very same nonconceptual content f, but

The argument developed in the preceding three paragraphs is an analogue, at the nonconceptual level, of points made about the updating of first person beliefs by Evans. In *The Varieties of Reference*, Evans discussed the relation between a later disposition to judge 'I was previously *F*' and its relation to a present tense judgement 'I am *F*' made at an earlier time. He wrote, 'as far as the "I"-idea is concerned, the later dispositions to judge flow out of the earlier dispositions to judge, without the need for any *skill* or *care* (not to lose track of something) on the part of the subject' (1982: 237). What the present discussion also adds is an explanation. I suggest that the explanation of the 'flowing out of the earlier dispositions' that Evans mentions here should be explained by the phenomenon of pure temporal updating of the subject file, together with the constitutive links between the nonconceptual first person and the conceptual '"I"-idea', of which there will be more discussion in Chapter IV.

Whenever an animal or a human has the ability to distinguish between the case in which the same object is now *F* and was *G*, as opposed to the case in which a different object was *F* from that which is now *G*, there must be some explanation of how the animal or human has this discriminative ability. In the case of objects perceptually given, Pylyshyn's FINSTS provide us with a possible and plausible explanation of the discriminative capacity. In the case of distinguishing from the first person point of view whether it was oneself who was recently *F*, pure temporal updating of the subject file, as part of the mechanism that places past tense contents in the subject file, can explain the capacity.

In each of these two very different kinds of case, the underlying explanation of the ability in question involves a sensitivity to identity without requiring at the explaining level a further representation of identity. We do not have to check, at the conscious personal level, whether or not it's the same FINST as earlier that's doing the pointing. That way infinite regress lies: for how would the system determine sameness of FINST? That itself is another identity question, and it is a

---

something subpersonally reconstructed from more directly remembered elements of the original perceptual present tense representation 'is *f* now'. The location of the boundary between the directly remembered and the subpersonally reconstructed is an empirical matter. There is, however, a good case to be made that genuine memory must involved some representational elements that are not reconstructed.

mistake to think that it is a question the system must somehow address. These questions must come to an end at some point if they are ever to be answered by the system. It is sensitivity without further representation that makes this possible.

The same applies to the operation of entry mechanisms for past tense predicates into the subject's file on himself. There is no question of the subject, at the personal and conscious level, checking whether the pure temporal updating is being done correctly, or is being done on the file with the right labeling. Again, that way regress lies, a regress that is entirely avoidable. And once again, a mechanism that is sensitive to identity does not need to have some independent test or criterion for identity.

None of these mechanisms is infallible. They may all fail or misfire in various circumstances, in which cases they respectively fail to represent, or misrepresent.

In an effort to make clear the central difference between the updating of the subject file on the one hand and perceptual object files on the other, I have used the simple notation 'f' for the predicative component of a nonconceptual content. The simplicity of the notation should not mislead. In a wide range of cases, the representations that enter the subject's file on itself will be those appropriate to the distinctive rich spatial contents of perception and action-awareness. Just as these states and events have spatial content that I tried in earlier writing to capture by the notion of scenario content (1992: Chapter 3), so too do autobiographical memories of these very states. So a subject's file on itself should not be thought of as some subpersonal analogue merely of a set of predicates, some with past-tense parameters. It should be thought of as including a rich array of imagistic representations. They will be prime candidates for representations that enjoy what Roger Shepard and Susan Chipman (1970) describe as standing in a second-order isomorphism with the reality they represent.

We can distinguish various categories of object file by what explains how a representation enters an object file of that category. For belief files associated with names (in a given connection), what explains a sentence entering that file is the thinker's acceptance of some sentence containing the name (in that connection). The sentence might be 'Paderewski played Chopin rather fast'. Such acceptance is something potentially under the subject's rational control, as the agent of his thinking; it is at the personal level; and it can be conscious.

By contrast, the conditions for entry of information into an object file in perception—as when information reaches it via one of Pylyshyn's FINSTS—are entirely unconscious, at the subpersonal level. These conditions, when they hold, explain facts about perception, something that simply happens to the subject at the personal level. The conditions for entry of information into the perceptual object file require that it be information from the FINST-tracked object, when all is functioning properly, and this concerns an unconscious, computational level of representation.

A subject's phenomenological file on itself is equally constructed below the level of conscious mental action, and below the level of consciousness altogether. The seemings of perception, memory, emotion, and the rest are events that, at the conscious level, commonly just happen to the thinker. Subject-reflexive perceptual seemings whose content concerns *de jure* the thinker himself are just a special case of this more general fact.

An account somewhat analogous to that given here for the first person can also be given for the case of conscious events and states with present tense contents. The account would refer to a 'now' file on a time. The same applies again to conscious states and events that represent something as happening or being the case *here*. Representations of these states and events would be collected in a 'here' file.

There is a further respect in which a subject's file on itself has a distinctive status. A time can exist without representing itself and having a file on itself, the idea makes no sense. The same applies to places. By contrast, a subject may represent itself, and when it does, it must have a file on itself, a subject file.

There can be an integrating apparatus in an individual that is not conscious at all, an integrating apparatus that forwards representations to the individual's file on itself. There can be nonconscious states with *de se* contents, even in entirely nonconscious individuals. The presence of an integrating apparatus and a self-file are merely necessary constitutive subpersonal conditions for the existence of conscious subjects. They are not sufficient conditions.

Even when we are concerned with a conscious subject, such a subject's primitive file on itself should not be regarded as integrating representations that already exist as the basis of conscious phenomenal events. You may be aware of your having both the properties of having a pond to your left and of walking straight ahead. This should not be described as your operating, at the conscious personal level, on two already existing conscious events to somehow make them co-conscious. Your total state of integrated awareness is not a result of your conscious mental action upon some more primitive, events and states that were already conscious prior to the supposed mental action. Your total state of subjective consciousness is not generated by your conscious mental action at all (though of course it may have mental actions as a component). The subject's file on itself, if it is to contribute to the explanation of subjectivity, must be regarded as operating on representations which are precursors of the representations that underlie conscious events and states, on pain of misrepresenting consciousness and phenomenology.

In this respect what is integrated in the subject's file on itself is very different from the case in which we have inferential integration that moves at the personal level from the two judgements *I am F* and *I am G* to the conjunctive *I am both F and G*. That inferential integration operates on conscious judgements at the personal level; the subject's file on itself does not. This means that we have to distinguish two kinds of subject file. There is the more primitive one I have recently been discussing, a file which helps to explain how things seem, nonconceptually, to the subject. But there is also, at the level of judgement, something that can still fairly be described as the subject's file on himself, that functions to integrate the contents of conceptual judgements. In cases in which a subject rejects the content of his more primitive, pre-judgemental phenomenology—for example, in the case in which he knows that he is looking at a perfect *trompe l'œil* or hologram—the contents of the more primitive subject file and the personal-level file at the level of judgement will not be in accord with one another. The more primitive one will contain some representation of the content of the illusion. The subject file at the level of judgement will overrule the illusion.

The operation of taking materials from precursors of conscious mental events and integrating them to form the contents of a subject's file on itself may seem in certain respects to resemble the operation of transcendental apperception in Kant's critical philosophy. Some of the resemblances are real, and could be pursued as an independent (and complex) topic. But there are also important differences. Precisely because the operations inserting material into the subject's file on itself are applied to non-conscious precursors of conscious event, they should not be regarded as operating on Kantian intuitions, if those intuitions are regarded as involving even a primitive form of consciousness. Mechanisms that insert something into a subject's file on itself are also not merely open to investigation by a scientific psychology, but that mode of research is essential to understanding how they work.

Despite these differences (and others), there is an undeniable Kantian streak in the position I am outlining. I am concerned to formulate the constitutive conditions of first person content and subjecthood. That is a goal that overlaps with Kant's. The goal is partly realized in the same way. The idea of a subject's file on itself, though very differently elaborated in these very different approaches, needs to play a role in both accounts.

The characteristic of a conscious subject-reflexive state or event, that its predicative content is carried through, in central cases, to a subject's file on itself, seems to me to be a resource on which we should draw in addressing two closely related constitutive philosophical questions.

First, we can cite this characteristic in answering the question 'What is it for a conscious state or event, such as an experience, to have a content concerning a subject that is also capable of enjoying other conscious states and events?' Without the psychologically real possibility of predicative integration with the contents of other subject-reflexive events and states, it would be hard to answer this question. It is because some representation of the content of an experience enters the subject's file on itself, a file that can also contain other materials, that it can concern a subject capable of being in other mental states too.

Second, I suggest that having a nonconceptual self-representation involves having an object file for oneself into which representations of the predicative contents of subject-reflexive conscious states and events are normally placed. At this level, these three properties are all instantiated:

having an object-file on oneself that takes in the relevant predicative contents;
being capable of subject-reflexive mental events and states; and
having a nonconceptual self-representation.

With these interconnections and their grounds, we begin to move from a mere description of subject-reflexivity, as given in the earlier characterizations, to the beginnings of an explanation of its possibility and its nature.

One apparent attraction of this approach to primitive self-representation is that it gives priority neither to a particular form of perception, nor to the content of thought, nor to action, nor to sensation in its account of primitive self-representation. A subject that has perception, but no action-awareness, can meet this condition. So can a Helen Keller. It is natural to compare this with the parallel attractions of an account of the full-fledged first person concept, according to which its reference is fundamentally determined by the rule that any use of the concept *I* in thinking refers to the thinker, the agent of that thinking. This rule gives priority neither to perceptual input, as Evans (1982) did, nor to intention and action, as Brandom (1994: Chapter 3) does, but rather sees these important connections with perception, intention, and action as consequential from a fundamental reference rule for *I* that in itself gives priority to neither.

It is reasonable to expect that the subpersonal mental representations involved in enjoying a subject-reflexive state or event contain or have some functional analogue of a symbol indicating the self-representation. It could be the presence of this symbol that normally pulls the predicative content of the subject-reflexive representation into the subject file. It then becomes natural to ask how this subpersonal symbol, or functional analogue thereof, differs from a subpersonal representation for the first-person concept itself. I would answer by emphasizing some of the points I have already made. The phenomena and the states and events I have been discussing so far, at the level of perception, memory, and action-awareness, and registration of the contents thereof, can all be present below the level of judgement, a rational and potentially reflective mental activity. The notion of a concept is essentially that of something that features in the contents of judgements. If this connection does exist, then the primitive subject-reflexive states and events that I have been discussing so far need not involve concepts so conceived at all. The integration of the contents of subject-reflexive states, the proper updating of object-files, and the rest can all be present in the mental states of a being that does not make judgements that are made reasonable, but not forced, by these various non-judgmental states. Similarly, if you hold that critical thinking is essential to possession of a concept, that too is a capacity additional to anything so far cited in this discussion of subjects and subject-reflexive states and events. Finally, many of the contents in which a primitive form of subject representation is involved may be scenario contents of the sort I discussed in *A Study of Concepts* (1992), a species of nonconceptual content. In short, we have been operating so far at a level below the kind of rationality and reasons involved in making judgements. In fact, it is precisely because we are below that level that, as I will argue in a later chapter, we can use this material in elucidation of the first-person representation that is genuinely conceptual.

There are many legitimate queries about mental files, some about their status, some about their explanatory powers, some about the propriety of appealing to them in addressing philosophical, constitutive questions. I take first an issue about their general status.

We can draw a distinction between two ways of conceiving of the relation of mental files to the level of sense and notions. On what I will call the complementary conception of this relation, mental files are complementary to the level of sense and notions. They are used in the explanation of various phenomena, such as those discussed earlier in this section, but they do not in any way replace or analyse away the level of sense and notions. Indeed, if some of the mental files are taken to be labeled with senses or notions themselves, they are not well equipped to function in such a proposed replacement. The discussion so far of mental files is committed to no more than this complementary conception of the relation between mental files and the level of sense and notions.

A second, more radical, view of the relation between mental files and senses or notions is that senses and notions can, or can in some restricted class of cases, actually be reduced to or analysed in terms of mental files. Recanati expresses this more radical view when he writes, 'A non-descriptive mode of presentation, I claim, is nothing but a mental file' (2012: 34). Whether this more radical view can be sustained for our topic of the first person mode of presentation is an issue to which I will return in Chapter V, Section 2. The interest and significance of mental files in this area is, however, independent of this more radical view.

Whether the complementary or the more radical conception is right, there may still be doubts about the alleged explanatory power of mental files in a philosophical enterprise. Can talk of two representations of entering the same mental file really be explanatory? Does it push some important questions back, in a regressive fashion? And should a philosopher really be involved in speculation about mental files at all?[8]

We need to be clear about what the appeal to mental files is intended to explain in the present discussion. The question is not what it is for a subject, something at the level of reference, to have a property. If that is a question that has any kind of general answer at all, it is a question in the metaphysics of the possession of properties, rather than anything to do with the nature and properties of *de se* representation which is my topic. Nor is the question what it is for nonconceptual *de se* content to be true. We do not need to appeal to mental files to answer that question. If an intentional content is individuated by the fundamental condition for something to be its reference, as I would hold, then we already have an answer to the question of what it is for a *de se* intentional content to be true. For the *de se* content $f(i)$ to be true as employed in a given context is for the entity referred by i, as determined by its fundamental reference rule, applied in the context, to have the property referred to by the content f, as determined by its fundamental reference rule, applied in that same context. This truth condition does not need to mention mental files.

Mental files contribute rather to the explanation of *grasp* of a certain kind of nonconceptual intentional content. The explanation involving mental files contributes to an answer to a how-question: how is the subject capable of being in states with *de se* nonconceptual contents? In these formulations, I am using the notion of grasping a content in ways that parallel the use of the notion of grasp at the conceptual level. A subject grasps an intentional content, be it conceptual or nonconceptual, just in case it enters the content of some of the subject's mental states and events. There is a factive notion of what I shall call *cognizing* a nonconceptual content that is in certain respects the analogue at this more primitive level of the notion of knowing a conceptual content. (A good case can be made that a notion of cognizing a nonconceptual content plausibly underlies the notion of knowing a corresponding conceptual content.) Grasp of a particular component of complete nonconceptual contents and the capacity to come to cognize certain complete nonconceptual contents containing that component are internally related. Grasp

[8] I thank Jonathan Lear for pressing the first two of these questions about explanation and regress in discussions in Chicago.

constitutively involves the capacity to come to cognize certain complete nonconceptual contents in certain circumstances. If we offer an explanation of how we come to cognize certain contents (including *de se* contents), that explanation should, prima facie, respect our pretheoretical understanding of how we in fact come to cognize those contents. Those explanations must not mention informational sources not apparently involved in our normal cognizing of nonconceptual contents; they must not treat the noninferential as inferential; when the proposed explanations do mention conscious states and events, the explanation must prima face mention the conscious states and events we take to be operative in the formation of the cognition of nonconceptual contents. The limited amount I have said so far about the operation of subject files in a subject's attainment of cognition of *de se* contents has been intended to respect these constraints, and to respect an internal connection between grasp of the *de se* and certain modes of coming to cognize *de se* intentional contents.

These points about the aim of a certain kind of explanation apply equally to perceptual object files too. The predicative contents involved in shape perception and the predicative contents involved in colour perception are integrated into perception of a single object as having both the shape and colour properties in question. The object is perceptually given as having a certain egocentric location, and some representation of that egocentric location labels the perceptual object file. The mental file contributes to an explanation of the subject's ability to perceive an object as having both the colour and the shape property. The explanation is not addressing the metaphysical question of what it is for the object to have shape and colour properties. Nor is it addressing the question of what it is for a perceptual-demonstrative nonconceptual content to be true, a question again answered by the fundamental reference rules for the constituents of that content. As in the *de se* case, it is plausible here too that there is no such thing as grasping these perceptual demonstrative nonconceptual contents without being able to cognize contents in which these perceptual demonstratives are predicatively combined with observational nonconceptual notions. The question about explanation that is addressed by citing perceptual object files is equally a question about grasp. The perceptual object files contribute to answering the question 'What explains a subject's grasp of perceptual modes of presentation of objects and events?'

When two predicative representations are entered into the same file, what is involved in its being the *same* file? It is the same file when it has the same (token) label. What in turn is the significance of that? It has a content-involving functional significance. When representations of properties are all in a single file with a given label, the subject represents something (given in the way determined by the intentional content of the file's label) as having all those properties. This in turn will have consequences for action and the creation of other representations. What those consequences are will depend, as always, on what other states the subject is in. Just as there is no one-one mapping of an accepted, or even a known, conceptual content onto particular consequences for a thinker's thought or action, so a similar point applies to the registration of non-conceptual contents. There is no one-one mapping from the registration of nonconceptual contents to the registration of other contents, or to actions, independently of what other contents are registered (amongst other factors).

What would be vacuous or circular would be to try to elucidate the explanatory significance, for an intentional psychology, of representing two properties as holding of the same object in terms of certain representations of those properties being in the same mental file. That is the reverse order of explanation on the present account. Mental files can contribute to the explanation of grasp, and of cognizing grasped contents, but the kind of explanation given above simply takes for granted the notion of a subject representing an object, given in a particular way, as having a pair of properties.

It may be helpful, in considering these issues about the direction and nature of the explanation in question, to think about a normal system for filing papers, in manila files hanging in a cabinet. There is a nonintentional characterization of a hanging file, but the functional significance of being in the same file is given by the identity that is registered by that relation when all is functioning properly. If the file collects all the author's notes on a given topic, the significance is that the author is representing the topic as having all the properties specified in the papers in the file. If the file collects all of an employer's records about a given employee, then it records the employer's representation of the relevant contents as all applying to the same employee; and so forth. The file may contain pictures as well as verbal documents. We can imagine asking of the output of some administrative office: how does it do things so effectively, how does it manage not to lose track of which bits of information are about which employee? Citing the filing system in answer to this question is not vacuous; it may be part of a true answer.

The same points apply to a subject's file on itself. The explanation of how a subject is able to cognize both that there is a pond to his left and that he is running straight ahead can appeal to its subject file and the normal sources of the information in that file from perception and action awareness of that very subject's properties. Such an explanation underpins both the subject's cognizing of the *de se* content and thereby what is constitutive of grasp of that content.

Is the existence of mental files properly within the purview of philosophy? The constitutive in general, and as applied to particular domains, would be widely agreed to be part of the classical subject matter of philosophy. Tracing out the consequences of true constitutive claims about a subject matter may involve the identification of empirical conditions in the world that are required if ordinary, uncontroversial truths about that subject matter are to hold. We have become familiar with such a state of affairs in other domains, a familiar case being that of the notion of linguistic understanding of semantically complex expressions. It is a constitutive claim, highly plausible, that understanding a complex expression requires understanding of its semantic constituents. It is equally plausible that the understanding of the complex expression is causally explained by a language user's understanding of the relevant constituents. Our ordinary conception of linguistic understanding, if it is instantiated, thereby substantially constrains what causal (and, I would say, computational) processes occur in the mind of one who understands the language. So constitutive claims about the nature of linguistic understanding require the existence of computational processes in understanders, processes open to further empirical scientific investigation. None of this seems to me intrinsically problematic, or to throw in doubt the constitutive claim about the understanding of complex expressions, nor of the legitimacy of philosophy's making such constitutive claims.

The same seems to me to be true of claims about nonconceptual *de se* intentional content. Grasp of such content is constitutively tied to the capacity to cognize various basic *de se* contents. Such cognition is possible only if there is integration of information from various sources into something functioning as a *de se* file, so labeled. The notion of such a file is a partially functional notion, so its realization need not be something highly localized in the brain. It will plausibly involve interconnections across regions, given the nature of the information in the representations that enter it. It is not clear to me that we have any alternative conception of how the states of a psychological economy involving states with *de se* content could exist without such a functional *de se* file. If there are plausible proposals for alternatives, they should certainly be considered. I do not know what they would be.

An alternative line of criticism is that I have overlooked a level. The critic may agree, on the problem of integration, that states of consciousness with nonconceptual *de se* contents such as *there is a pond to my left and i am running straight ahead* cannot be reached on the model of conceptualized inferences of conjunction-introduction. But, the critic may ask, will not nonconceptual content have its own distinctive logic? Why has this level been overlooked? Can't we answer questions about integrated *de se* contents at this level, without invoking mental files at all?

Logic in the conceptual case generates norms, norms to which rational judgement is answerable. The transitions leading up to perception and action awareness are not mental actions at all; and so any system of norms is irrelevant to it. However, this point shows only that the objection has been overstated. For any transition that involves states with content at all, even nonconceptual content, we can still assess that transition for soundness, even if making the transition between states with those contents is not a mental action subject to norms. So the objector still seems to have a point. Have I not overlooked a system, somewhat structurally analogous to logic, that explicates soundness relations between nonconceptual contents, and which could explain the phenomena of integration?

I reply that the occurrence of an experience of a pond to one's left and of running straight ahead does not stand in the relevantly same relations as a belief in a conjunction stands to two beliefs in the conjuncts from which the conjunctive content is inferred. When reached by inference, the conjunctive belief's existence is caused by the existence of belief in the two conjuncts; and the beliefs in the conjuncts could have existed without the conjunction-introduction inference occurring at all. But a complex state of consciousness is not a causal consequence of two independently existing consciousnesses, one of a pond to the left, another of running straight ahead. The complex consciousness is not merely causally related to the experience of the pond and to the awareness of running straight ahead. The complex state involves those two consciousnesses constitutively, not causally. It involves the unity of consciousness that is discussed below in Chapter III, Section 3 (b). The idea of explicating a soundness relation for nonconceptual contents is a good one, and has its place in other projects. It will not help with the explanation of complex states of *de se* consciousness in way that makes it analogous to logical inference in the conceptual case.

3. Three Degrees of Self-Representation

We can distinguish three degrees of self-representation. The three degrees are defined by the way, if any, in which the subject represents itself as being in the world. At what we can call Degree 0, the subject does not enjoy mental states with *de se* contents. The subject itself really is an element of reality, but it does not represent itself as such. This is a limitation on the content of the subject's representations, not on the existence of the subject. Here is an example. There could be a creature, let us take it to be a spherical underwater creature, whose perceptual apparatus is positioned in such a way that it cannot perceive its own body. It is moved passively through the fluid. It enjoys perceptions of objects and events around its location. It perceives spatial, material and temporal properties and relations of these objects and events. Its perceptual states display some of the perceptual constancies for such properties as shape, colour, size, texture, and the like. This creature remains at Degree 0, however, because it never represents anything as standing in certain relations to itself. None of its perceptual states have *de se* contents of such forms as *that thing is that direction from me*. Rather, they have *here*-contents, such as *that thing is that direction from here*.

This creature has needs and desires, but it does not represent them as its needs and desires. Its needs and desires explain its actions, which consist not in bodily movements, but in such matters as change of colour, or electric charge, or the release of chemicals for attack or defence. It absorbs foodstuffs in the liquid as it passes through regions that are nutritious. If it is moved towards a dangerous object, it releases attacking or defensive chemicals. It is compatible with all this that the creature at Degree 0 has a cognitive map of the world around it, and keeps track of where *here* is on this map. Its map has, so to say, not a *de se* pointer *I am here*, but rather one saying *this place on the map is here*. This creature may by use of this map distinguish between qualitatively indistinguishable regions. It may keep track of how the spatial world changes over time. It may have memories of how things were at earlier times. But it does not place itself on the map, and its memories have contents not of such forms as *I was at a place that was f*, but rather of such forms as *that place was f*. There are no features of its actions that are explained by its content-involving states that can be accounted for only by attributing *de se* contents. The above indexical and demonstrative contents—*here, now, that event, that thing*—together with the predicative and relational notions with which they can be combined suffice for the explanation of its actions. The *here* in these contents is (a fortiori) not equivalent to *the place where I am*, which would be a *de se* content after all. It is rather a *here* explicated in more detail by something akin to, though not identical with, the nonconceptual scenario contents of *A Study of Concepts* (Peacocke 1992). The *here* that is in play in cases of Degree 0 does not need to have the origin in the scenario content labeled by any kind of relation to a body. In ordinary visual experience, for instance, there is a location from which the world is experienced. An experience can be as of the world from that location without having a *de se* content. As we might put it: the experience can have a centre, internal to the subjective character of the experience, without the subject thereby having to engage in self-representation.

As far as I can see, there is nothing incoherent in this description of a subject at Degree 0 who perceives the world but does not self-represent. The case as described does sever any tight connection between the presence of spatial content in perception and spatial bodily action by the creature. The envisaged creature does not engage in actions that are bodily movements. The case does not, however, sever a weaker but still plausibly important connection, that between enjoying perceptual states with spatial content and the capacity to perform actions which have an explanation under a spatial description. When our creature releases some chemical because it is very close to an object of a certain shape, where such objects are recognized as dangerous, the action of releasing the substance is explained under the description 'release when close to an object of such-and-such shape', and indeed under the relational description 'release because close to that object of such-and-such shape'. So the possibility of cases at Degree 0 does not involve a total abandonment of constraints linking perceptual content with action.

Are these cases of Degree 0 simply ones in which the reference to the subject is merely implicit in the subject's mental states? The implicit/explicit distinction is an important one, but it cuts across the distinction crucial to characterizing Degree 0. A subject at this Degree 0 may employ, for example, a representation with the content *pond to the left*, and that may indeed involve implicit elements. But the implicit reference is, in this case, to a place—to the location of what is in fact the perceiving subject—and not to a subject or person. The implicit/explicit distinction classifies representations, be they mental representations, or sentences, or utterances, rather than what is represented. The difference between Degree 0 cases and others concerns what is represented together with the way it is represented (the notion used), not the vehicle of representation.

The distinction between creatures at Degree 0 and creatures at Degree 1 is necessarily a distinction both in respect of expressive power of the contents of mental states enjoyed at Degree 1, and in respect of the explanatory role of the states of a creature at Degree 1. The creature at Degree 0 has a (partial) atlas of the world around a location, and may have a history of the world in the form of a time series of time-indexed atlases, specifying how the world was in the past. By contrast, the creature at Degree 1 has, when all is working properly, a line connecting locations on successive time-indexed atlases, indicating his potentially changing location over time. This increase in expressive power brings in the possibility of further significant representational enhancements unavailable to a creature at Degree 0. The creature at Degree 1 can represent his having been at certain locations when asleep, something a perceptual experience or perception-based memory cannot in itself supply. The creature at Degree 1 can represent that some other agent is benevolent or hostile to *him* (as opposed to being benevolent or hostile in general). The creature at Degree 1 has the basic representational resources that make possible the experience of emotions with *de se* content.

The attribution of greater expressive power to mental states is answerable to the explanatory role of those states. When the mental states of a creature have *de se* content, as opposed to the contents available at Degree 0, there must be the real possibility of those *de se* states interacting with the subject's other states, desires, appetites, and emotions, to explain actions that would not be explained merely by states with contents that are not *de se*. The legitimacy of the richer attributions and the real possibility of such explanations are internally connected, and in the nature of the case are either both present or both absent. The attribution of representational contents of a certain type to a subject's mental states is always answerable to the explanatory powers of those states in the subject's psychological economy. Indeed, though throughout this book I will frequently be concentrating on the representational content of states and events that just happen to subjects, the distinctions I will be drawing always, and in the nature of the case, have significance for the explanation of the actions of the subject.

The existence of cases in which there is Degree 0 of subject-involvement in the representation of the objective world bears on several positions that have been put forward in the literature. First, the existence of the cases offers support for an even more radical version of the claim that, way back in *A Study of Concepts*, I called 'the Autonomy Thesis'. The Autonomy Thesis states that a subject might enjoy a set of events and states with nonconceptual contents without possessing a set of genuine concepts at all. This Autonomy Thesis is denied by those (including me in the past) who think that any content at all, even the nonconceptual kind, must have connections with states with first-personal conceptual contents. The denial of the Autonomy Thesis sometimes rests on a failure to recognize that any supposed connections between content in general and the first person can be connections not with the first person concept, but rather with a nonconceptual *de se* that has the sort of links we have been discussing with a subject's file on itself, and with subject-reflexive events. But if these Degree 0 cases exist, then even the idea of a constitutively autonomous level of nonconceptual content operative in the minds of animals and in our own less sophisticated representations understates the independence of nonconceptual content from the first person and the *de se*. If Degree 0 cases exist, then the sort of sensitivity to changing relations as one moves (or is moved) in the spatial word may be a sensitivity that does not require that one represent what is in fact one's current location as one's current location. The location may be represented simply as *here*. Not even a nonconceptual first person is required for representation of an objective spatial world.

Second, if examples at Degree 0 exist, then it is not true that the nonconceptual indexical types *here, I, now* constitute a little local holism no element of which can exist in the content of a thinker's mental states unless the others exist too. If cases of Degree 0 exist, then *here* and *now* can feature in the content of a subject's mental states without *I* featuring in those states.[9]

In a popular lecture, Vilayanur Ramachandran writes, 'the self, almost by its very nature, is capable of reflection—being aware of itself. A self that's unaware of itself is an oxymoron' (2004: 97). If there can be cases of Degree 0, as I have argued, then there can be conscious subjects who do not self-represent. A fortiori such subjects are unaware of themselves. One can restrict the term 'self' stipulatively to subjects who do self-represent, and then drain Ramachandran's claim of any substance. (The phrase 'almost by its very nature' suggests however that that this was not at all Ramachandran's intention, otherwise his 'almost' would not be there.) Perhaps Ramachandran would distinguish between subjects, in the sense in which I have been writing about them, and selves, who make use of the conceptual first person. I endorse that terminology (I will be using it myself); but a restriction to selves so understood would again drain the claim that selves must self-represent of substance. It is trivial that any subject that employs the first person concept self-represents, and the reason that holds is not something deep about subjects or selves. There are other interesting and important theses of the form 'Subjects that have property P must also self-represent', but I think their interest and importance comes from the specification of the property P and its importance. It would be a different matter to obtain such nontrivial theses simply by reflection on the notion of a subject itself. Possibly the intended force of Ramachandran's remark is captured more by his talk of 'reflection', which is certainly something stronger than self-representation or even than some forms of self-awareness. I discuss reflective self-consciousness in Chapter IX (and some of Ramachandran's own related views in Chapter VIII, Section 3).

The representational contents of the mental states of a subject who is only at Degree 0 of subject-representation are in the literal sense, and in respect of the subject itself, 'nonpositional', a word that occurs in the natural translation of Sartre's phrase 'conscience non positionelle de soi' (Sartre 2003: 136). It is natural to say that the consciousness of what is in fact its location on the part of a creature at Degree 0 is one example of

---

[9] The thesis of such a local holism for the conceptual *Here* and the conceptual first person *I* was endorsed by Evans (1982: 6.3, 7.1, 7.6).

Sartrean nonpositional consciousness. The subject at Degree 0 does not think of itself as having a position, since that would be *de se* content of the sort he does not grasp. Sartre also held that all positional consciousness of an object is necessarily nonpositional consciousness of oneself ('Toute conscience positionelle d'objet est nécessairement conscience non positionelle de soi').[10] Whether or not there is a neat mapping of Degree 0 onto Sartre's distinction—a matter for some interesting scholarship—it is certainly plausible that the states enjoyed by creatures with this Degree 0 involvement of subject-representation in the objective world are states that make possible all the richer degrees of subject-representation we will mention later.[11]

The third bearing of subjects at Degree 0 is upon the Kantian thesis that consciousness of objects has to involve self-consciousness. If conscious subjects at Degree 0 are possible, then there can be consciousness of objects without self-consciousness, without even the most minimal form of nonconceptual *de se* content. The cases at Degree 0 will provide counterexamples to many standard formulations of that Kantian thesis. That may be consistent with the correctness of some of the considerations that motivate the Kantian thesis. But what is right in those considerations cannot carry one as far as the full Kantian thesis itself, if cases of Degree 0 are possible. I return to some of these Kantian issues in Chapter VII, Section 2.

The next degree of subject involvement in representation of the world, Degree 1, is exhibited by a subject who enjoys states with nonconceptual content that is objective, and which represent the subject as standing in spatial relations to other objects and events in the spatial world. The

[10] Sartre (2003: 136). I am not, however, at all in agreement with Sartre's other theses about nonpositional consciousness, which seem to involve a form of no-ownership thesis about mental states and events. Nonpositional consciousness at Degree 0 does not imply a no-ownership account. The mental events of a subject at Degree 0 are owned by a subject. If the theses of Chapter III are correct, then those mental events are individuated in part by their relations to that subject, even if its consciousness is nonpositional. There is extended discussion of these points in Chapter III and in Chapter IX, Section 2.

[11] The existence of cases at Degree 0 bears on the Fichtean thesis that 'the self posits itself'. Taken in isolation, this dictum has two readings. (i) It might be saying that there is a subject, which has a nature that is philosophically prior to any positing, and that subject can go on to posit itself. This is a true claim if Degree 0 cases are possible. (ii) The dictum might be saying that part of what it is to be a subject at all is to posit itself. I would not dare to pronounce on the question of which reading, if either, Fichte intended. Under this reading, the dictum is contradicted by the possibility of cases of Degree 0.

subject perceives a tree as in front of him (*de se* content); the sun to his right; and so forth. Such *de se* perceptions are often accompanied by perception of the subject's own body, possibly by internal proprioception, possibly by visual perception of some of the subject's own body parts. But perception of one's own body is not required for perceptual states with *de se* content. Even if your body is anaesthetized, and sight and sound are your only senses, and if you cannot see any part of your own body, a perceptual state can still (unlike the states of a creature at Degree 0) represent you, *de se*, as located in a field, with a row of trees ahead of you, and so forth. J.J. Gibson gives many examples of perceptual states with *de se* content.[12] The examples are ones in which body parts such as the subject's nose, feet, lower legs, hands, and forearm are also seen. But it is inessential to something being seen as straight ahead, or a certain distance away, or a certain angle off to the left, that these body parts are seen, experienced, or represented in the content of consciousness at all. The *de se* spatial content is still present when these bodily contents of the perception are deleted.

Grasp of some complete truth-evaluable intentional contents containing a *de se* component is founded the subject's enjoyment of states that exist in Degree 0 cases. One such foundation is given by the distinctive *here* contents at Degree 0 made available, with their particular reference, by the subject in fact having a particular location. When perception has a content *there's snow straight ahead*, a perception that can feature at Degree 0, then correspondingly a creature at Degree 1 will perceptually register the *de se* content *there's snow straight ahead of me*. That connection generalizes to other spatial properties. It provides an elaboration of the neo-Sartrean point that such positional self-representation is founded in states that do not involve self-representation. The perceiver operating at Degree 1 will also be capable of registering contents not attained by such simple rules relating the *de se* to the lower level, such as *i was here during the night*, registered even though the subject was asleep all night. A subject operating at Degree 1 also has the resources for thinking of his own history and past path through space.

If there can be subjects with only Degree 0 of involvement of self-representation in its representations of the objective world, there are

----

[12]   Gibson (1986: Chapter 7, 'The Optical Information for Self-Perception').

some important conclusions to be drawn about the most basic structures underlying the existence of a subject. It is not correct to speak of the existence of a subject file in cases of Degree 0, at least in the specific sense I have been using that term. The subject file is meant to include predicates the subject represents as holding of himself; but the subject at Degree 0 does not represent himself at all. Instead of a subject file at Degree 0, we have just an even more primitive integration of representations, such as the perceptual representation of something heard on the right with something seen straight ahead, to generate a perceptual content of the form *there's such-and-such on the right and so-and-so straight ahead*. These more primitive states and their integration must exist if there is to be a subject at all. At Degree 1, the integration function and the realization of a simple kind of *de se* representation are intertwined. But the integration and the representational functions can in principle come apart, if cases of Degree 0 are possible.

At Degree 2 of subject involvement in the representation of the objective world we have use by the subject of the conceptual first person (the concept expressed in English by 'I', by inflection of the verb in some languages) and the enjoyment of states that conceptually represent the subject as located in the spatial world. Just as the states enjoyed by a creature at Degree 0 make possible the nonconceptual *de se* states enjoyed at Degree 1, so similarly the states at Degree 1 make possible the conceptual states enjoyed at Degree 2. I discuss this dependence further in Chapter IV below.

The existence of these three separate degrees of self-representation means that there is intelligible room for two different kinds of theory of acquisition of self-representation. There is room for a theory of how a subject moves from Degree 0 to Degree 1. That would be a theory of acquisition of the nonconceptual first person. There is also room for a theory of how a subject moves from Degree 1 to Degree 2. That would be a theory of acquisition of the conceptual first person. The possibility of acquisition of a nonconceptual notion of oneself by an already existing subject that does not yet possess it makes sense only if we distinguish these levels. In addition to theories of the acquisition of notions and concepts, we should of course always distinguish all of the above from how successful a subject may be in articulating the contents of states involving those notions in his natural language utterances. That is a further task for empirical theory.

It will occasionally be convenient to have a term restricted to subjects who have attained some specific one of these Degrees of subject-involvement in the content of their mental states. I will continue to use 'subject' (in accord with English, as it seems to me) to apply to any possessor of mental states and events at all, at whatever Degree, potentially including subjects capable only of nonrepresentational mental states, should such be possible. Subjects who employ the conceptual first person I will call 'selves', in accord with some philosophers' use of talk of 'the self'. Conceptual content is present only at the distinctive level at which subjects' actions, both mental and non-mental, are explained in terms of their reasons. So this use of 'self' coincides with its use by those who are primarily motivated by considerations in the philosophy of rational action. John Searle is a prominent example.[13]

When we come to discuss Descartes and Kant, it is clear that their focus is on thinkers who think of themselves using the first person concept *I*. So that discussion concerns selves in the sense specified. Subjects who self-represent, but only in nonconceptual forms, could be called egos. With this terminology, a topic for further discussion is the relation between egos and selves: some of the issues involved will be discussed in Chapter IV.

The points I have been making about nonconceptual self-representation are neutral on the question of whether subjects must, in some central or fundamental case, be embodied. In fact in distinguishing the three Degrees above I considered only embodied subjects, even if, as in the cases at Degree 0, some of the subjects fail to think of any body as their body (those subjects do not think of themselves *de se* at all). Those who think that subjects must, in the fundamental and explanatorily central cases, have a body can consistently endorse the legitimacy, interest, and importance of the concepts of *de se* content and of subject-reflexive events and states. Those theorists could very properly insist that embodied subjects may enjoy subject-reflexive states as characterized here. But so also could those who deny that subjects must, in some central cases, be embodied, even if they have to have something like a brain, or a central physical system for integrating information. The

---

[13] Searle writes, 'Agency is not enough for rational action. The agent must be a self' (2001: 92); 'It is a formal requirement on rational action that there must be a self who acts' (2001: 93).

concepts of *de se* content and of subject-reflexive states can by themselves serve several radically different ontological views.

Nonetheless, it is striking that the notion of nonconceptual self-representation has been explained here in terms that do not in any obvious or immediate way involve embodiment of the subject. The notion of nonconceptual *de se* content can dovetail with a conception of subjects that does not fundamentally conceive of subjects as embodied, even if it is agreed that subjects must involve some physical item that functions as brains function for humans. The later chapters of this book will bear on the intelligibility of that conception of subjects.

III

The Metaphysics of Conscious Subjects

1. Consciousness and Conscious Subjects: An Interdependence

The nature of conscious subjects and the nature of conscious states and events are ontologically interdependent. In one direction, there is a dependence because:

> what makes something a conscious state or event is that there is something it is like for the subject of that state or event to be in that state, or to be the subject of that event.

'Conscious state or event' here means: phenomenally conscious state or event, in the sense intended by Ned Block (2007). The displayed statement of dependence is simply a slight modification of the classical characterization of Thomas Nagel, who wrote 'organism' where I have 'subject' (1974).[1] This modified characterization entails that conscious mental events and states have subjects. The characterization does not in itself say anything about what it is for a mental event or state to have a subject. We do not need for present purposes to place much weight on the phrase 'what it is like', for it is not capable of bearing much. As Paul Snowdon writes, the phrase legitimately occurs in 'what it is like to be bankrupt', and this can mean: what it is like for the subject—not owning a credit card, and so forth—and it need not allude specifically to experiences (2010). Since our task at the moment is not some noncircular

---

[1] 'But fundamentally an organism has conscious mental states if and only if there is something that it is like to *be* that organism—something it is like *for* the organism' (1974: 436). Whether any subject must be an organism is a substantive question. The version with 'subject' instead of 'organism' seems less controversial.

characterization of consciousness, it would equally serve the purpose if 'something it is like' in the displayed characterization were expanded to 'something it is like subjectively'. More specifically, we are concerned with what it is like subjectively strictly in virtue of being in the state in question, which is not a person-relative notion. I take the importance of the characterization to be the link it states between consciousness and subjects of consciousness. What I do recommend is that we look at the displayed intuitive characterization of consciousness as one part of an account of the ontological interdependence of mental events and their conscious subjects. As Frege said, 'It seems absurd to us that a pain, a mood, a wish should go around the world without an owner, independently. A sensation is impossible without a sentient being. The inner world presupposes somebody whose inner world it is'. In contrast, 'Things of the outer world are on the contrary independent', and do not need any bearer.[2] The claim of ontological interdependence disputes the view Hume formulates when he says of 'particular perceptions' that 'All these . . . may exist separately, and have no need of anything else to support their existence'.[3]

I am defending the principle that what makes something a conscious state or event is that there is something it is like for the subject of that state or event to be in that state. This is a metaphysical principle about the nature of the property of being conscious. It makes a claim about a certain type of event or state. The formulation of the claim in natural language runs: it is in the nature of the property of being a conscious occurrence that for anything with that property, there is some subject who enjoys (or suffers) that occurrence.[4]

---

[2] These translations are from P. Geach and R. Stoothof (Frege 1977: 14).

[3] *A Treatise of Human Nature* Book I, Part iv, Section 6, third paragraph.

[4] The notion of something holding in virtue of the nature of a certain entity or entities has been investigated and formalized by Kit Fine. Fine (1995) employs the notation $\Box_F A$, which is to be read as: A is true in virtue of the nature of the objects which F. Let C be the property of being a conscious event or occurrence. Then the claim I am making about that property is that:

(i) $\Box_{\lambda P(P\ =\ C)}\ \forall x(Cx \rightarrow \exists y(y$ is the subject who enjoys (suffers) x)).

For a range of individual (nonsocial) mental events, it may be in the nature of any such event e that it has its particular subject essentially. That further claim, using Fine's notation, is that for any such event e,

(ii) If s is the subject of e, then $\Box_{\lambda x(x\ =\ e)}(s$ is the subject of e).

There is an equally plausible dependence in the other direction, a dependence of the nature of conscious subjects on conscious states. The dependence is captured in this principle:

what makes something a conscious subject is that it is capable of being in conscious states and of being the subject of conscious events.

Here, despite some disagreements with him later in these lectures, I am in agreement with Sartre (or at least with the spirit of his claim) when he writes that consciousness is the subject's dimension of being: 'la conscience', he says, is 'la dimension d'être du sujet' (2003: 136).

It is also plausible that the property of being a subject is a subject's most fundamental substantive kind. Anything that is a subject is essentially a subject.

Such a conception of ontological interdependence between conscious subjects and the capacity for being in conscious states is not intrinsically a Cartesian conception. It is entirely consistent with this ontological interdependence that both subjects and their conscious states require some material realization.

The ontological interdependence does not, or at least does not obviously, imply that subjects are essentially or fundamentally embodied. The interdependence does not, or at least does not obviously, imply that subjects are essentially or fundamentally living animals. If embodiment is in some fundamental way necessary to being a conscious subject, that necessity needs to be shown by further arguments. So too would the claim of mere contingency of embodiment.

It may be asked why a particular pain or other mental event isn't individuated in the same way as any other particular event, by (perhaps) its particular causes and effects, as in Donald Davidson (2001), or by some other account of particular events. I answer that there is no incompatibility between such a view of the individuation of particular, token events and the claim I am making of the interdependence of conscious events and their subjects. The claim of interdependence is a claim about types or kinds: what makes something a pain, for example, is

---

The proposition with the converse relation embedded in the 'nature of' operator is false. It is not in the nature of s that e be one of its mental events. The conscious subject s could have existed and had a different mental life, one in which e does not exist at all. So,

(iii) If s is the subject of e, then $\sim\square_{\lambda x(x\,=\,s)}(s$ is the subject of e).

that it bears a certain relation to a subject that suffers it. That is something concerning its kind (and no doubt its most fundamental kind), rather than its identity as a particular, for which some further account may be correct.

The distinction between the nature of the kind and the individuation of the particular member of the kind applies to events quite generally, whether conscious or not, whether mental or not. Consider, for instance, explosions. What makes an event a member of that kind is that it is, roughly, a flying apart of some object or mass of material caused by forces acting from within that object or mass. That account of the nature of the kind is entirely consistent with there being some additional account of the individuation of any particular explosion occurring at a particular time.

The interdependent conception I am offering is, by contrast, definitely opposed to no-ownership views of mental states and events. On the approach I am advocating, it is not only essential to conscious states and events that they have subjects, but this possession by a subject is also involved in what makes them conscious events and states. It is this notion of a subject, distinct from Cartesian conceptions, from conceptions of essential embodiment, and from the constructed subjects of no-ownership views, that I will argue is also crucial for the philosophical elucidation of such matters as self-consciousness and the nature of first-person thought.

Subjects can normally sense, perceive, and they may be able to think. Normally, they can act physically and act mentally. These sensings, perceptions, thinkings, and actions are conscious states and events of the subject. Subjects also persist through time. Some conscious states are experienced by their subjects as continuing conscious states. Subjects can remember some of their previous conscious states and events; and some subjects are capable of thinking about their future states and events. Many of these mental states and events each have correctness conditions concerning the subject of that very state or event. These will be the states with the *de se* contents considered in the preceding chapter.

There are at least two views that can be taken of these principles of interdependence between subjects of consciousness and conscious states and events. The more extreme view is that this is the only notion of a subject of mental states. A variant extreme view is that any other notion of a subject of mental states is somehow parasitic on it, or derivative from the notion of a conscious subject. The more moderate view is that these principles specify an interdependence that exists for subjects of consciousness, but that the category of conscious subjects is a subspecies of a more general category of subjects of mental states.

The more moderate view has considerable plausibility. There certainly seems to be a notion of subject that has application when we consider the almost certainly unconscious states of arthropods and other creatures with mental representational states. This more general notion of a subject must involve some kind of integration of states and events, and a control system for action linked to that integrating apparatus. The difference from the case of conscious subjects is that the integration does not result in the occurrence of a conscious state or event. The integration has rather informational and explanatory significance. My concern in this work is with conscious subjects, but I do register here that there is evidently much more to be said at some point about the nature of subjects in general, whether conscious or not, and it cannot but bear on the notion of a conscious subject. Indeed, it seems to me equally plausible that nonconscious personal level mental events, such as the perceptual states of the older dorsal system in humans, must have subjects too. The attribution of any mental events with content, even unconscious events, is answerable ultimately to their role in the explanation of actual and potential actions. Those actions must be actions of a subject, who is also the subject of the unconscious event. A natural hypothesis is that the interdependence between conscious events and conscious subjects is an interdependence that relates consciousness to subjects of a more general kind, a kind that can have unconscious instances. Under this approach, whatever is involved in the evolution from merely unconscious subjects with unconscious perceptual states to conscious subjects, we have a case of subjects of one very general underlying kind, capable of action and perception, evolving to have richer properties. There is an austere, general notion of a subject that can have both conscious and unconscious instances.

2. A Response to Hume

Hume famously remarked, 'when I enter most intimately into what I call *myself*, I always stumble on some particular perception or other, of heat or cold, light or shade, love or hatred, pain or pleasure. I never can catch *myself* at any time without a perception, and never can observe anything but the perception'.[5] Russell, at least in 1914, agreed: 'We can easily become aware of our own experiences, but we seem never to become aware of the subject itself' (1966: 163). I will argue that there is something right in Hume's view that he can never catch himself, and that the sense in which he is right is something that holds for reasons of principle. Catching himself is not something that might be achieved 'by great exertion' by 'some rare person', as Russell puts it in a passage whose status as irony is unclear (1966: 164). But I will also argue that what is right in Hume's view does not in any way tell against an ontology of subjects, of the kind for which I have been arguing, equally for reasons of principle. Let me take first what seems to be right in Hume's view.

Hume was surely well aware that he could attend to his own body, either by looking down, or by looking in a mirror. This would ordinarily and unproblematically be described as Hume's looking at himself. It seems to me certain that Hume would not have taken this obvious fact as any kind of counterexample to what he meant when he wrote that he could never catch himself when he enters most intimately into himself. So how then should we formulate what he meant? I suggest that Hume's point should be expounded in terms of a distinction between what I will call *original attention* and *derivative attention*. Here is the intuitive distinction, stated initially with very little in the way of theory. When you attend to yourself by attending to yourself in a mirror, you attend to yourself by attending to something not given in a first person way, but rather to something given in visual perception as *that person*. When you look down at your hand, you are attending to something given in vision as *that hand*. When you attend to your hand with your eyes closed, by attending to your body part as given in proprioception, by means of experiences of tension or relaxation in your hand, and sensations of warmth or cold, you are attending to something as *this limb*, as given in proprioception. In all of these cases, you are attending to yourself by attending to something given in a way distinct from the first person way. We are willing to say something of the form 'you are attending to yourself' only because you are attending to something given in something other than the purely first person way. That is why I say these are cases of derivative attention to yourself.

---

[5] *Treatise of Human Nature*, Book I, Section VI 'Of Personal Identity'.

By contrast, when you attend to the road in driving, or to the traffic light, you do not do that by attending to something given as anything other than the road, or as the traffic light, as presented in these cases in visual perception. When you attend to one of your throbbing pains, you do not do that by attending to something given in some way other than as that very pain. When you attend to the road, or the pain, or the light, these are cases of original attention. You are attending to the road, given as the road, to the pain given as the pain, and so forth.

The Humean thesis that you cannot attend to yourself should more properly be formulated as the thesis that a case of attending to yourself cannot be a case of original attention. It can be only a case of derivative attention. The Humean thesis so formulated seems to me to be true. Attending to your body or your hand do not provide counterexamples to that formulation of the thesis.

Attending is a relation between a subject and an entity (an object, event, property-instance . . .), the very entity to which the subject is attending. But whenever a subject is attending to an entity, the subject is attending to the entity as given in a certain way. Whenever s is attending to x, there is some way m such that s is attending to x as given in way m. There does not seem to be any such thing as attending to an entity except insofar as the entity is given in a certain way. (This is of course an instance of a much more general principle about the intentional content of mental states.) It should also be clear that one and the same thing can be attended to in two different ways, corresponding to different ways in which one and the same object is given. Consider a version of John Perry's example, of what is in fact a huge aircraft carrier seen through one window, and an aircraft carrier seen through a second window, where in fact the same carrier is seen through both windows. It makes sense to say that someone is attending to the aircraft carrier as presented through the window to the left, as opposed to the attending to the aircraft carrier as presented through the window to the right.

It matters that, in our use of the intuitive locution 'attending to one entity by attending to something given in a different way', that locution should be understood as follows: attending to an entity given in one way m by attending to an entity given in a distinct *way m'*. So attending to an entity given in a different way does not necessarily mean attending to a different entity. It would not in fact be a different object in the example of the aircraft carrier. What matters is that the ways are distinct, not that the entities given in the two ways are distinct. The ways *that person in the mirror* and *I* are certainly distinct. That suffices for correct application of the distinction between original and derivative attention, and its use in discussing Hume's point. The distinction between the two sorts of attention by itself leaves entirely open the question of whether the entity given in the first person way is the same thing as the entity given as *that person in the mirror.*

It follows that the formulation of Hume's thesis in terms of the distinction between original and derivative attention can be endorsed even by someone who thinks that you are essentially embodied, or holds that you are in some way individuated by your body (or, much less plausibly, holds that you are identical with your body). This way of finding something right in Hume's thesis in no way presupposes that your existence is something utterly distinct from the existence of your body. The formulation can certainly be endorsed by anyone who holds what seems to be a platitude: that when you are perceiving your body, you are perceiving yourself, and that when you are attending to your body, you are attending to yourself.

In a case in which we say that you are attending to yourself by attending to something given in some way other than the pure first person, there need not be two acts of attention. There can be just one act of attention. That you are attending to yourself is true in virtue of your attending to something not given in a purely first personal way. Here there are two truths, not two acts.

Attending is a very specific notion, applicable in perception, sensation, and arguably in certain kinds of personal memory. The kind of thesis we have formulated for Hume for the first person in connection with such attention would not, for instance, hold for thinking in general. There is no plausibility in the claim that in thinking of myself in the first person way, I must be doing so in virtue of thinking of myself in some other, non-first-personal way. A first person thought can be a first person thought in its own right, without reliance on the presence of some other thought that is not in the first person.

The distinction between derivative and original attention takes us a certain distance in understanding what Hume's thesis is. We should, however, demand much more by way of explanation if we are to attain any appreciation of why, so construed, it holds. Why do some cases of attention fall on one side of the distinction, and others fall differently? *Why* is there apparently no such thing as attending to oneself originally?

An immediate answer is that to be an object of attention, the object or event must be given in perception, sensation, or perhaps in certain kinds of sensory imagination or memory; and to be given in one of those ways is not to be given as oneself. Again, that seems fine as far as it goes. The explanatory question, however, is just pushed back. *Why* is there no such thing as being given as oneself in perception, sensation, or certain kinds of sensory imagination or memory? To ask the question in compressed form and only slightly oversimplified form: why can't the subject be an object of perception? *That* it cannot was also noted by Wittgenstein in an entry in his *Notebooks* when he wrote: 'I objectively confront every object. But not the I.'[6] This of course is still at the level of the description of the phenomenon. It is not yet an explanation of why I cannot objectively confront 'the I'.

In the previous chapter, I suggested that the nonconceptual *de se* notion ('*i*') is individuated by the condition that in any mental state, event or process in whose content it features, it refers *de jure* to the subject (the possessor) of that state, event, or process. No further condition is involved. By contrast, anything that is given in perception or sensation (or perhaps in imagination) is thereby given in a way that is individuated by a condition of the following form: the reference of the way, in the context in question, is the thing that stands in a certain relation to the perceptual experience, to the sensory experience, or to the imagining in question. In the case of perception it is a relation that involves causation of the experience; in the case of sensation, it is the relation of being the mental event of which the sensation is an experience; and so forth. These relations are different from the relation of being the subject of the experience in question. Since ways are individuated by the conditions for entities to be their references, it follows that nothing which is an entity that is perceived or sensed or imagined can in that very experience be given solely as oneself. It must be given in some other way too. Whenever one attends to something, in the nature of the case one will be attending to it as given in some perceptual, sensational, or possibly memory- or imagination-based way.

The source of these points is the very nature of the nonconceptual notions involved in perception, sensation, imagination, on the one hand,

---

[6] This is the entry for 11 August 1916 (Wittgenstein 1961: 80e).

and the nature of *de se* content on the other. So it is neither a contingent nor a merely an a posteriori fact that Hume could not find himself in any of his impressions. Hume says, with heavy irony, that another person 'may, perhaps, perceive something simple and continu'd, which he calls himself; tho' I am certain there is no such principle in me' (*Treatise* I iv 6). We need to be explicit about what would justify the irony, to establish that Hume's observation is not merely one about some individual's empirical and contingent psychology. On the position I have been proposing, the impossibility of original attention to oneself follows from three things jointly—the nature of attention, the nature of the ways in which entities are given in perception, sensation and imagination, and the nature of the *de se*. This explanation means that the case for the impossibility of original attention to oneself goes far beyond anything that is confined to what one can or cannot introspect in one's own case.

It may be helpful here to compare the first person in this respect with the nonconceptual present tense notion *now*. It displays some relevantly parallel phenomena. I argued in the previous chapter that when *now* features in the content of any perception or other mental state, event, or process, it refers *de jure* and nondescriptively to the time of occurrence of that state, event, or process. This is what makes it the intentional content it is. Consider a perception which involves the representation of other events, as for instance when a television producer sees many screens simultaneously. Some of the televised events on the screens may be of past events, some may be of present events. But none of the televised events is given, in the producer's experience of the screens, as happening now (as opposed to the displayed images being given as occurring now, which of course they are). The time of occurrence of an event represented on one of the screen is given as 'the time of this screened event', or even *that time*, if an image on a TV screen is allowed to ground a demonstrative mode presentation of a time.[7] Both of these ways, 'the

---

[7] The way in which the time of the events is represented on the TV screens need not be thought of as a mixed descriptive-demonstrative content. It can be a demonstrative *that time* (made available by the TV image), its reference fixed as the time of the presented event, analogous to the demonstratives discussed in Peacocke (1983: 125–6, 144ff.). In that work, in [that T time], T is an experience-type; but we can invent demonstratives related to TV images in which T is type of image, and the whole demonstrative refers, in a given context that fixes a particular TV image at a particular time, to the time of occurrence of the events represented in that image. That demonstrative is still distinct from *now*.

time of this screened event' and such a demonstrative as *that time*, are distinct from the pure present tense *now* that features in the content of the producer's perception.

None of the points I am making about what is right in Hume's thought depend upon some kind of merely stipulative restriction of attention to perceptual and sensational attention. Suppose, for the sake of argument, it is left entirely open whether perceptual and sensational attention are subspecies of some more general category of attention, perhaps even including intellectual attention (discussed below). Even if we do so leave open that issue, it remains a substantive thesis that for perceptual and sensational attention, there is no such thing as attending to something given in a purely first personal way. The object must also be given in some way that is not purely first personal to be an object of perceptual or sensational attention. It would not at all have satisfied Hume for him to reflect that he himself is an object of his intellectual attention. That he was thinking about himself was not something he was questioning. What he could not find was anything given in perception or sensation as himself, and I have been finding something right in that thought, if it is carefully formulated.

Because nothing given in perception is thereby given purely as oneself, and because this holds whatever perception may be in question, a temptation may exist to say that the subject is not in the world, or that the subject is merely the limit of the world. Neither proposition follows. The fact that the subject is not given purely in perception as being in the world does not imply that the subject is not in the world. The fact about the impossibility of perceiving something as oneself is a fact about the way in which something is given. This should not be confused with a fact about the entity so given.

Wittgenstein arguably did succumb to the temptation when, in a much discussed passage of the *Tractatus*, he wrote:

5.632 The subject does not belong to the world: rather, it is a limit of the world.
5.633 Where *in* the world is a metaphysical subject to be found?
You will say that this is exactly like the case of the eye and the visual field. But really you do *not* see the eye.[8]

---

[8]   This is the translation of D. Pears and B. McGuinness (Wittgenstein 2001).

The points I have been making supply a reading of Wittgenstein's remarks as based on a genuine insight (also in Schopenhauer) about a distinctive way of representing themselves that is available to subjects, the *de se* way. Agreed, anything one perceives or senses would be in the world, mental or non-mental. But really nothing follows from these insights about subjects not being in the world. The insight concerns purely *de se* content, and its relation to perceptual states. This is one of several junctures at which the insights of the *Tractatus* would have been formulated very differently if Wittgenstein had made use of Frege's distinction between sense and reference, and had applied it at every level of representation, both conceptual and nonconceptual.

I have said, somewhat cautiously, that nothing is given purely as oneself in perception, sensation, or in states parasitic upon perception and sensation (such as memory and imagination). Some things are given in perception and in sensation in ways that do essentially involve the *de se*, and in respects that go far beyond their being represented as standing in certain spatial relations to the subject. You experience your seen right hand as yours, as belonging to you—a *de se* content. It is certainly not sufficient for a hand to be experienced as yours that it be hand-like and stand in a certain spatial relation to your point of view on the world. The rubber hand illusion shows that a hand-like object standing in the same spatial relation as your hand normally stands to your point of view may or may not be experienced as belonging to you. It will be so experienced when certain kinds of stimulations are applied, and otherwise not (Botvinick and Cohen 1998). A hand's being experienced as yours is part of the phenomenology of ordinary human experience. As elsewhere, this phenomenology should not be identified with any kind of judgement of a content 'that's mine'. That judgement is not made (in fact, it is rejected) when a subject knows that he is experiencing the rubber hand illusion, but he still experiences the rubber hand as his. Similarly your own pains are not merely yours, in normal circumstances they are experienced as yours. It seems equally right to say that each normal human's experience of his or her body has the content that it is his or her own body.

None of these important points about the experience of ownership and its *de se* content undermine the applicability of the distinction between original and derivative attention. Even when something is experienced as being yours—or even, perhaps, in the case of partially proprioceptive experience of your own body, is experienced as being you—you can attend to the thing or event so given only by attending to it in some perceptual, sensational, memory- or imagination-based way that is not purely first personal. That reading of Hume's point still stands.

To summarize, I am endorsing the thesis that for any conscious state in which a subject x is given *de se* and can be a potential object of attention, there is also some mode of presentation δ distinct from the *de se* and such that in the conscious state, x is given under the mode of presentation δ. This thesis is consistent with the proposition that some conscious states are such that although they have *de se* content, the subject is not given in them as a potential object of attention. Such conscious states include seeing something as coming towards oneself, even when there is no experience of one's own body in any sense modality, including proprioception. They also include the conscious state of experiencing a thinking as one's own. (Though the case is more complex, they may also include the case of experiencing pain in a merely apparent bodily part, as in the case of pain in a phantom limb.) So I am not endorsing the thesis that in every conscious state with *de se* content, the subject must be a potential object of attention under some mode of presentation δ distinct from the first person. The subject may not be a potential object of attention in that experience at all.

Let us take stock at this stage of the discussion. I argued at the start of this chapter that conscious mental events must have subjects, for funda-mental metaphysical reasons. I have found something in Hume's argu-ments in which he claimed he could not find his self. Obviously I am committed to saying that Hume drew incorrect ontological conclusions from what was right in his premises. But can we give some further diagnosis of the situation, beyond mere attribution of a non sequitur, of the transition from a truth about the impossibility of a certain kind of attention to the conclusion that there are no subjects of consciousness?

I suggest that Hume's reasoning highlights the fact that what G. E. Moore called the 'diaphanous' character of conscious events and states applies equally to the subject itself. Moore described the diaphan-ous character of consciousness thus: 'the moment we try to fix our attention upon consciousness and to see *what*, distinctly, it is, it seems to vanish: it seems as if we had before us a mere emptiness. When we try to introspect the sensation of blue, all we can see is the blue: the other element is as if it were diaphanous' (Moore 1993: 41). In conscious states and events, the subject is diaphanous in the way in which Moore rightly says the consciousness or awareness is diaphanous. In enjoying an experience or any other conscious event, we can equally say of the subject of the conscious event that 'the moment we try to fix our attention upon the subject and to see *what*, distinctly, it is, it seems to vanish'. The correct response to Hume's position is that he, the subject, no more needs to be an object of awareness and attention to exist and to be involved in his current conscious states and events than consciousness itself needs to be an object of awareness to be involved in his current conscious states and events. The ontological status of the subject is no more impugned by the phenomenon of diaphanousness than is consciousness itself.

Hume did not draw the same conclusion about consciousness itself as he drew about the subject of experience. Almost everyone would regard it as a *reductio ad absurdum* of his form of reasoning if he were to have done so. So we have to avoid a double standard that applies to subjects a treatment that it does not apply to consciousness. Hume's line of thought gives no reason to dismiss an ontology of subjects that would not apparently equally apply to consciousness itself.

Suppose we write (very crudely, and ignoring distinctions important for other purposes) the basic form of attribution of a conscious state as

(1) subject x enjoys event e of conscious kind K with intentional content C.

What we are aware of in enjoying a conscious state or event is what is referred to in the intentional content C in the mental event or state of kind K. The awareness is, for fundamental metaphysical reasons, an awareness belonging to a subject. The four elements—the subject of the awareness x, the conscious state or event e, the intentional content C, and what at the level of reference is given in C—are equally and essentially involved in this state of affairs. But neither the subject, nor the consciousness, nor indeed the intentional content C, is involved by being something on which the subject can fix his attention in original fashion.

I do not mean to imply that whenever a subject is in a conscious state, the subject has some awareness of himself as being in that state. That would collapse the distinction between consciousness and self-consciousness (the topic of Chapters VIII through X below). We are concerned here with a subject's having a mental event or being in a mental state, rather than with the subject representing something as being his own in enjoying that event or state. The thesis is only that in any case of a conscious event or state, there is a subject who enjoys that state or event, and that it is a non sequitur to argue from the fact that one cannot attend to or be aware of the subject in a certain way to the conclusion that the subject is not so involved. But I do add that even when a subject is aware of his being in a conscious state, as when you are aware of your seeing a red traffic light, you need not be given to yourself in a way which allows you to attend originally to yourself.

In the case of the impossibility of attending to oneself as given in a purely first personal way, I offered an explanation, an explanation drawing both on the nature of the *de se* intentional content, and on the nature of attention. If both consciousness and the self are diaphanous in Moore's sense, there ought equally to be an explanation of the fact that one cannot attend to one's own consciousness, at least in the way that Moore emphasized. So what precisely is the impossibility explanandum in the case of consciousness? And what is the explanation of that impossibility in the case of consciousness?

If there is a brain realization of the consciousness of some event or state, then I suppose it could be said that a subject can attend to his own consciousness by looking at a real-time scan of his brain. That is clearly not something Moore meant to deny. It is not what is in question when we are inclined to insist that there is some significant respect in which we cannot attend to our own consciousness. So just what is in question, and why is it impossible?

What seems to be impossible is that you should attend to your own consciousness, given as your own consciousness, where your own consciousness itself is the object of your attention, as opposed to your attention being directed to the objects of your consciousness. A full discussion of this would take us into territory too far from the self and self-representation, but here is a starting point for the explanation of this apparent impossibility.

First, in any conscious event, we can distinguish the consciousness from what it is consciousness of—as it may be, of a car, a door's slamming, one of one's own pains. In any conscious event, attention can be directed within that event only to the object of consciousness, to the car, the door's slamming, to the pain event. It seems that attention has to have something to operate on, something as given in a certain way in the conscious event.

This first point, if correct, establishes only that a subject's own consciousness in an event, given as such, cannot be the object of that subject's attention in the very same event. Why, it could be asked, should that consciousness not be the object of attention in some other mental event enjoyed by the subject? This is a deep issue about attention, and a preliminary answer would be that in any conscious event which is of such a kind that one can attend to now one object in its content, now to another, what is attended to is always given demonstratively in the form *that* or *that F*. But being given demonstratively in that form, and certainly in perception or sensation, is not apparently compatible with the object of attention also being given as one's own consciousness.

As I said, there is much more to be done on this on some other occasion. But if this suggested explanation is at least in the right direction, or drawing on the right materials, it is certainly an explanation turning on the special features of attention, consciousness, and the relations in which they stand.

There is such a thing as a way of thinking of a particular conscious event that is made available to you by the occurrence to you of that particular event. At a conceptualized level, there is a consciousness-based demonstrative available in thought *this particular consciousness*, where the demonstrative latches on to (and is individuated by) a particular conscious event or state you are enjoying. But that particular demonstrative is available to you because you are enjoying the experience, not because your consciousness is an object of your attention. Insofar as attention is present in the conscious experience and has an object, the attention is directed to what the conscious event is a consciousness *of*. Attention seems in its very nature to be directed to what the consciousness is of, not the consciousness itself. 'Consciousness of an object cannot also be an object of that same consciousness' is one compact (and continental) way of formulating part of the point. But that is not quite the full force of the point. The formulation above of the impossibility implies that consciousness, given as one's own consciousness, cannot be the object of attention of *any* conscious state or event, not just of the original mental event in question.

You can also pay attention to what you are thinking about your current conscious states and events. Equally, your thinking about that or any other subject matter can occupy your attention. But neither of these things involves your consciousness being an object of perceptual or sensory attention.

But is it not yet another platitude that one can be conscious of one's particular state of consciousness? It is; but that does not imply that consciousness can be the object of one's perceptual or sensory attention. It seems to me that consciousness of one's own consciousness is a matter of conscious knowledge of one's lower-level consciousness. It is knowledge attained in rational response to that very consciousness itself. (It is not attained by inference, by observation, or by testimony.) This kind of consciousness of one's consciousness does not involve attending to one's consciousness in a way that makes the consciousness, as one's own consciousness, an object of attention.

There is such a thing as intellectual attention, exercised in thinking about something. One may exercise intellectual attention in judging carefully what one's conscious states are like. I do not object to saying that one's lower-level attention may be the object of one's intellectual attention, as can anything else one is capable of thinking about. There is still a distinction between the intellectual attention and the lower-level attention it is about. We would not, in admitting intellectual attention, have any counterexample to the thesis that in any event of consciousness, the consciousness that makes available a certain object of attention cannot also itself be an object of attention, given as a state or event of the subject's own consciousness.[9]

I leave these interesting but diverting topics, and step back to consider the point we have now reached. I have now identified things of three very different kinds, each of which cannot, in the respects I have outlined, be the object of attention. They are (i) the subject, as given in a purely *de se* or first personal way; (ii) the consciousness involved in a given event or state; and (iii), as noted above but not discussed in any detail, the intentional content of a conscious event or state. Though each of these three cases has its own special features, there is a common thread

---

[9] At one point, the otherwise excellent Geach and Stootfhof translation of Frege's 'Der Gedanke' makes it sound as Frege was confusing the notions of the object of awareness and the object of thought: their translation reads 'the object of my awareness, of my thought, . . . ' (Frege 1977: 22). The original German reads 'das Gegenstand meiner Betrachtung, meines Denkens'—see Frege (1967: 357). 'Betrachtung' in this occurrence would be better translated by 'contemplation', 'consideration', 'reflection', or some such cognate. Frege does not confuse intellectual attention with being an object of attentional awareness.

running through these several impossibilities. That common thread is that attention (non-intellectual attention), when it has an object, has to be directed at something given in perception or sensation (or possibly in memory or imagination). This characteristic rules out (i) attention to the subject as given in a purely first personal way, since perceptual and sensational (memory/imagination) modes of presentation cannot be purely first personal; it rules out (ii) such attention to consciousness itself, since one's own consciousness of an event or object is not something given (as such) as an object of consciousness; and it rules out (iii) attention to the intentional content of the mental state or event, since intentional contents as abstract objects or types are the wrong kinds of entity to be objects of perceptual or sensational attention. If this is correct, then what is right in each of Hume's and Moore's points about what one cannot attend to is something that can be generalized to a range of cases. Their insights have a common source in the nature of attention, and its nexus of relations to the *de se* and to the structure of consciousness.

3. The Consequences of Interdependence

I now turn to a series of issues upon which this conception of subjects has a bearing: issues of reductionism, of the unity of consciousness, of materialism, and of a seems/is distinction for identity of subjects over time.

(a) On the position I am developing here, conscious subjects and conscious events are ontologically coeval. Specifying the nature of either one involves mention of the other. So mental events already involve subjects, and not just as a way of talking. The position I am advocating is not consistent with the view that the existence of a subject consists in the existence of various mental events and other entities. I am taking it that in such a neo-Humean view, 'consists in' is supposed to be an asymmetrical relation. If 'consists in' is an asymmetrical relation, my position is incompatible with the neo-Humean thesis that the existence of a subject consists in the existence of mental events and other entities that allegedly do not involve subjects.

Derek Parfit formulates his famous view of these matters as the thesis that a subject is not a 'separately existing entity, distinct from a brain and a body, and a series of physical and mental events' (1987: 223). Suppose

'*A* exists separately from the *Bs*' is understood to imply 'The existence of *A* is not settled by or determined by the existence of *Bs*'. Then of course I would have to agree that in that sense a subject of experience is not an entity existing separately from mental events. But this agreement is not an agreement to a form of reductionism or constructionism about subjects. A subject does not 'separately exist' on this understanding of the phrase 'separate existence' because mental events, on the present view, already involve subjects. So the existence of the subject *is* in one sense settled by the existence of mental events and states.

It follows that the formulation in the quotation I gave from Parfit does not fully capture his intention, the intention to formulate a species of moderate reductionism about subjects of experience. The issue of reductionism should really be formulated in terms of individuation and the ontological priority, or otherwise, of mental events and states vis à vis the subjects that enjoy them. The issue at stake in the reductionism in which Parfit is interested is that of whether mental events and states are ontologically prior to the subjects who enjoy them.

Since the fundamental issues are metaphysical, it also follows that we should be careful not to formulate the issues in terms of what is describable without explicitly mentioning subjects. We can conceive of what Derek Parfit calls an 'impersonal' description of mental events, bodily events, and physical objects and events, and their properties and relations, a description that does not explicitly mention subjects (1987: 225). This does not at all mean that there is no commitment in such a description to the existence of subjects. As a comparison: we cannot establish relationism about space simply by giving a description of everything we want to say in terms of spatial relations between material things and events. If a case in metaphysics can be made that spatial relations between material things themselves consist in relations between the places at which the things are located, then the availability of the place-free description fails to establish relationism about space. The same applies to the impersonal description mentioned by Parfit. If the events and the properties of events mentioned in the description cannot be elucidated without mentioning subjects, then all we have in such a description is something that does not make explicit the full ontology to which it is committed.

As it happens, Parfit himself mentions a parallel with space and time in *Reasons and Persons*: 'Descartes' view may be compared with

Newton's belief in Absolute Space and Time. Newton believed that any physical event had its particular position solely in virtue of its relation to these two independent realities, Space and Time. We now believe that a physical event has its particular spatio-temporal position in virtue of its various relations to the other physical events that occur' (1987: 252). Contemporary formulations of physical theory do not at all supply a reduction of spatio-temporal location to relations between events. They simply quantify over place-times, and take that ontology as primitive.[10] Even in a world in which the laws are Newtonian, there can be recognition of events as having spatio-temporal locations without treating space and time as absolute in Newton's sense. The locations can be locations in neo-Newtonian spacetime, in which the notion of spatial coincidence holds only for simultaneous place-times.[11] I agree with Parfit there is some justice in comparing unconstrained Cartesian egos with Newtonian absolute space and time. Both seem to float free of any empirical constraint whatsoever. However, there can be empirically constrained conceptions of place-times without a collapse into pure relationism about space-time. Similarly I have been arguing for a conception of a subject of experience on which the notion is empirically constrained, and grounded in relations to integrating apparatus, without at all being reducible to mental events and other matters that (allegedly) do not involve subjects of experience.

That any such philosophical elucidation of mental events and their properties, in particular the property of being a conscious event, must involve subjects is precisely what I have been arguing. For someone who thinks that talk of subjects is a mere *façon de parler*, there must be some replacement for the characterization of a conscious state as one such that there is something it is like to be in it for the subject of that state. I have no idea what this replacement could be.

There is, not at all surprisingly, an analogous problem for a view of action that parallels Hume's view about conscious events. We can imagine a theorist who holds that there is no subject who is the agent of actions, 'existing separately' from the actions themselves and other events and entities. Actually we do not have to imagine such a theorist,

---

[10] For a typical example, see J. Anderson (1967: 4): 'The common feature of all space-time theories is the use of the concept of the *space-time point*.'

[11] See for instance, Sklar (1976: 202–6).

for Nietzsche held precisely this view of agents. In the First Essay in *The Genealogy of Morals* Nietzsche wrote, 'For just as the popular mind separates the lightning from the flash and takes the latter for an *action*, for the operation of a subject called lightning, so popular morality also separates strength from expression of strength, as if there were a neutral substratum behind the strong man, which was *free* to express strength or not to do so. But there is no such substratum; there is no "being" behind doing, effecting, becoming; "the doer" is merely a fiction added to the deed–the deed is everything' (2000: 481). A few lines later he adds, 'our entire science still lies under the misleading influence of language and has not disposed of that little changeling, the "subject" (the atom, for example, is such a changeling, as is the Kantian "thing-in-itself")'.

The problem for this view is that what makes something an action is that some subject does it; just as what makes something a conscious mental event is that there's a subject for which there is something it's like to experience (or enjoy) the event. Just as neo-Humeans face the challenge of saying what it would be for an event to be one in consciousness without any commitment to an ontology of subjects, so Nietzsche faces the challenge of saying what it would be for an event to be an action without any commitment to an ontology of agents. I equally have no idea what Nietzsche's replacement account of what makes an event an action, an account that does not make reference to agents, could possibly be.

I suggest that there is not merely a parallel between conscious states and actions, but that the metaphysical interdependence between conscious states and conscious subjects is part of a wider metaphysical interdependence between all three of conscious states, conscious subjects, and conscious actions. What makes something a conscious state, and what makes something a conscious action, are in part their relations to a conscious subject. The nature of any one element of this trio can be explained only by reference to the other two.

It is natural to conjecture that this interdependence contributes to the explanation of the plausible view that consciousness of a state involves direct and global availability of that state for control of various actions and processes.[12] Consciousness is constitutively the consciousness of a subject, a subject which can act, and which can make the occurrence of

---

[12] See Chalmers (2010), esp. Chapter 1, 'Facing Up to the Problem of Consciousness', and Chapter 4, 'On the Search for the Neural Correlate of Consciousness'.

actions sensitive to the occurrence of particular kinds of conscious states. The actions may be mental, physical, or both.

To endorse the irreducibility of subjects of experience is not to say that fission is impossible for such subjects, nor is it to say implausible things about fission. The material integrating apparatus that is the basis of the identity of a given subject might in principle divide. If that is possible, then subjects might divide too. The irreducibility of subjects that I have been defending does not imply that in such a case of fission, the original subject is unknowably identical with only one of the post-fission subjects. Nor does it imply that the original subject should care in a special way about only one, or neither, of the post-fission subjects. The possibility of fission no way shows that experiences are possible independently of an irreducible ontology of subjects.

(b) The issue of the reducibility or otherwise of subjects of consciousness has consequences for the intelligibility of other alleged possibilities with which it has not always been connected. Michael Lockwood (1989) and Susan Hurley (1994) have suggested, in somewhat different ways, that the relation of co-consciousness need not be transitive. On their view, two events a and b may be co-conscious, and events b and c may be co-conscious, without a and c being co-conscious. So, for instance, on this view someone could hear the note middle C sounded and hear the note E two tones above it, in one conscious state; the same person could simultaneously hear the note E and the G a tone and one half above it in another conscious state; and yet the same person, at that time, may not hear anything as the triad C-E-G. We find this hard to imagine from the inside. If a subject is experiencing b and a, and also experiencing b and c, how can his total experience fail to include both a and c, and doesn't that mean the last two must after all be co-conscious?

This puzzlement can be justified by a plausible principle (CC) about what co-consciousness consists in:

(CC) Co-consciousness of mental events a and b occurring at the same time consists in a and b being events in the awareness of one subject, as elements of that subject's single total state of consciousness at that time.

That statement about what co-consciousness consists in would not be available to the reductionist about subjects. On the reductionist's view, the statement has the relation of consisting-in the wrong way round. The reductionist about subjects will say rather that facts about subjects must be explained in terms of mental events, their relations, including co-consciousness amongst others. Nonetheless, the principle (CC) is very plausible in itself.

Is there some explanation of why (CC) is true? It seems to me that its truth is founded in the nature of what it is like for a conscious subject. There cannot, apparently, be a subject for whom the event a contributes to what it is like consciously for that subject, and for whom the event b contributes to what it is like consciously for the same subject, and yet for whom a and b are not co-conscious for that subject. Specifications of what it is like are additive in this sense. The notion of what it's consciously like for a subject is essential in characterizing what the impossibility consists in.

This is one clear sense in which we can say that the unity of consciousness exists. What I am offering an explanation of here is equivalent to what Tim Bayne and David Chalmers call the 'unity thesis', and I am in agreement with them that its denial seems to be inconceivable (2003: 55–7). The elaboration of the impossibility in terms of an ontology of subjects contrasts with explanations of the unity of consciousness that is offered by theories that regard selves as virtual objects (Bayne 2010). I consider some of these theories later in Section 4 of this chapter.

In the context of other plausible principles, (CC) implies that co-consciousness is transitive. It implies that if a and b are co-conscious, then they are events in the total state of consciousness of a single subject, and a total state of consciousness of a subject involves the co-consciousness of all events that are elements of that total state. So any third mental event c co-conscious with any event that is an element in that total state will be co-conscious with any other event in that total state. The underlying general principle here is that for any individual conscious mental event e, there is a unique subject who enjoys it, and who is in a total conscious state, all elements of which are co-conscious, and which includes the event e. This general principle implies that co-consciousness is transitive.

This transitivity is, incidentally, a necessary condition of the notion of a subject's phenomenological file on itself playing the role it did in the previous chapter. If co-consciousness were nontransitive, there would have to be multiple files even in the case of ordinary subjects, and the relationship between, and operation of, these multiple files on the one hand, and the subject's consciousness on the other, would become quite obscure.

So, if we find it unintuitive that co-consciousness could be non-transitive, it is not clear how we could explain the apparent impossibility of non-transitivity under reductionism about subjects of consciousness. The above explanations certainly seem to presuppose an ontology of subjects. Maybe it will be said that we are puzzled by the idea that co-consciousness could be non-transitive simply because any conscious event must be an element in a total conscious state all elements of which are co-conscious. It seems to me, however, that the reason any conscious event must be an element in a total conscious state all elements of which are co-conscious takes us back to a subject of consciousness. The requirement of membership in such a total state exists because it is consequential upon what is involved in a single subject enjoying all the events in that total state of consciousness. We have no conception of what it would be like for a single subject to enjoy two conscious events at a given time, while that subject is not also in a state of awareness of both.

Perhaps it will be replied that the reductionist can accept a very slightly modified form of the principle (CC), the modification being a replacement of the asymmetrical relation 'consists in' with 'holds iff' (with consequent grammatical changes). Why, it may be asked, should the reductionist not treat this modified form as an additional axiom, an axiom to which any construction of subjects out of mental events and their relations must conform?

The reply must be that it does not seem intelligible to suppose that the general principle is simply an optional add-on, as opposed to something more fundamental about the very nature of consciousness and conscious mental events. If the principle were an optional add-on, it ought to be possible that there should be something like subjects, say 'subject*s', which are just like subjects, except that their experiences fail to conform to the transitivity of co-consciousness. But this stipulative move does not at all help us to make sense of the possibility of something like a subject of experience, a subject*, who hears the notes C and E, hears the notes E and G, but does not have an experience of hearing the triad. The unintelligibility seems to lie in the very nature of conscious states and events themselves. Transitivity of co-consciousness does not seem to have the status of a definitional restriction of some wider domain that is both still one of conscious states and events, and one in which transitivity fails.

This position I am advocating ends up very close to the excellent discussion of Bayne and Chalmers, with one amendment. They consider two approaches to explaining what they call the unity thesis, one of them attempting to start from 'our concept of a subject' (56), the other from the concept of consciousness. They say that the approach that starts with the concept of a subject cannot explain the unity. But they develop that approach only in combination with a bundle theory of the subject. In fact my preceding paragraphs imply agreement with them on the proposition that under a neo-Humean treatment of subjects, we will have no explanation of that unity. We can however involve subjects in the explanation without commitment to a bundle theory of subjects. I have already argued that mental events are not ontologically prior to the existence of subjects. If we take the existence of subjects as co-ordinate with mental states and events, and not as some kind of construct, we can still take the relations between the nature of subjecthood and the nature of what it is like to be in a conscious states as the ground of the truth of the unity thesis. The unintelligibility, from the first person point of view, of the nontransitivity of co-consciousness can be endorsed without commitment to a reductionist view of subjects. For further discussion of the unity of consciousness and theories of virtual subjects or selves, see Section 4 of this chapter, below.

Sometimes what is meant by 'the unity of consciousness' is a kind of unity concerned with internal connections within the content of a subject's experience at a given time, a unification plausibly effected by the nature of the subject's capacity to represent a spatial and temporal framework. That is clearly an interesting subject matter, claims about which go far beyond the rather minimal point that has been exercising me in recent paragraphs, that co-consciousness at a given time is an equivalence relation. Nothing here is meant to preclude the interest and value of the investigation of further respects in which experience can be said to be unified. Those investigations may indeed give some further insight into the basis of the unity of consciousness in the rather austere sense discussed in this section.

(c) To say that the ontology of subjects and the ontology of mental states and events are interdependent is not at all to imply that subjects are immaterial things. On the contrary, such interdependence may imply just the opposite. If various aspects of the mental states and events with which the ontology of subjects is interdependent themselves require certain relations to the nonmental world, that fact will have implications for the material status of subjects too. Just that seems to be the case. The mental states and events have multifarious constitutive connections with the material world. A sensation of pain must be experienced as in some part of some apparent body. What it is for it to be experienced as in some part of an apparent body cannot be elucidated independently of the relation of the pain-event to such a body part, when the subject has a body with such a part. What it is for a visual experience to represent something as being a certain distance and direction from the subject cannot be elucidated independently of the causal powers of things at certain distances and directions from the subject, when the subject is properly connected to the world, to explain the occurrence of such experiences—and so forth, for myriad other examples.

If something is in states that are individuated in part by their relations to material objects, properties, and relations, it seems as a matter of general metaphysics that it must have some realization in material objects and events. This is true of domains at some distance from our present subject matter. It is true of a financial institution such as a bank, of which it is constitutive that it can stand in loan, credit, and debit relations. The transactions of a bank must be materially realized, even those of an internet bank. We have, apparently, no conception of how something could stand in these material relations without itself having a material realization. The same seems to me to be true of subjects of conscious states and events. So Cartesian immateriality not only need not be, but also should not be, any part of the conception of subjects for which I am arguing. For this reason, I also think that the conception of subjects for which I am arguing is consistent with Kripke's famous views on the essence of origin for persons and, by extension, subjects (1980).

The identity of a subject over time is something to be explained partly in material terms. That a subject has some material realization plausibly follows from these considerations about the material realization of states that are themselves individuated by their relations to material things and events. More specifically, I suggest that the identity of a subject over time consists in the identity of the apparatus that integrates states and events in such a way that a single subject has, or may have, perceptions, sensations, thoughts, action-awareness, and the rest, both at a time and over time.

What matters is the identity of the integrating apparatus, not the identity of the particular pieces of apparatus whose states are integrated to yield states of the subject. Your perceptual apparatus may be entirely replaced consistently with your continued existence, provided that the states produced by the new apparatus are properly integrated by some continuing apparatus with your other conscious states and events. Like any other material object, the matter constituting the integrating apparatus may also change over time. This partial account of identity of subjects over time provides a connection between what makes something a subject—its ability to enjoy a range of kinds of conscious states and events—and the role of the material integrating apparatus in which the identity of a given subject consists.

The claim for which I have been arguing is that subject x is identical with subject y if and only if x and y have the same material integrating apparatus. Having an integrating apparatus is not the same as being an integrating apparatus. It is not my view that a subject is identical with an integrating apparatus. A subject's integrating apparatus has many properties that the subject does not. The integrating apparatus may, for instance, be concentrated in a certain set of regions in his brain. The subject is not concentrated in a certain set of regions of his brain; and similarly for a range of other properties possessed by the integrating apparatus, but not by the subject.

The requirement, for a subject's existence, of the existence of a material, integrating apparatus is weaker than the requirement that the subject have a body and be capable of bodily movements. The experiences of the subject might, for instance, simply be auditory experiences of events in the world, and the subject, though it has some perceptual apparatus, is not capable of moving the material object in which this perceptual apparatus, and its integrating apparatus, are housed. Though perception has, constitutively, to have some explanatory connection with action (see the discussion of the Degree 0 case in Chapter I), those actions need not involve bodily movement. They may consist in change in electric charge, alterations in colour, and so forth.

Some thinkers hold that a subject does not persist if all its memories and beliefs are destroyed. For these thinkers, continued existence of the integrating apparatus in which a subject's existence is partially realized does not amount to continued existence of the subject itself. I myself do not share this intuition about the case. But for those who do, all that matters for present purposes is that identity of integrating apparatus is a necessary condition for continued existence of a subject, even if it is not sufficient. Further conditions can be added to reach sufficiency if such conditions are thought to be needed.

The integrating apparatus provides the realization of the subject's file on itself, the file discussed in the preceding chapter on primitive self-representation. This is one of several connections between the theses on representation in that chapter and the metaphysics of subjects outlined here.

There is also a connection between the metaphysical interdependence of conscious events and subjects, on the one hand, and the correct description of the operation of the subject's phenomenological file on itself. I emphasized that the file should not be regarded as collecting together predicates determined by events that are already conscious. If the events were already conscious, it certainly seems that there could be conscious events that could exist both temporally and ontologically prior to there being a subject who enjoys them, since the subject file is the causal basis of the subject's being in a number of co-conscious states. The subject's phenomenological file on itself must have inputs from non-conscious states and events if there is a metaphysical interdependence between subjects and conscious states and events. So on the present view, the correct conception of the subject's phenomenological file on itself and the ontological interdependence of conscious states and events go hand-in-hand.

(d) Kant famously, and as it seems to me correctly, objected to one conception of conscious subjects for the reason that it fails to distinguish between the existence of one continuing subject on the one hand, and a succession of distinct shorter-lived subjects which pass memories of their states on to their immediate successors, which in turn are ignorant of the change in identity. Kant wrote:

An elastic ball that strikes another one in a straight line communicates to the latter its whole motion, hence its whole state (if one looks only at their positions in space). Now assuming substances, on the analogy with such bodies in which representations, together with consciousness of them, flow from one to another, a whole series of these substances may be thought, of which the first would communicate its state, together with that of the previous substance, to a third substance, and this in turn would share the states of all the previous ones, together with their consciousness and its own. The last substance would thus be conscious of all the states of all the previously altered substances as its own states, because these states have been carried over to it, together with the consciousness of them; and in spite of this it would not have been the very same person in all these states. (Kant 1998: A364, p.423)

Kant's point need not be construed as verificationist. It can be regarded as a constitutive challenge to the conception of subjects in question. If the ontology of subjects is legitimate, what is the difference between being sensitive to genuine identity over time as opposed to apparent identity realized in a succession of subjects? The question is analogous to non-verificationist objections to classical Newtonian absolute space.[13] When construed as a constitutive challenge, Kant's demand seems to me justified.

I think the constitutive question is well posed against any position that makes genuine identity consist in seeming-identity. But the present account is not such a position. On the present account, genuine identity of subject consists in real identity of the material integrating apparatus in which a subject is realized. There could in extreme, distant counterfactual cases be transmissions of memories through a succession of distinct underlying physical pieces of integrating apparatus. That really would involve an illusion of identity over time on the part of the subjects in the later parts of the series. If two experiences are not realized in the same integrating apparatus, they are not experiences of the same subject. So apparent identity (even by reliable causes) by no means ensures genuine identity on the present view. The account meets Kant's justified demand.[14]

4. Contemporary Differences: A Historical Affinity

The metaphysics of subjects that I have offered can be located more precisely by relating it to some contemporary, and to some historic, views on this matter. The positive account of subjects that I have offered

---

[13]   See the discussion in Peacocke (1988).

[14]   I have not attempted a point-by-point discussion of Parfit's very extensive writings on these topics. I hope it is easy to derive a statement from the above account of the issues on which we diverge. 'Teletransportation' that destroys a subject's integrating apparatus is, on the account above, not something a subject will survive. Some of the other cases devised by Parfit are the analogues, for a brain or for an integrating apparatus, of the ship of Theseus.

contrasts sharply with two other prominent contemporary views, the narrative oriented view of Daniel Dennett and the animal oriented view of Paul Snowdon. These two views are radically different from one another, but in both cases the contrast with the treatment I am offering turns on the distinctive nature of the ontology of subjects that I am proposing.

I quote two paragraphs from the highly quotable Dennett:

Our fundamental tactic of self-protection, self-control, and self-definition is not spinning webs or building dams, but telling stories, and more particularly concocting and controlling the story we tell others–and ourselves–about who we are. And just as spiders don't have to think, consciously and deliberately, about how to spin their webs, and just as beavers, unlike professional human engineers, do not consciously and deliberately plan the structures they build, we (unlike *professional* human storytellers) do not consciously and deliberately figure out what narratives to tell and how to tell them. Our tales are spun, but for the most part we don't spin them: they spin us. Our human consciousness, and our narrative selfhood, is their product, not their source.

These strings or streams of narrative issue forth *as if* from a single source–not just in the obvious physical sense of flowing from just one mouth, or one pencil or pen, but in a more subtle sense: their effect on any audience is to encourage them to (try to) posit a unified agent whose words they are, about whom they are: in short, to posit a *center of narrative gravity*. Physicists appreciate the enormous simplification you get when you posit a center of gravity for an object, a single point relative to which all gravitational forces may be calculated. We hetero-phenomenologists appreciate the enormous simplification you get when you posit a center of narrative gravity for a narrative-spinning human body. Like the biological self, this psychological or narrative self is yet another abstraction, not a thing in the brain, but still a remarkably robust and almost tangible attractor of properties, the "owner of record" of whatever items and features are lying about unclaimed. Who owns your car? You do. Who owns your clothes? You do. Then who owns your body? You do! When you say

This is *my* body

you certainly aren't taken as saying

This body owns itself.

But what can you be saying, then? If what you say is neither a bizarre and pointless tautology (this body is its own owner, or something like that) nor the claim that you are an immaterial soul or ghost puppeteer who owns and operates

See the later parts of Parfit (1987: Appendix D, 'Nagel's Brain'). In those cases, I think our intuitions about identity of subjects march in step with those about identity of integrating apparatus. We are liable to have conflicting intuitions about identity in any case that is structurally analogous to that of Theseus's ship.

this body the way you own and operate your car, what else could you mean? (Dennett 1993: 418)

If the ontology of subjects I have described is real, the analogy with the physicists' centres of gravity does not go through. What it is for something to be a material object does not have to be explained fundamentally in terms of its relations to a centre of gravity. (This is consistent with every material object having a centre of gravity). There is no ontological interdependence between being a centre of gravity and being a material object—indeed that is part of Dennett's case for selves as real but derivative entities. But I have argued that there is precisely such interdependence, at the level of kinds, between subjects, conceived of as nonderivative, and conscious events. What it is to be a conscious event or state has to be explained, constitutively, in terms of relations to a subject. It seems to me that the relations of ontological priority in this domain have a structure incompatible with the conception of subjects as derivative entities.

Dennett seems to me to be talking about an important subject matter, but a different subject matter, when he writes 'Our tales are spun, but for the most part, we don't spin them; they spin us'. In my view, much of what Dennett says in his discussion of these issues applies to what writers mean when they speak of the motivational, interpersonal, social, cultural, racial, national, or class identity a subject conceives himself as possessing. Some of these are what would be classified as individual identity in ordinary discourse, some are what would be classified as kinds or types under which the individual conceives himself as falling. Dennett is right that it is an important insight that we often do not take identities of any of these sorts under our own control. This is a phenomenon at the level of the web of judgements, beliefs, emotions, and other propositional attitudes, just as Dennett says. It is a phenomenon at the level of thought, not at the more primitive nonconceptual level of perceptual experience and other subjective states I discussed earlier. It makes sense to say to someone 'You ought to shake off such-and-such cultural identity; its values and presuppositions are wrong'. A subject who reflects on whether he ought to abandon certain values and presuppositions of necessity uses the first person in his reflections. He asks, 'Should I really think that way? Ought I to identify so closely with my old College/my ethnic group/my nation/my co-religionists?' The first person is a way of thinking and representing that in the nature of the case refers to the subject engaged in these reflections quite independently of any values and presuppositions he may currently possess. One and the same subject could shake off such an identity, without ceasing to exist. To summarize a complex and fascinating topic that deserves much more treatment in its own right, I would say: the notion of a centre of narrative gravity is psychologically important, in the ways Dennett describes; but there is a subject who has such an identity, and who has that identity (so conceived) contingently, and whose existence is not to be explained as a centre of narrative gravity.

The same applies more specifically when we consider ordinary empirical beliefs about oneself, the web of first person beliefs that do not involve values or emotional identification. The first person has an identity as a way of thinking or representing oneself that is independent of, can be detached from, almost everything in this web. To take an example to which I will return in each of the next two chapters, the subject Neo in the movie *The Matrix* comes to discover that almost everything he at first believed about the world apparently around him, the world in which he seems to have woken up and lived (and taken phone calls) for many years, is illusory. This is far from equivalent to discovering that he does not exist. He still takes himself to exist, and rightly so, after the discovery. After the discovery, he learns what he really is, and what the real physical world is like, and what relations he stands in to the real world. He needs the first person to express these discoveries. He also employs the first person essentially in formulating the project of finding out what, physically, he really is.

There is also a question about the reference of thoughts apparently about oneself on Dennett's view. Dennett says that talk of a centre of narrative gravity is talk about how someone is representing himself as being. Now the contents of these first person thoughts must have a reference as well as a sense if they are to be assessed as true or as false. The question of the nature of their reference is one that arises for Dennett's view. Is the reference merely to an intentional object, something whose nature is given simply by the subject's attitudes about it? This intentional object could be regarded as like a Meinongian object under Terence Parsons's elegant treatment (1974). Under Parsons' proposal, Meinongian objects are sets of properties. When Meinong speaks of the 'the golden mountain', he is, under Parsons' treatment, referring to the set of properties {being golden, being a mountain}. If we apply this apparatus to Dennett's centres of narrative gravity, we could say that a subject is the set of all properties (relational and nonrelational) that a person attributes to himself or herself, using the first person. But that would leave it problematic how we are to make sense of the idea, which seems intelligible, that someone's conception of himself may be errone-ous (like Neo's, in an extreme case). If a self-conception can be errone-ous, there must be some subject who has it and whose nature is given independently of that conception. That is the just the kind of view for which I have been arguing. The ontology of intentional objects is attained without great expense, but the low price also fails to secure an adequate conception of the level of genuine reference. It is at the level of reference that the notions of correctness and incorrectness get a grip.

I strongly agree with Dennett that the thought 'This is my body' is not a 'pointless tautology', and that its truth does not require immaterial objects or 'brain-pearls' (1993: 430). But these agreed points can be explained without commitment to subjects as centres of narrative grav-ity. 'This is my body' means: this body is the one that is controlled by the subject that is me, and/or is the body from which the subject that I am is perceiving. The subject of which this is true can be a subject meeting the interdependent conception I offered. No one body is uniquely my body if one body meets the condition on action, and a different body meets the condition on perception—a circumstance describable in detail using points beautifully deployed by Dennett himself in his essay 'Where Am I?' (1978).

At one point Dennett writes that 'Thus do we build up a defining story about ourselves, organized around a sort of basic blip of self-representation. . . . . . What makes one blip the *me* blip and another blip just a *he-* or *she-* or *it-*blip is not what it looks like, but what it is used for. It gathers and organizes the information on the topic of *me* in the same way other structures in my brain keep track of information on Boston, or Reagan, or ice cream' (1993: 428–9). With the last two sentences of course I have a large measure of agreement, for they make the self-'blip' sound very much like the subject file I talk about. But if we have identified something as the object about which the blip tracks information, inde-pendently of whether that information is correct, then we cannot also say that the story the blip tells about the subject is a 'defining' story, as Dennett does in the early part of this quotation. If on the other hand we have not, independently of the information in question, philosophically identified something as the object about which the blip is tracking information, then we have not done justice to what is distinctive of first person representation. Yet such an independent identification of something as the object about which the blip is tracking information (or misinformation) is what one would expect if the parallel with keeping track of information about Boston, or Reagan, is sound.

Dennett also considers cases of multiple personality disorder. Those are cases in which I would say the brain's integrating apparatus realizes, at different times, different subject files, only one of which is dominant and operative at any one time. That last condition explains why recognition of multiple personality disorder does not reopen the possibility of nontransitive co-consciousness. Multiple personality disorder is consistent with the view of subjects I have been proposing. In general, I conjecture that if Dennett had recognized the option of a materialist ontology of subjects of the sort I have been offering as a fourth option, he could still have said much of what he wanted to maintain in his discussion, without needing the conception of selves as centres of narrative gravity.[15]

Dennett's is not the only theory to treat subjects of consciousness as intentional entities. Another theory that does so is that of Tim Bayne (2010: Section 12.5). Bayne's approach is of particular interest for two reasons. First, unlike Dennett's treatment, Bayne's concerns the level of conscious states and events below conceptualized propositional attitudes. Second, Bayne's approach aims to respect the link between subjects and the unity of consciousness, something I have also strongly endorsed. Bayne writes, 'We need a notion of the self according to which the relationship between the self and the unity of consciousness is *constitutive*' (2010: 281). Concerning that constitutive relationship on which we agree: Bayne thinks it is best respected by a theory of the self as intentional entity, while I have argued for it in the context of a theory under which subjects are not merely intentional entities. So this is a significant disagreement worth further investigation.

---

[15] There is a further issue about subjects as centres of narrative gravity. Dennett mentions the Chaplin twins (1993: 422), who act as if—but only as if—they have a single mind. Since the twins apparently require only a single centre of narrative gravity, but are still two subjects, the case—or one suitably adjusted—seems to be a counterexample to Dennett's view. We do not really want to say that in the Chaplin twins we have only one conscious subject with two bodies. There are two conscious subjects, coordinated in remarkable respects.

The approach Bayne favours is not what he calls a 'naïve phenomen-alism' that identifies subjects with streams of consciousness. Rather, Bayne writes of the self as 'the virtual object that is brought into being by *de se* representation' (2010: 289). Bayne's view is that this idea not merely respects, it actually 'forges' (2010: 289) the constitutive connec-tion between the unity of consciousness and selves: 'for the cognitive architecture underlying consciousness ensures that any *de se* representa-tions that occur within a single phenomenal field will be coreferential. For phenomenal selves, the rule is one subjective perspective at a time, for *de se* thought cannot bridge gaps between phenomenal fields. The functional role of *de se* representation guarantees that the boundaries of the virtual self are limned by the boundaries of the phenomenal field (at least, at a time)' (2010: 289).

It seems to me that this cannot be a fully general explanation of the unity of consciousness, because unity of consciousness is (and must be) present even when a creature's conscious mental states and events lack *de se* content. Consider the beings at Degree 0 of subject-representation, as discussed above in Chapter II, Section 3, who have conscious perceptual states, with indexical content concerning objects and events, but whose states have no *de se* content. The suggestion that they have non-transitive co-consciousness seems to me to be just as unintelligible as it is for beings that do have states with *de se* content. It is intrinsic to consciousness and to subjecthood that they conform to the unity of consciousness, whether or not the kind of consciousness in question has *de se* content. In my view, unity of consciousness is distinctively a feature of consciousness, not of any particular type of content of consciousness.

This argument would likely not cut any ice with Bayne, since he says 'I do think that a case can be made on broadly Kantian grounds for the view that *de se* content must inform the representations of any creature whose experiences purport to represent an objective world' (2010: 290). So further discussion of this first objection would have to address the coherence of examples of creatures at the envisaged Degree 0 of self-representation. Yet even beings, like us, who sometimes enjoy conscious states with *de se* content also sometimes enjoy states and events whose content is not *de se*. Monaurally hearing a middle C, with the E and the G just above it, does not obviously need to have a *de se* content. But as I argued above, a failure of unity of consciousness in such cases seems equally unintelligible. If unity flows from the nature of consciousness itself, that is what one would expect.[16] In any case, there are further problems I would raise for Bayne's position that do not rely on the possibility of cases at that Degree 0, nor on conscious states and events that lack *de se* content.

The correctness condition for a state or event with *de se* content must concern the reference of the *de se* component of its intentional content. Whether your apparent memory of being in Athens is correct depends on whether the reference of that first person content was in Athens. We need a genuine reference for this condition to be fulfilled; a 'virtual object' by itself is not enough. (Contrast Bayne 'the reference of an I-thought is nothing other than an intentional object' (2010: 290).) I suggested earlier that getting the truth conditions of states and events with *de se* content right would take one back to identity of integrating apparatus, conceived as realizing a subject that is not merely an intentional object, and whose states respect the unity of consciousness. Bayne could of course equally formulate the truth conditions of these *de se* contents in terms of the relation of his virtual objects to physical entities, brains, and indeed integrating apparatuses. I suggest that if this is done in a way that secures the right truth conditions for the states and events, we will already be using materials that suffice for the construction of a theory of real, and not merely virtual, subjects.

I also think that the theory of subjects as virtual objects will still be open to some of the objections to what Bayne calls 'naïve phenomenalism' about the self. We can make sense of idea that in the night you had an experience of which you have no memories. The experience has no consciousness relations to your other mental states. On my view, on which subjects are realized in an integrating apparatus, the nighttime experience can be yours because it was realized in the same integrating apparatus as is involved in realizing your current experiences.[17]

---

[16] If there can be beings whose conscious mental life is wholly non-representational (on which, see Chapter VII, Section 2), that it seems to me that thesis of the unity of consciousness applies to them too.

[17] If *de se* content legitimizes subjects as virtual objects, then does the present tense, *de nunc*, content of experience equally legitimize times as virtual objects? It seems equally impossible for current events A and B to seem simultaneous and occurring now, and current events B and C to seem simultaneous and occurring now, yet for A and C not to seem simultaneous and occurring now to a given subject. Even if we did introduce virtual times as intentional objects, it is not clear that they would serve any purpose not served by

I turn to a different metaphysical issue that I have left unaddressed. The positive view I have been advocating earlier is certainly materialistic. Is it in fact also consistent with the claim that subjects are animals? As far as I can see, everything in the positive conception of subjects I have offered is consistent with the possibility that subjects could be created in some future AI laboratory. So it is not necessary that all subjects are animals. Is it then at least the case that all human subjects are necessarily animals? This is Paul Snowdon's position (1996). Well, does an animal still exist after brain damage that destroys its cognitive functions, but leaves its respiratory and other bodily functions intact? If the animal does still exist, then the subject is not an animal, for in that case the animal exists but the subject does not. But perhaps it is no accident that we describe this as a vegetative state, so that in these circumstances, the animal no longer exists either. Certainly the animal in a vegetative state is not a properly functioning animal, and Snowdon's animalist position can use that point to classify the case correctly. I myself am inclined to think that what makes something an animal is, in part, its being a subject as conceived earlier in this material. Being a subject would then be metaphysically prior to being an animal, something constitutive of it. But since appeal to the notion of a properly functioning animal is open to the animalist, nothing so far tells conclusively against the position that human subjects are animals.

I am, evidently, in agreement with Snowdon's conclusion that 'Animals . . . have no claim to be, of necessity, the unique possessors of mental states, nor, therefore, to be the only persons' (1996: 45). I am committed also to agreement with his view that the philosophical tradition on these issues has overlooked some options. Nonetheless, Snowdon and I are proceeding in quite different directions. Snowdon is tempted by the two views that I am fundamentally an animal, and that I am not fundamentally a person (where 'person' has what he calls a psychological interpretation). My own view is that I am fundamentally a subject. What that implies about embodiment, or a philosophical explanation of my existence in terms of possible embodiment, depends further on a constitutive account of the mental states that a subject enjoys. In general, the available options for revising the philosophical tradition on

present tense intentional contents; and in any case we would need to explain their relations to real times. The case has many structural analogies with that of subjects.

these issues should be formulated using not only the notion of a person, but that of a subject too.

The most difficult cases for the animalist are those split brain examples it is most plausible to classify as examples in which there is one animal whose brain realizes two different subjects.[18] No animal can be identical with subjects that are distinct from one another. The animalist, if he says that the subject of consciousness is the animal, is committed to saying that consciousness can be disunified, that the unity of consciousness we discussed and endorsed earlier in Section 3(b) of this chapter does not need to obtain. It remains very hard to conceive of how a subject can be conscious of mental event e_1, and conscious of mental event e_2, without those two events being co-conscious. It seems to be constitutive of being a subject that in those circumstances the events are co-conscious. (This is of course not a theorem of logic, it is rather something distinctive of subjects and mental events.) An equivalent way of emphasizing this point is to say: for any token experience, it will have a unique subject such that what it's like for that subject is fully determined by what is co-conscious with that token experience. If animals are subjects and are vulnerable to split brain cases, then this principle would not be true. It is of course open to the animalist to say that the split brain cases show that our ordinary conception of subjects as having unified consciousnesses is something that applies only in familiar circumstances, and that extraordinary circumstances show that that conception is sometimes erroneous. But I am inclined to think that if we can develop a metaphysics of subjects on which it there is no contradiction in the brain of one animal realizing two subjects of consciousness, we not have to abandon our intuitive conception of a subject of consciousness. I do not think we have any conception of what it would be like to be an alleged subject with a disunified consciousness.[19]

The philosopher to whose views the treatment I have offered is closest, though by no means identical, is John Locke.[20] Locke's account of 'what

---

[18] These cases became known to many philosophers through Nagel's famous paper 'Brain Bisection and the Unity of Consciousness' (1971), which also contains some references to some leading literature of that time.

[19] For more extensive discussions of animalism, see van Inwagen (1990) and Bayne (2010: 12.2).

[20] I thank Rory Madden for noting this, and prompting me to think further about these relations to Locke.

Person stands for' includes the requirement that a person 'can consider itself as itself, the same thinking thing in different times and places; which it does only by that consciousness, which is inseparable from thinking, and as it seems to me essential to it'.[21] I said in the Introduction to this book that a fourth option had been overlooked in the literature, an option that regards subjects as not fundamentally embodied persons, not Cartesian immaterial entities, and not as logical constructs from allegedly unowned mental events. There are several respects in which Locke does meet this specification of the fourth option. First, Locke was definitely not an immaterialist about persons. He has a formidable critique of immaterialist entities as incapable of sustaining the identity of persons, a critique on whose main lines it would be hard to improve today (Bk. II, Ch. XXVII, §§13–15). Locke seems to have had no Cartesian tendencies in this area. Second, Locke did not emphasize the role of bodily identity in identity of person: just the opposite, in fact, in his famous discussion of the prince and the cobbler (Bk. II, Ch. XXVII, §17ff.). Third, as far as I can tell, there no signs of a fundamentally no-ownership view in Locke's discussion of persons.

There are two differences from Locke that block the claim that the fourth option I am offering is actually identical with Locke's position. I omitted from the quotation above from Locke his further requirement that a person must be 'a thinking intelligent Being, that has reason and reflection' (Bk. II, Ch. XXVII, §9). This places persons at the level of rational, reflective, conceptual thought. This may well be right for the notion of a person. But not all subjects of consciousness are persons in this sense. Subjects of consciousness exist also solely at a more primitive level, with mental states and events that have only nonconceptual content, and without necessarily having any capacity for reflective thought. Locke also famously remarked that '*Person*' is 'a Forensick Term appropriating Actions and their Merit; and so belongs only to intelligent Agents capable of a Law' (Bk. II, Ch. XXVII, §26). This forensic conception further emphasizes the distance between his target notion of reflective beings and the more general notion of a subject of consciousness.

The other difference between the fourth option and Locke's account concerns Locke's problematic noun phrase 'same consciousness'. This

---

[21] *An Essay Concerning Human Understanding* Book II, Chapter XXVII, §9; subsequent references in the text to Locke are to this work.

term, much used by Locke, evidently does not mean 'same conscious event', because he says it holds of people at two widely separated times. So what does it mean? Locke often writes as if 'same consciousness' is more fundamental than, and explanatory of, identity of self. Thus he writes: 'as far as this consciousness can be extended backwards to any past Action or Thought, so far reaches the Identity of that *Person*' (Bk. II, Ch. XXVII, §9). He employs, revealingly, the constitutive vocabulary of 'makes' and 'depends': 'For it being the same consciousness that makes a Man be himself to himself, *personal Identity* depends on that only' (Bk. II, Ch. XXVII, §12). That sentence occurs in a section with the title 'Consciousness makes personal Identity'. What then is involved in such sameness of consciousness? We might try explicating it in terms of sameness of process, for there is a notion, in good standing, of an individual particular process with an identity over time. But it does not seem that it could serve Locke's purposes at this point. Transmission of merely apparent memories between different subjects, as in Kant's example discussed in the preceding chapter, is equally a process. Locke's thesis that 'Consciousness makes personal Identity' will work only if sameness of consciousness has already to mean or involve same subject of consciousness. So Locke's discussion needs some account of the nature of this 'same consciousness' over time that answers the complaint that this might involve mere psychological continuity, without genuine identity of subject (or of person). Locke could appeal to identity of integrating apparatus to meet this demand. This revised account would then overlap with mine.

The relation between my position and that of Descartes is much more complex and theoretically more interesting. I argued earlier that subjects must be materially realized. So the position for which I am arguing is not with Descartes on the issue of immateriality. There are, however, other Cartesian theses with which it strongly agrees. One of course is that mental states and events must have subjects, and that this is a fundamental metaphysical truth. I will return to this and other Cartesian issues in Chapter VI, once we have done more on the first person concept.

IV

The First Person Concept and its Nonconceptual Parent

Philosophers from at least Augustine onwards have been fascinated by phenomena apparently distinctive of the first person concept. These phenomena are diverse, having to do variously with distinctive features of the first person in epistemology, in psychological explanation, the emotions, and interpersonal relations. Our task should be not merely to characterize these phenomena—a substantive exercise in itself—but also to explain them.

Explanations of the phenomena have to draw on a positive account of the nature of the first person concept. Explanations that draw in part on the nature of the concept can supply us not only with an understanding of those phenomena themselves, but also of why one and the same concept, that of the first person, should be involved in all these various phenomena.

The nature of the first person concept is to be elucidated in part in terms of its relations to the nonconceptual *de se*, understood as referring to a subject of the sort discussed in preceding chapters. That is what I will be arguing in this chapter. In the next, I will draw on this account in offering an explanation of some distinctive epistemic phenomena involving the first person concept.

My case will be an instance of an argument to the best explanation. We can best explain four particular features of the first person concept if we both recognize a nonconceptual *de se* notion, and give an account of the conceptual *I* whose significance rests in part on its relations to states involving that more primitive notion.

1. Some Background on Concepts

The first person concept is expressed by the word 'I' in English, by the first person pronoun in other languages, and by inflection of the verb in yet others. Claims about the first person concept are to be assessed in the first instance against the evidence of various properties (truth conditions, evidential relations, psychological role) of first person sentences and contents as uttered or thought in various circumstances. But to make good some philosophical claim about the nature of the first person concept, such as the one with which I have introduced this chapter, a theorist needs to draw on some positive theory of concepts in general. Only with such a general theory as background is one in a position to substantiate or refute claims about the nature of any specific concept.

I will be taking it that a concept is individuated by its fundamental rule of reference. Intuitively, the fundamental rule of reference for a concept states the condition that makes something the reference of the concept. This is the approach to concepts that I offered in *Truly Understood* (2008), and I will be taking it for granted here. The approach is broadly Fregean in several respects. It respects the idea, so sharply formulated in Frege's *Grundgesetze*, that senses are individuated by the contribution they make to the truth-conditions of complete Thoughts. It also respects the idea that a concept is a way of thinking of something. The approach contrasts sharply with views according to which a concept is individuated by some kind of canonical evidence for certain contents containing the concept, or by some kind of canonical consequences of the holding of certain contents containing the concept.

Concepts, as indicated in Chapter II, I also take to be constituents of the contents of judgements, which thinkers may make rationally or irrationally, but which in any case can be made for reasons. Nonconceptual contents also have their reference conditions, and are in my view equally individuated by their fundamental reference conditions. The reference condition of a nonconceptual content does not, however, have anything intrinsically to do with the level of reasons and the mental activity of making judgements. These nonconceptual contents feature in the contents of such states as perception, memory, and certain kinds of action awareness (amongst others), and these are states and events that subjects do not enjoy as a result of the operation of their own reasons at all. Entering one of these states, or enjoying one of these events, is not itself a mental action, though it may be the intended result, brought about by some other mental action.

The case of states with conceptual content is very different. As I argued in *Truly Understood*, the psychological significance of the fundamental rule of reference for a concept lies in part at least in the contribution it makes, in combination with the rest of a thinker's information, in helping to determine what are, and what are not, good reasons for judging contents containing the concept. That is a statement of the link between concepts and reasons that is formulated in terms of the general approach to concepts that I myself favour. But a fundamental link between concepts and reasons can certainly be acknowledged on other approaches to concepts too.[1]

Given our present concern with the first person, we need more specifically a formulation of the relation between concepts and fundamental reference rules that takes into account the context of the use of a concept, and thus applies to indexical and demonstrative concepts too. When we take context into account, we should say, as a first approximation: the fundamental reference rule for a concept states, for any given thinker and time, what relation something has to stand in to the thinker at that time to be the reference of that concept, as used by that thinker at that time. Suppose we are concerned with a concept C, and the relation in which a thinker has to stand to something for it to be the reference of the concept C at a given time is R_C. Then the abstract general form of a rule of reference for a concept C is this, approximately:

$$\forall \text{thinker } \tau \; \forall \text{time } t \; \forall x\text{: } x \text{ is the reference of } C \text{ as used by } \tau \text{ at } t \text{ iff } R_C\,(x, \tau, t).$$

I call this an approximation because for some concepts, the fundamental reference rule will need to mention more, or different, parameters besides the thinker and the time.

Here are some plausible examples of fundamental reference rules. As in previous writings, I use square brackets to indicate indexical or demonstrative types. Suppose that last Monday at twelve noon you

---

[1] For a very different approach to the relation between rules of reference on the one hand and conceptual intentional content, see the writings of John McDowell, especially his 'In Defense of Modesty' (1998). McDowell does not believe in the existence of personal level nonconceptual content at all; but his position on the nature of conceptual content, and its link with rationality and reasons, a link with which I agree, is independent of that denial.

thought 'It's sunny now', and that last Tuesday at twelve noon you thought 'It's not sunny now'. The type [now] is the unique temporal indexical type an instance of which was employed by you at twelve noon last Monday, and an instance of which was also employed by you at twelve noon last Tuesday in these two events of thinking. The fundamental reference rule for the type [now] is the relatively uncontroversial:

$\forall$thinker τ $\forall x$ $\forall$event θ of thinking by τ: x is the reference of an instance of the [now] type as used by τ at t iff x is the time of occurrence of the event θ of thinking·

For a perceptual demonstrative type [that F_W], such as 'that building', where the perceptual demonstrative is fixed by a particular way W in which something is given in perception, the rule is:

$\forall$thinker τ $\forall$time t $\forall x$: x is the reference of an instance of the type [that F_W] as used by thinker τ at t iff x is the F perceived in way W by x at t.

As always, whether x is perceived in way W is partly a matter of the causal relations in which x stands to the perception in question.

Formulations of fundamental reference rules become more controversial as we proceed beyond such cases. For the case of the first person concept, I would defend this formulation of the fundamental reference rule for the first person type [self]:

$\forall x$ $\forall$event of thinking θ: x is the reference of a use of an instance of the [self] type in the event θ of thinking iff x is the producer (agent) of that event θ of thinking.

I will call this a statement of the 'the thinker-rule' for [self], or, equivalently, for the I-concept.

Philosophers who disagree on other aspects of what is involved in first person thought may nevertheless agree that the thinker-rule is true. My thesis is that the thinker-rule is, in the presence of other plausible claims about subjects and mental states and their contents, all that needs to be said by way of specification of the nature of the first person concept. Others, notably Evans in his chapter on self-identification in *The Varieties of Reference* (1982), and some neo-Kantian writers, would say that more needs to be said about the nature of the concept itself, including the capacity to self-locate in space. The claim that the thinker-rule individuates the first person concept is also in competition with the thesis, found in some parts of John Perry's writings, that we do not need the idea of a distinctively first person concept (Perry 2002a) to explain first person phenomena. I will return to that issue in the Chapter V.

A theory of concepts needs to be accompanied by a theory of what it is to grasp those concepts, to be capable of having propositional attitudes with contents containing those concepts as components. My own view, again as argued in *Truly Understood*, is that grasp of a concept consists in tacit knowledge of its fundamental reference rule. The knowledge may be incomplete.

It is not true that anyone employing a concept in thought must thereby be thinking of its reference as something that meets the condition given in the fundamental reference rule for the concept. There are obvious counterexamples to that generalization. A child may not have the concept of perceptual experience, but can still use perceptual demonstratives such as 'that ball', 'this toy' extensively. The child can also employ the first person in thought without having the concept of mental events that are thinkings. The important point is that a thinker can meet the condition for something to be the reference of one of his concepts without thereby conceptualizing the condition that something has to meet to be the reference. What makes something the reference is one thing. Whether the thinker has the resources to conceptualize that condition, or additionally to formulate it correctly, is something else.

These points apply to the discussion of the first person in Saul Kripke's paper 'The First Person', in which he writes, 'it is a rule of the common language that each of us fixes the reference of "I" by the description "the subject"' (2011a: 305). I regard the role of the description 'the subject' in fixing the reference of the first person as something that operates at the level of the individuation of a way of thinking of something, rather than as a description employed in thought by someone capable of first person representational states and events. But Kripke too I would expect to draw, if not precisely that distinction, then at least something analogous. As Kripke's paper proceeds, it becomes clear that what matters for him in grasp of the first person is not a thinker's use of some definite description *the thinker*, but rather the thinker's standing in a relation of acquaintance to himself that is made available by his being the subject of certain mental events and states. He writes, 'Each one of us can fix the reference of the word "I" by means of acquaintance with oneself, self-acquaintance' (302); and 'No one can grasp the rule for "I" stated in the common language except by means of one's own self-acquaintance' (302). I return to discuss acquaintance relations, and their connection with the thinker-rule above, in the final section of this chapter.

This distinction between conceptualizing a relation, and that relation being involved in the account of what makes something the reference of a given notion, concept or expression, is not taken into account in the otherwise excellent discussion in the first chapter of Sebastian Rödl's book *Self-Consciousness* (2007). He considers this reference rule for the first person pronoun: 'I' is used to refer to the person who is using it (2007: 1). He complains that this rule specifies only a reference, and not a sense. His objections to the rule as specifying a sense all turn on the fact that the phrases 'the person uttering "I"' and 'I' are not cognitively equivalent. Agreed, they are not equivalent, and for many reasons. To give just one reason they are not cognitively equivalent: if I am profoundly deaf, I may, when I suspect I have lost my voice, not know whether I have uttered the sentence 'I am hungry'. I may well know that I am hungry; but I may neither know nor believe that the person uttering 'I am hungry' is hungry. However, the claim that a concept or a sense is individuated by its fundamental reference rule does not imply any such equivalence of 'I' with 'the person uttering "I"'.

As always, the limited parallel between the first person and the present tense is helpful in making the point. The phrase 'the time at which a certain token of the word "now" is uttered' is not cognitively equivalent to 'now'. (As evidence, we could adduce parallel considerations about a deaf utterer.) Consider the rule: 'now' is used on any occasion of utterance to refer to the time of occurrence of the utterance. It is very plausible that there really is no more to the meaning of 'now' than is given by this rule, modulo some provision about the temporal boundaries of the time referred to. That suggests that there must be something wrong with the corresponding reasoning about 'I'. What is wrong with the reasoning, in both cases, is that insofar as a fundamental reference rule is meant to individuate a sense, the cognitive properties distinctive of a sense will flow from the relation in which an entity has to stand to a thinker when the thinker is thinking of it using that sense, rather than from the thinker's conceptualization (if any) of the referent's standing in that relation.

Rödl's own positive account of the first person concept is one under which 'First person reference depends on a knowledge-providing relationship with the object' (2007: 8). I agree with Rödl that it is an important point that relations which provide knowledge are distinctive of first person thought, as indeed they arguably are so distinctive for all other genuinely indexical and demonstrative concepts. But as we proceed, I will be arguing that, in the case of the first person concept, this connection with knowledge is explained by the relations between the first person concept and the more primitive nonconceptual *de se* notion.

2. Explaining Four Phenomena

With this much by way of background, I return to the argument for the thesis that the nature of the first person concept is to be explained in part in terms of its relations to the nonconceptual *de se*, and that nonconceptual first person's reference to a subject of a certain kind. If this thesis is true, it should be possible to argue for it from materials we have already presented. For I have already suggested substantive accounts of both the first person concept and the nonconceptual *de se*. The first person concept is individuated by the thinker-rule, and the nonconceptual *de se* is individuated by its fundamental reference rule, that in any occurrence in a mental state or event, it refers to the subject of that state or event. So the relations between the conceptual first person *I* and the nonconceptual *de se i* will be determined as consequences of these two reference rules, when taken in combination with auxiliary principles.

Some consequences follow immediately from those two individuating reference rules, in combination with uncontroversial principles. The agent who makes a judgement is the same subject who enjoys certain perceptions, memories, and action awareness. It follows then from the thinker-rule that the reference of the conceptual first person *I* on a particular occasion, that is, the agent making the judgement, is the same subject as is represented as having various properties and standing in various relations by perceptual experiences with a *de se* content.

Not only do these identities hold, it is obvious to the subject that they hold. In ordinary, non-pathological cases in which a thinker makes a first person judgement (or any other judgement for that matter), he is aware that he is making the judgement. This is action awareness in the case in which the action is a mental action. So if he grasps the first person concept, our thinker will be aware that in judging *I'm F*, he is thinking about himself, the same person who is represented as being a certain way in his perceptions, and as having been a certain way in his memories.

The thinker-rule does not itself explicitly mention states with non-conceptual *de se* contents. But a normal human who grasps the first person concept, as individuated by the thinker-rule, will rationally take the correctness of his I-thoughts to be answerable, in various defeasible ways, to the *de se* nonconceptual contents of his perceptions and other representational states. It is only because of these connections of the conceptual first person with the nonconceptual *de se* that someone who understands *I*, as governed by the thinker-rule, has an empirically usable conception of what is involved in the truth of first person thoughts.

This anchoring of first person conceptual content in states with non-conceptual *de se* content may be seen as an instance of an entirely general thesis about the relations between conceptual and nonconceptual content. It is arguable that conceptual content, whose nature is tied to good reasons for being in states with such content, must be individuated eventually by its relations to states with nonconceptual content, of a sort characteristic of states that simply happen to thinkers, states, and events that thinkers do not enjoy for reasons at all. The argument for such a general thesis would take the form that only such a grounding of conceptual content in nonconceptual content would avoid an individuative regress, and would avoid ungroundedness in an explanation of what can be a good reason for being in a state with conceptual content. Such a general thesis has to deal with an array of possible replies and even potential counterexamples. My own view is that these apparent obstacles can be overcome, but it would divert us too far off the main course of this book to pursue the general issue here. At this point, I just note that if a good case can be made for that general thesis about the grounding of the conceptual in the nonconceptual, then the recent point about the grounding of the conceptual first person in the nonconceptual *de se* is an elaboration of how, in more specific detail, the first person concept meets a condition that must be met by any concept whatsoever.

As I said, my main task in this section is to argue, by inference to the best explanation, for the general thesis that the conceptual first person is to be understood philosophically in part in terms of its relations, as just described, to the nonconceptual *de se*. Here are four features of the conceptual first person that can be explained if that thesis is true.

Feature (1): The Linguistic Expression of Nonconceptual States. A first intuitive reason for thinking that the first person concept is to be elucidated in part in terms of its relation to the nonconceptual first person concerns the linguistic expression of nonconceptual states. When we want to express in language the content of a state with a nonconceptual *de se* representational content, we naturally use the first person pronoun. A person says 'I see the cyclist coming towards me', or simply 'The cyclist is coming towards me', where the judgement so expressed is based on a subject-reflexive perception with a *de se* content, one in which the cyclist, given as such, is represented as coming toward the subject. A similar point about linguistic expression applies to ascriptions based on memory and on action awareness. We say, 'I remember tripping over', 'I am raising my arm now'. The naturalness of such linguistic expressions is entirely to be expected if the grasped truth conditions of conceptualized first person contents are conceived of as concerning the same subject that is the reference of the *de se* element in the nonconceptual awarenesses that are expressed. But that identity of reference and subject is what is implied by the fundamental reference rules for the conceptual first person and for *i* (the nonconceptual *de se*), given that the thinker of the first person thought in question is enjoying the relevant perception, memory or action awareness.

Feature (2): The Description of Nonconceptual States. What applies to expression, as in Feature (1), also applies to description. A second reason for thinking that the nonconceptual *de se* contributes to the explanation of the nature of the first person concept is its ability to explain our pre-reflective inclination to use the first person concept in specifying the content of subject-reflexive states and events. We say it looks to the dog as if the bone is in front of him, and that it sounds to the dog as if the bang occurred behind him. These are *de se* uses of 'him' that we use confidently and without reflection to articulate what it is like for the dog. As I said at the start of the discussion of primitive self-representation, we do not think that we thereby attribute first person conceptual representations to the dog. This descriptive practice too is entirely understandable and justifiable if the links I have been trying to articulate really do exist. For those who do possess the first person concept, the subject-reflexive states and events involving the nonconceptual first person give reasons for making judgements containing the first person. So it is natural to pick out subject-reflexive perceptual states and events by means of this link with the first person concept. We can identify the states by means of that relation to the first person concept without commitment to the states and events themselves containing first person conceptual contents. We use the first person concept in identifying these states and events because of the special connection of these states and events with what makes rational certain first person judgements (on which, more below). But we can say what feature it is of these events and states—viz. the presence of the nonconceptual *de se* in their content—that gives them this connection, without implying that they themselves have first person conceptual content.

It is highly intuitive that there are subjects who are not yet capable of conceptual thought and making judgements for reasons, but who nonetheless represent themselves as having various spatial and material properties. That is to say, in the terms of Chapter II, there are subjects at Degree 1 of subject involvement in the representation of the objective world. If the only form of self-representation were to involve the first-person concept, we would be at an impasse in trying to explain how such subjects are capable of self-representation. The notion of the nonconceptual *de se* and of subject-reflexive events and states provides a way around this apparent obstacle. The nonconceptual *de se* and subject-reflexivity, together with their subpersonal realizations, explain how self-representation is possible for subjects who do not possess conceptual capacities.

I have been presenting these links between subject-reflexivity and the first person concept in the context of an approach under which concepts are individuated by their fundamental reference rules. But links of the same general character could be formulated under other treatments of conceptual content too. Suppose you favour a pure conceptual role theory of concepts, and treat concepts as individuated independently of considerations of reference and truth. This is the approach of Brandom (1994) and of Harman (1999a, 1999b). You would then be adopting what I called a 'Level 0' theory in Chapter 1 of *Truly Understood*. This is a treatment with which I am not in agreement, for reasons presented in that book. Nonetheless, under the pure conceptual role approach, you could still say that the individuating conceptual role of the first person concept is to be given in part by specifying the subject-reflexive events and states that give reasons, in normal circumstances, for accepting conceptual contents containing the first person concept. The relevance of subject-reflexive states and their relation to the first person concept is not restricted to referential and truth-conditional theories of concepts.

Feature (3): Satisfaction of the Conditions for Genuine Indexicality and for Corresponding Awareness. There is a substantive requirement for a kind of intentional content in mental states to be genuinely indexical or demonstrative, a requirement that goes beyond mere dependence of reference upon context. We can highlight the requirement by considering a hypothetical expression 'thar', which, we stipulate, when used by a thinker on earth refers to the location on the other side of the earth from his current location. So, used at the North Pole, 'thar' refers to the South Pole. Used in London, it refers to a location somewhere near New Zealand; and so forth. The word 'thar' can be semantically and syntactically unstructured, but that cannot be enough for it to express an unstructured genuinely indexical *concept*. In thought, 'thar' expresses the complex concept 'the polar opposite location on the surface of the earth from here'. 'Thar' is certainly an indexical expression, for its reference on any given occasion of use depends upon the location at which it is used. Intuitively, however, the concept expressed by 'thar' is a mixed descriptive-indexical concept *the polar opposite location on the earth from here*. At the level of concepts, this is not a genuinely indexical concept, on any given occasion, of the polar opposite location. Rather, it involves a descriptive functor concept applied to the genuinely indexical content *here*. Now why do we find this classification of the case plausible?

Is it plausible because we as users of 'thar' are not in conscious states whose intentional contents nondescriptively concern the place that is the polar opposite of our current location? It is true and important that we do not enjoy such conscious states, in the way that we really do enjoy conscious perceptual states with nondescriptive intentional contents concerning the things we currently perceive. However, the presence of any such conscious states cannot be what is critical to genuinely nondescriptive intentional content, because the nonconscious states and events involved in the older, dorsal system that controls human reaching must certainly have genuinely indexical intentional contents.[2] They will have correctness conditions concerning objects as given with certain locations egocentrically identified. So an event or state's being conscious

---

[2] For a description of some of the phenomena and plausible explanations, see Milner and Goodale (2006).

is not a necessary condition for it to have genuinely indexical or demonstrative intentional content.

It does seems to be a requirement for a state to have a nondescriptive intentional content concerning an entity in the spatiotemporal world that there exist an information link between the state and the entity, as Evans (1982) said. The information link will have its conditions of operation; it need not be operative in all circumstances. Both conscious and unconscious states can meet this requirement of an information link. But only conscious states and events can give a thinker reasons for making judgements. The unconscious indexical perceptual states of the older, dorsal perceptual system do not give us reasons for making judgements. They do not enter awareness at all. Maybe we could flesh out a possible example in which there does exist a conscious state that meets the requirements, and whose presence gives a thinker a reason for judging a genuinely nondescriptive content expressed by the invented expression 'thar'. If we could flesh out the example, then in such a world, what is expressed by 'thar' would be indexical, if the example is properly developed.

Now intuitively the first person concept is genuinely indexical, and, unlike the actual sense of 'thar', the first person concept does not consist of a descriptive functor applied to some other element. What explains this third feature of the first person concept, the fact that it satisfies the requirements at the level of intentional content for being genuinely nondescriptive? I suggest the explanation is that the fundamental reference rule for the first person has it refer, on any occasion of use, to a subject, a subject who is in conscious states with *de se* nonconceptual contents. We noted that the ordinary user of the first person concept is in a position to know that he is thinking about the same thing that is the reference of the *de se* component of the content of his perceptions, memories, and action awareness. His first person judgements are rationally answerable to the content of these states. These states meet the requirements for having nondescriptive contents concerning the subject itself. The existence of these states means that we are in very different situation in relation to the first person concept than we are to the invented concept *thar*, for which there in fact no such corresponding states for ordinary humans. How states with nonconceptual *de se* content can concern the subject itself was the concern of Chapter II. The presence of an integrating apparatus that provides input to a subject's file on itself helps to explain how all this can be the case, and how the informational requirements for genuinely indexical content are thereby met.

Since I will be diverging from his views later on, I would like to emphasize here the areas of agreement with what I have said so far, and the position outlined in John Perry's paper 'The Self, Self-Knowledge, and Self-Notions' (2002a). Perry's position is best given in his own words: 'I shall say that there are "normally here-informative" ways of getting information and "normally here-dependent, here-directed, and here-effecting" ways of acting. [....] I shall call relations between an agent and another object—including places, material objects, and other persons—that support such special ways of knowing and acting "epistemic/pragmatic relations." The relation of *being at*, that holds between people and places, is an epistemic/pragmatic relation. There are many others. There are special ways to know about the material objects and people *in front of* one (open your eyes and look, reach out and touch) and special ways of dealing with them. [....] Where *R* is an epistemic/pragmatic relation, we may speak of "normally *R*-informative ways of perceiving" and "normally *R*-directed/dependent/effecting ways of acting"' (2002a: 200). So, on Perry's conception, certain relations between an object and the thinker support what he calls normally *m*-informative ways of getting information, for various ways *m* of thinking of objects (2002a: 200). These epistemic-pragmatic relations fulfill in Perry's account the role that must be fulfilled, on the account I have offered, for an intentional content to be genuinely indexical or demonstrative.

When we confine our attention to conscious states and events that can give reasons for making judgements of contents containing the conceptual first person *I*, we need some further restrictions on the epistemic-pragmatic relations Perry is discussing. In both of the examples in given in the preceding quotation, it is only a restriction of the relations *being at* and *being in front of* that support the relevant distinctive *m*-informative ways of coming to judge rationally, and know, a conceptual content. Being at a place supports the special way of getting information rationally usable by the conscious thinker in conceptual thought only if one is in one way or another perceptually aware of the place at which one is located. Similarly, only objects that stand in the relation of being in front of one and are also perceived by one sustain especially informative ways of getting information about those objects that is usable in rational conceptualized judgement. (I would not expect Perry to disagree.) The more restricted relations incorporate an awareness requirement.

Perry also says, 'Identity is an epistemic/pragmatic relation' (2002a: 202, 204), and Recanati follows him in this in classifying identity as an epistemically rewarding relation (2012: 35–6). On first reading, this may be puzzling. How can simply standing in the relation of identity to the thinker support any distinctively informative ways of getting information? When, however, one looks at the example Perry offers in illustration of this thesis, the example seems rather to focus on a relation that allows a subject to gain information about himself from a conscious state with *de se* content. Perry immediately follows the claim that identity is an epistemic/pragmatic relation with the point 'Feeling one's face flush is a way of registering the information that the person identical with the feeler is blushing' (2002a: 204). The role of identity in this formulation is apparently redundant—the quoted sentence is equivalent to 'Feeling one's face flush is a way of registering the information that the feeler is blushing'. This understates what is registered, for it omits the content that the feeler is oneself. This is again a form of the point made in connection with Tim Bayne, back in Chapter II, Section 1, that descriptive functors applied to an experience-based demonstrative do not capture the content that the experience is *mine*. The full content normally registered when one is blushing is that one is blushing oneself. We capture the relevant relation more accurately by saying: there is a relation in which a thinker stands to his own face when he perceives it from the inside (proprioceptively) as flushing, and this relation makes available knowledge that he himself is blushing. This specification of the relation goes beyond mere identity to include a relation of informational awareness, of perception of the face from the inside, in a way available normally only to the person whose face it is. I would also say that a normal subject who experiences the flushing experiences his own face (*de se*) as flushing, a nonconceptual conscious state with a subject-reflexive content.[3]

---

[3] There may here be a diagnosis of Perry's formulation employing the complex term 'the person identical with the feeler'. Perry may take the blushing example as a case that illustrates the proposed role of identity as an epistemic/pragmatic relation because he appreciates that it involves some registration of the information that the feeler is me. But I am not sure how this can be properly captured without attributing *de se* content to the experience of blushing.

Perry says, 'We might think of our notions as forming a multileveled system' (2002a: 201). At the top level, he places notions that are maximally independent of relationships to us, what we might call maximally nonindexical ways of thinking of things. 'The lower levels contain buffers for various relationship to us, associated with various epistemic/pragmatic relations' (2002a: 201). We pass information up when we rely on the epistemic/pragmatic relations in which we stand. We pass information down when, for instance, we recognize an object and draw on information about properties we know it had in the past.

I am, then, at this point suggesting two revisions to Perry's structure. One revision is that the relevant buffers for the conceptual level, insofar as it involves rational judgement, are constrained to be based on relations of informational awareness. The other revision is that the lower levels of which Perry writes are not the lowest, but are rather themselves underlain by files of nonconceptual information, including nonconceptual information with a *de se* content about the subject. And to return to the main theme of this part of the discussion: I also suggest that it is the presence of a nonconceptual form of the first person in conscious states of perception, memory, and action awareness that makes possible a first person concept that is genuinely nondescriptive, and is implicated in a full statement of the role of Perry's epistemic/pragmatic relations.

Feature (4): Explaining Specific Rational Links. A fourth reason for thinking that the nonconceptual first person contributes to the nature of the first person concept is that under the hypothesis that it does so, we can explain some facts about the rationality of certain first person judgements. Consider a subject's informational state when the state of his nonconceptual file on himself represents him as f (say, as in front of a tree). I continue to use the notation of lower-case italics for nonconceptual contents, and so in particular to use the notation *i am f* for the nonconceptual first person content just considered. So let us suppose that a subject accepts the nonconceptual content *i am in front of a tree*. Now consider the conceptual first person way of thinking, *I*. Consider also a predicative concept F whose nature is such that if an object falls under the nonconceptual f, it also falls under the predicative concept F. The nonconceptual contents of perceptual experience are related to observational predicative concepts in this way. Suppose the subject's representational state containing the nonconceptual *de se* content *i am f* is correct, and suppose too that the subject judges the conceptual content *I am F*, and does so rationally because he is in that nonconceptual state. Then, since the subject that is *f* is the subject who is judging, the judger will have property *f*. But the judger is the reference of *I*, by the reference-rule for the first-person concept. Hence the subject's judgement of the conceptual content *I am F* will be a true judgement (by choice of *F* and its relation to *f*). That is: the correctness of the judged content follows in these circumstances from the reference rule for the first person concept, and the fact that the subject who represents himself as *f* is also the subject who judges the conceptual contents.

The correctness, in these circumstances, of the judgement *I am F* does not rely on any further empirical information about the subject or his mental states. The truth of the judged content *I am F* when the subject possesses the correct representation with the nonconceptual content *i am f* follows from the nature of the contents involved. Now in other cases, when the truth-preserving character of a transition is founded in the nature of the contents involved, without reliance on further empirical or other non-obvious information about the concepts, that is apparently a sufficient explanation of the rationality of the transition. This was the general position for which I argued in *The Realm of Reason* (2004). I suggest that structurally the same explanation applies here too. So under this approach, the rationality of certain first person judgements is properly grounded in the acceptance of the contents of events and states with nonconceptual *de se* contents.

In the discussion in this section so far, we have been concerned with nonconceptual *de se* states that represent the thinker as having a particular location in the spatial world. But the thinker-rule for the concept *I* can still get a grip when the subject, though having a brain, does not have a body. If the first person concept, as used on any particular occasion, refers to a subject of this sort, there will not, contrary to many other theories of these matters, be any intrinsic difficulty in the idea of a subject who thinks about himself using the first person concept, and coherently wonders whether he has a body. He may speculate truly that he does not. He may speculate that some illusion is being produced in him. His speculation is true if the thinker, the subject, producing this very thinking does not have a body. Similarly, consider the subject in Daniel Dennett's (1978) fantasy, the subject whose brain is in Houston and is connected with now one, now another, and sometimes with no, distant body. This subject may wonder, in thought using the first person concept, 'Will I have a body today? If so, I wonder which one it will be?' This subject's later experience could supply a clear answer to this apparently entirely intelligible question. I suggest that to explain its intelligibility and the bearing of later experience, we need all three of the thinker-rule for the first person concept, the notion of subject-reflexive conscious states, and the constitutive links between the nonconceptual and the conceptual forms of the first person that will later be relied upon when the subject is hooked up to a particular body that day.

Now we can return to Evans' and Rödl's claim that first person reference 'depends on a knowledge-providing relationship with an object'. That the availability of a genuine first person concept will imply the existence of a knowledge-providing relationship with an object is something that follows from the various constraints and claims I have made. The operation of an integrating apparatus will in normal circumstances, when all is functioning properly, cause a subject to be in nonconceptual states with a *de se* content that are reliable in what they represent as holding of that very same subject. These nonconceptual states can make rational first person judgements by the subject.

When the conceptual contents of those judgements are appropriately related to the nonconceptual contents of the rationalizing states in the ways we have just been discussing, the judgements will be knowledge. On this approach it is right to see an internal connection between grasp of the first person conceptual content and first person knowledge, but the nature of that connection is derivative from the following sources: the fundamental reference rules for conceptual first person content; the fundamental reference rule for nonconceptual *de se* content; and the relations, including those involving the integrating apparatus, between *de se* content and the subject whose *de se* states they are.

I conjecture that these links, in the special case of the first person and ways of coming to know first person contents, are an instance of something much more general. For a wide range of concepts and ways of coming to know contents containing those concepts, the status of those ways as ways of gaining knowledge can be explained as derivative from the condition for grasping the concept. If this general conjecture is correct, the attempt given here to explain these connections between the first person and ways of coming to know should be seen as carrying through a derivation of a sort we should be able to do in many other cases too.

Some writers are very sceptical that we can learn much about first person thought by considering conscious states that can be present in subjects that are not capable of first person thought. Here are two pertinent passages from Sebastian Rödl. Note that in these passages by 'self-consciousness' Rödl means the capacity to employ the first person concept. (We will be using that word with a more restricted application in later chapters. The present issue is not at all terminological.) In the case of one particular class of conscious events, sensations, Rödl writes, 'Reflection on the nature of sensation cannot reveal how it is that sensation is represented in first person thought, because sensation is present in animals that are not self-conscious. If, in animals with thought, sensation is represented first personally, then this is because, first, the power of thought includes a power of first person knowledge and, secondly, sensation is caught up in thought in such a way as to be brought within the purview of this power. Therefore, the first thing we must consider in order to understand self-consciousness is thought, not sensation' (2007: 11).

Before considering the particular case of sensation, I want to consider a partially parallel argument about perception that would run thus: 'Reflection on the nature of perceptual content cannot reveal anything about first person conceptual content, because perception is present in animals that are not self-conscious. If, in animals with thought, perception does have a first person content, then this is because, first, the power of thought includes a power of first person knowledge and secondly, the content of perception is caught up in thought in such a way as to be brought within the purview of this power. Therefore, the first thing we must consider in order to understand self-consciousness is thought, not perception'. As I said, this is really is only a partial parallel. (The strict parallel would be with the representation of perception itself in thought.) But it is a general form of reasoning I want to consider. It seems to me that in this partially parallel reasoning, there are various true premises: that perception is present in animals who lack the first person concept; the power of thought includes a power of first person knowledge; and the content of perception is caught up in thought in such a way as to be brought within the purview of the power of thought. But if what I have said earlier in this material is along the right lines, the conclusion is false. We can learn a great deal about the nature of the first person concept by considering its relations to the more primitive nonconceptual *de se*. The true premises in this partially parallel reasoning here do not at all undermine that conclusion. They do not do so, because it may be that one cannot understand philosophically the nature of the first person concept without considering its various constitutive relations to the nonconceptual *de se* intentional content.

In the particular case of sensations that Rödl is addressing, I agree that the power to self-ascribe sensations must be elucidated by a theory of first person thought. But it does not follow that the nature of sensation, or of conscious states more generally, is irrelevant to a theory of such knowledgeable self-ascription. On the position I have offered, the sensation must be a sensation of a subject; the sensation as a conscious event (part of its nature) can be a reason for applying a sensation concept to oneself, using the first person concept; and the subject to which the first person refers is the same subject who enjoys the sensation. It seems to me that drawing on the nature of first person thought and drawing on the nature of conscious states and events that are available also to fully nonconceptual subjects in elucidating present tense first person ascriptions are in no way exclusive approaches. It seems to me that we need to draw on both.

Rödl also writes, 'sensation does not constitute the kind of subjectivity we call self-consciousness' (12). I agree of course that having the capacity for first person thought goes beyond merely being a subject with sensations (and being a subject who enjoys other states with nonconceptual content). But it does not follow that a subject who in fact has concepts, including the first person concept, in enjoying a sensation is not in one of the same subjective states as a subject who does not have concepts and is enjoying the sensation. As far as I can tell, Rödl seems to think that it does follow. He writes, 'Acts of sensibility of a thinking subject are part of the content of her self-consciousness, which shows that, in her, the nexus of subject and sensation has a different form from the one it has in an animal without thought' (12). I would say on the contrary that that last-mentioned nexus—that between subject and sensation—is the same in the thinking subject and in the animal without thought. There is no need to deny this to acknowledge what is special about first person thought. The additional layer of thought and conceptualized *de se* consciousness is built upon a nexus common to the conceptual and to the nonconceptual cases.[4]

---

[4] Though the formulation is not essential to Rödl's point, I myself would not write of 'acts of sensibility'. Sensibility is passive: sensations, and perceptual experiences too, are not

We can acknowledge this provided we recognize a notion of a subject of consciousness that is, philosophically, explanatorily prior to the notion of first person thought. It is this more primitive notion of a subject that is employed in the modified Nagelian characterization of consciousness, in terms of there being something it's like for the subject. As before, if this more primitive notion of a subject is rejected, I do not know on what notion of consciousness both the animals without thought and concept-using creatures are uniformly counted as conscious, in the same sense.

That concludes the discussion of the four phenomena—the expression and description of nonconceptual *de se* states, the genuinely indexical character of the *I* concepts, and its specific rational links—that can be explained if we take it that the nature of the first person concept is to be elucidated in part by its relation to the nonconceptual *de se*. I suggest, for these reasons, that it should be so elucidated.

3. Issues of Acquaintance

This discussion has so far left hanging the issue of whether a relation of acquaintance is playing any part in this account of the *de se*. We already saw that Kripke holds that self-acquaintance plays an essential part in understanding the first person pronoun. Kripke also writes, 'The doctrine of acquaintance is much less explicit in Frege than in Russell, but I have long believed that it is needed for a proper understanding of him' (2011b: 289).

For what it is worth, I think Frege's own writings are neutral on this issue if we operate *au pied de la lettre*. The famous sentence in 'Der Gedanke' says 'Nur ist jeder sich selbst in einer besonderen und ursprünglichen Weise gegeben'—now everyone is given to himself in a particular and original way (1967: 350). The talk of being given in a certain way is something Frege uses quite generally for all senses, including those that are clearly descriptive, such the sense of 'the intersection of lines *a* and *b*'. The passage in which he introduces the notion of sense in general, in 'Über Sinn und Bedeutung', speaks of a 'kind of being given': 'was ich den Sinn des Zeichens nennen möchte, worin die Art des

---

mental acts. This means that the explanation of their occurrence on particular occasions is something of a different kind from those events that are mental acts, which are done for reasons.

Gegebenseins enthalten ist' (1967: 144). Immediately following that sentence he mentions, as an example of two different ways of 'being given', the senses associated with 'the intersection of a and b' and 'the intersection of b and c'. Those are descriptive senses. It would be quite implausible to claim that acquaintance with the relevant intersections is required to grasp these definite descriptions. So the famous sentence 'Nur ist jeder . . . ' seems to be using an entirely general notion of a way of being given, a general notion that covers all of descriptive, indexical, and demonstrative senses. All the same, nothing excludes combining what Frege actually says with an acquaintance-based account of the nature of first person sense, and perhaps we really ought to do so. The combination certainly has the potential to explain why it should be the case that, as Frege says, the thinker is given to no one else in that distinctive way, 'wie er keinem andern gegeben ist' (1967: 350). So, let us address the question: whatever is actually in Frege's texts, should we think of acquaintance as the relation which makes available *de se* content in thought and other mental states?

'Acquaintance' is a term of art, and needs some substantive explication. David Lewis probably writes for many when he says of the relation of acquaintance that underlies cases of *de re* belief in general that 'in each case, I and the one of whom I have beliefs *de re* are so related that there is an extensive causal dependence of my states upon his; and this causal dependence is of a sort apt for the reliable transmission of information' (1979: 542). On the next page of the same article, he writes, 'Certainly identity is a relation of acquaintance par excellence. So belief *de se* falls under belief *de re*' (1979: 543). The condition of causal dependence of the thinker's states upon the object, and the aptness condition, work well for perceptual and memory-based ways in which an object may be given to a thinker. They can plausibly be adapted for recognitionally based ways. But how well does this account of acquaintance work for the case of the *de se* ways?

In some respects it seems a stretch. I do not doubt that many of your states, including your beliefs, are causally dependent upon your own earlier states, and are so in a way that meets Lewis's aptness condition. But is that what *makes* you capable of representing yourself in the first person way? In the perceptual case, we are very clear that when a perceptual experience, and corresponding perceptual beliefs, are not causally dependent upon the state and relations of a particular object, the experience is not of that object, and beliefs based upon the experience by taking it at face value are not about that object. Nothing quite like that seems to apply in the case of the first person. Precisely what Descartes emphasized was that even if my experiences are not caused by the states of my body, or even by my earlier mental states, any *de se* component they may have nevertheless still refers. Certainly for beliefs about one's physical states and relations, it seems that one can be radically mistaken, and those beliefs need not be causally dependent upon one's own physical states and relations for the *de se* component of the content of one's mental states to continue to refer, and to refer to oneself. A fortiori, if there is no such causal dependence of the beliefs, there is no causal dependence satisfying an aptness condition. I think Descartes was right in holding that while the evil demon could make it seem to you that certain perceptual demonstratives pick out objects in your environment, when in fact they do not, the evil demon could not produce an illusion that the *de se* content refers, when in fact it does not. Descartes was right that the *de se* contents of a mental state could not fail to refer (on which, more in Chapter VI). On any particular occasion, at least, causal linkages of your *de se* physical beliefs to your actual physical states do not seem to be required for the *de se* content to refer, and to refer to you.

The same seems to be true for the present tense way of being given, *now*, and the present time. I do not doubt that in fact a huge range of your present experiences with a present tense content, and a huge range of your present tense beliefs, are causally dependent on the way the world is now (or at least was a moment ago, a qualification I will ignore, though it raises significant issues). But we should ask again: is that causal dependence what *makes* your experiences and beliefs have a present tense content? The evil demon can deceive you extensively about what is the case right now, and make your present tense experiences and beliefs dependent on matters other than how the present time is. But your present tense beliefs would still be about the present time, be the causal dependence as it may. Though to the best of my knowledge he did not say so, Descartes could equally have argued 'I am thinking, therefore now, the present time, exists'.

An enthusiast for the account of acquaintance in terms of a certain kind of causal dependence might try to restrict the account, and give a special place to the dependence of a thinker's beliefs about his conscious mental states upon his actual mental states. But a thinker may still refer to himself using the first person even if he lacks any mental concepts, and has no beliefs about his physical properties caused by his possession of those properties. Neo, the character in the film *The Matrix*, may begin to suspect that nothing apparently around him is real. He may think, 'None of these things is real. So what am I, what kind of thing am I?' Here he still succeeds in referring to himself, but not because his beliefs about his physical states are caused by his physical states, and not because of his use of any concepts of the mental.

The cases of *The Matrix* and of Cartesian deception are extreme, but they serve to make vivid a point that also gets a grip in much less extreme cases. It seems to be the case that the *de se* way of thinking is always distinct from any way of thinking grounded in acquaintance relations that are a matter of causal dependence. As is famously the case, the thought *I am identical with that F*, where *that F* is either a perceptual demonstrative, or a memory demonstrative, or a recognitional notion or concept, seems always to be potentially informative, provided that the demonstrative or recognitional notion or concept does not embed the first person itself. The relations in virtue of which the first person has the reference it does are distinct from the causal-dependence relations that ground these other demonstrative and recognitional notions.

From these considerations it does not at all follow that an acquaintance-based account of the *de se* is false. It follows only that a mode of acquaintance that is explicated in terms of causal dependence on the model of perception, memory, and testimony is not the basis of the *de se*. There may be modes of acquaintance other than these paradigms. I conclude this chapter with some noncommittal reflections on how such a position might be developed.

One natural suggestion is that there is a constitutive mode of acquaintance, made available by consciousness. If a subject is in a conscious state, then by Thomas Nagel's modified characterization, there is something it is like for the subject of that state. We can distinguish a class of strictly conscious states such that the nature of those states is fully settled, constitutively, by what it is like to be in those states. These states do not consist of conscious states plus some further condition not involving consciousness of the subject in question. For these strictly conscious states, what it is like for the subject, when the subject is in such a state, settles as a constitutive and epistemic matter that he, thought of in the first person way, is in the relevant state, thought of in a certain canonical way. Here we seem to have something that is both a mode of acquaintance, but which also has constitutive elements, and in which causation is involved in a way that differs from the paradigms of perception, memory, and testimony.

It is a mode of acquaintance, because there is still a causal dependence of the thinker's judgements and beliefs about his strictly conscious states on those conscious states themselves. The mental states both cause and make rational the thinker's self-ascription of the strictly conscious states. But we also have a constitutive variety of acquaintance, in that what makes the judgement one about the subject is not the causal antecedents of the mental state that causes and makes rational the self-ascription of the mental state. There is a doubly constitutive feature here. First, the strictly conscious mental state must have a subject, as discussed in the metaphysics of the conscious at the start of Chapter III. Second, it follows from constitutive features of the first person that when a thinker makes a self-ascription of a conscious state on the basis of enjoying that conscious state, the agent of the self-ascription must be the subject enjoying that state, and so the first person must refer to the subject enjoying that state. The fact that the use of the first person refers to the subject enjoying the state is not at all rooted in the nature of the causal antecedents of the state. This is a kind of limiting, special case of acquaintance.

On this approach, the first person is always and constitutively a genuinely indexical way of thinking of a subject, because of this fulfillment of constitutive and epistemic conditions. States with first person content do often, but do not necessarily, have the informational links required to provide information about a particular living body. The first person may, but does not need to be, an indexical way of thinking about an embodied person.

Founding the *de se* in constitutive acquaintance also provides an explanation of Frege's second feature of *de se* content, that the subject is not given to anyone else in the distinctive way that he is given to himself. That follows, on the account of constitutive acquaintance, because no one else can stand to his strictly conscious mental states in the relation that their subject can.

This form of acquaintance does not involve any kind of perception of the subject by himself. All the features that distinguish perceptual ways of being given from the *de se* militate against such a view. The view that founds the *de se* in constitutive acquaintance also contributes to the explanation of the fact that even in the presence of the evil demon's activities, the *de se* still secures a reference, and one that the subject can know to have conscious properties; for it is by such conscious properties that the subject stands in a constitutive acquaintance relation to himself. It also contributes to the explanation of the difference between the *de se* way of being given and perception-based ways of being given in more ordinary, everyday cases.

Since this treatment is one on which constitutive acquaintance is more fundamental, in the order of philosophical explanation, than grasp of the *de se*, it is very naturally married to various further claims about understanding of the first person. One of those claims is that a subject's being in a certain kind of conscious state, or enjoying a conscious event of a certain kind, gives the subject good reason for self-ascribing (that is making a *de se* ascription) a state or event of that kind (under a canonical concept of that state or event-kind). Another such claim is that the principle about good reason for self-ascription stated in the first claim is something that is partially constitutive of grasp of the conceptual *de se* and the relevant concepts of psychological states and events. The marriage is natural, because these two claims relate the *de se*, something at the level of intentional content, to the possession of properties by the subject him or herself, something at the level of reference.

If this combination of views about constitutive acquaintance and the *de se* is correct, it positively supports another of Kripke's claims, that 'self-acquaintance is more fundamental than anything purely linguistic, and is the basis of our use of first person locutions' (320). To look forward to an issue we will pursue in more detail later, this combination of views also stands in contrast with the claims of those who try to explain ownership of a conscious mental event in terms of the possibility of *de se* ascription, such as Strawson in *The Bounds of Sense* (1966: 97–112, esp. p.100). The combination also contrasts with the rather different theorists, such as Anscombe, who say that for the first person concept, there is no reference, and that 'With "I" there is only the use' (1975: 59).[5]

---

[5] Strawson's views are discussed in more detail in chapter VIII below. There is a case to be made that Elizabeth Anscombe's various claims on the matter entail that self-ascription is philosophically more fundamental than the subject's possession of the property picked out by the concept self-ascribed. Although she held that 'I' does not refer, there is certainly for her such a thing as the use of 'I'; as noted in the text above, that is all there is, according to Anscombe. It is presumably in terms of this 'use' that locutions such as 'This experience belongs to me' are to be explained.

To say that a subject's ability to think of him or herself in a *de se* way is founded on an acquaintance relation elucidated in terms of conscious states is not to imply that the subject so thought about has only mental properties—is only a thinking thing, and not an extended thing, as Descartes might have put it. As I said earlier, if subjects also have physical properties such as location, then *de se* ascriptions of those properties will be correct, and are potentially knowable. Equally, to say that a perceptual mode of presentation is grounded in a perceptual relation is not at all to imply that the object perceived has only perceptible properties. What other properties an object given in a certain way may or may not have depends on the correct metaphysics of the object so given. That is not an epistemic or cognitive matter. No doubt the case of subjects is special in several interesting respects, but the general principle still applies.

As I said, I intend these remarks on a non-causal notion of acquaintance to be non-committal. Their truth or falsity is independent of the main claims of this book. But they do suggest a way in which a theorist who wants to give a central role to acquaintance in an account of the first person could integrate such a role into the main theses for which I have been arguing.

V

Explaining First Person Phenomena

So far I have proposed an account of first person content, both of the conceptual and the nonconceptual kinds, and discussed the metaphysics of the objects referred to by uses and occurrences of the first person. I now turn to putting these accounts to some explanatory work, in particular in epistemology.

Whenever there are phenomena distinctive of a given concept, a good theory of that concept should contribute to an explanation of those phenomena. This general point applies in the special case in which the phenomena are those that have come to be known as immunity to error through misidentification, and the concept in question is the first person concept *I*. The general point implies that there must exist an explanation of these immunity phenomena, an explanation that draws on a theory of the first person concept. My aim in this chapter is to offer such an explanation; and to consider some rivals to the proposed explanation.

Epistemological phenomena are not the only phenomena for which a theory of the first person must provide an account. Even within epistemology itself, there are further phenomena distinctive of the first person to be explained, beyond cases of immunity to error through misidentification. My hope is that the techniques and points used in the treatment of such immunity can also be employed more widely.

1. Explaining Immunity to Error through Misidentification

I will continue to take it that a concept is individuated by its fundamental reference rule, and that the first person concept *I* is individuated by the thinker-rule:

What makes someone the reference of *I* in a thinking is that he or she is the producer of that thinking.

The characterization of immunity to error through misidentification to be used in the explanation needs rather more discussion. A notion of immunity to error through misidentification, together with an appreciation of its generality and significance, was first introduced in philosophy by Sidney Shoemaker in his justly famous paper 'Self-Reference and Self-Awareness' (1968). Various forms of the notion were distinguished in Shoemaker's later writings, and their significance was discussed in Gareth Evans' *The Varieties of Reference*. The form of the notion pertinent here needs three relativizations. The relevant notion is that of a judgement with the content *Fa* being immune to error through misidentification

(a) relative to the particular occurrence of *a* in the content,
(b) when the judgement is reached in a certain way W, and
(c) in normal circumstances.

We will confine our attention here to first person contents containing only a single occurrence of the first person in the content. So we can dispense, for present purposes, with the relativization (a). We can then consider the following two tables of examples. In the first column of the first table, we have examples of judgements of contents which are immune in the intended sense to misidentification in normal circumstances, when they are made on the basis of the reasons or ways specified in second column:

Table 1

Content	Way
I feel hungry	Feeling of hunger
I'm in front of a desk	Perceptual experience of being in front of a desk
I once stood on a glacier	Personal memory of standing on a glacier
My arm is broken	Visual experience of your own broken arm, seen as part of your own body

As Shoemaker emphasized, immunity to error through misidentification does not have to involve infallibility or incorrigibility. The judgements that you are in front of a desk, that you once stood on a glacier, that your arm is broken, are none of them infallible when they come to be made in the ways indicated in the corresponding entries in the second column.

In the second table, we have judgements not immune to misidentification in normal circumstances, relative to the specified way:

Table 2

Content	Way
My arm is broken	Arm seen in tangle of limbs, post-accident
I have a Roman nose	Visual experience of silhouette of nose taken to be your own
My cellphone is ringing	Auditory experience of a cellphone ringing
I was in Athens	Seeing a photo of someone looking like you in front of the Acropolis

Shoemaker's original characterization of immunity to error through misidentification was in modal terms (1968: 557). Adapting his formulation, which was given in terms of language, to the case of thought, and restricting it to the first person, we obtain this characterization of the relevant immunity: it is not possible to reach the judgement *I'm F* in question in way W in normal circumstances and to be right thereby that something is *F*, but wrong about whether it is oneself that is *F*. Formulations that replace 'be right' with 'know' are also possible and illuminating. This modal criterion classifies a large number of examples correctly, including those Wittgenstein famously gave in *The Blue Book*, in which he distinguished uses of 'I' as subject (immune to misidentification) from uses of 'I' as object (not so immune) (1958: 66–7). When I see a broken arm in a tangle of arms post-accident, and judge *My arm is broken*, it is possible for me to be right that some arm is broken, but be wrong that my arm is broken. When I judge that I have a Roman nose on the basis of the shape of a seen shadow of a face in profile, I may be right that someone has a Roman nose, but be wrong that I have a Roman nose. By contrast, when in entirely normal circumstances, I have a perceptual experience as of being in front of a desk, it is not possible for me to be right that someone is in front of a desk, but wrong that it is me. It is not possible, when in entirely normal circumstances I have a feeling of hunger, that I am right that someone is hungry, but wrong that it is me.

All the same, the modal criterion is not quite right. Suppose, for one reason or another, that in normal circumstances mirrors were always entirely flat, and that they only reflected faces very close to the mirror, so that in those normal circumstances, for any person x, only x can see the face and head of x in the mirror. In those circumstances, it would not be possible for someone, basing his judgement on what he sees in the mirror, to be right that someone's hair is tidy, but wrong that his hair is tidy. Nonetheless this judgement still rests on acceptance of a substantive empirical identity, that that person seen in the mirror is he himself. So an improved criterion should include this requirement: the thinker's judgement *I'm F* is immune to error through misidentification when reached in way W only if there is no individual concept m distinct from I such that the thinker, in reaching the judgement in way W, relies on the thinker's identity belief $I = m$. Then, when mistakes about which thing is F are really possible, that will be so because it is a real possibility that the thinker's identity belief $I = m$ is false. But even when, as in the mirror case as just described, there is no real possibility that $I = m$ is false, nonetheless the thinker's belief *My hair is tidy* rests upon his belief *I am that person in the mirror*.

So let us take this as criterion for immunity to error through misidentification of a judgement *I'm F*, when reached in a certain way: a thinker can rationally come to make the judgement in that way without relying on some identity $I = m$, for some individual mode of presentation m distinct from the first person. This formulation is in terms of rationality, but plausibly equivalent formulations could be given in terms of knowledge, given the connections between rationality and knowledge. In paradigm cases of first person immunity to error through misidentification, you can know *I am F* without reliance on any substantive empirical identity involving yourself. Further refinements are possible, but they do not affect the explanation I will be offering of the *de se* epistemic phenomena. Our announced task then becomes that of explaining first person immunity to misidentification, so understood, from the nature of the first person concept, characterized as above.

Why should there be such an explanation? Could the kinds of cases in which there is first person immunity to misidentification simply be given by a list, not unified by any underlying principle? This would be a form of minimalist position about immunity to misidentification. Perhaps the most fundamental difficulty with such a minimalism is that the phenomena of immunity to misidentification do not seem to be arbitrary, unprincipled add-ons to first person thought. Once it is given that it is the first person concept that is being employed in a judgement, and that judgement is reached in a certain way in normal circumstances, it seems to be already settled, for instance in the examples listed in the table above, whether or not the judgement is vulnerable to error through misidentification. If someone claims there can be a use of the first person that is the same first person concept as ours, but claims that because of different conventions, judgements that we do not now classify as immune to misidentification would be so (or vice versa), it seems impossible to fill in any detail of such an alleged possibility.

There is here not merely a parallel, but an actual identity, with an argument that can be applied to the status of certain contents as a priori. Being a priori is evidently a matter of epistemic status. For the case of the a priori too, we can equally formulate a version of minimalism. And there too, the minimalism is faced with exactly the same problem it faces in the case of immunity to misidentification. It does not seem to be merely an add-on to a concept that certain contents containing it have an a priori status. It seems, rather, that once we have fixed the identity of the concept in question, the status of contents containing it as a priori or not is thereby settled. In both the case of the a priori and the case of immunity to misidentification, we have a philosophical obligation to say how it is so settled. In short, in both the case of immunity to misidentification and the case of the a priori, we should aim to give what I have called a metasemantic explanation of the phenomena (Peacocke 1993, 2000): an explanation that turns on the meanings or the intentional contents involved.

Here are two sample explanations of first person immunity to misidentification on a metasemantic view.

Example One: here the judgement is *I feel hungry*, made in normal circumstances, and on the rational basis of an experience as of hunger.

In such a case, the following hold:

(a) The judgement is true iff the thinker of the thought feels hungry (by the fundamental reference rule for the first person).

(b) The concept *feels hungry* is such that an experience as of hunger makes reasonable self-ascription of the concept by a subject having such an experience.

Hence, an experience of hunger, in the very same subject who is making the judgement, makes reasonable his judgement *I feel hungry*.

In being a concept whose instantiation makes reasonable a self-ascription by the subject, the concept *feels hungry* is one of several kinds that are in a more general sense anchored in the subject. (This more general sense I discuss further in Chapter VIII, Section 2 below.) The displayed explanation of the rationality of the judgement does not at any point appeal to the rationality of a judgement on the part of the thinker $I = m$, for some mode of presentation m distinct from the first person concept. So the explanation accounts for the immunity to error through misidentification of *I feel hungry*, when made as specified, under the characterization of such immunity on which we settled a few paragraphs back.

A corresponding explanation can also be given of why the judgement is true when it comes to be made in this way. The explanation involves the point that an experience as of hunger is sufficient for feeling hungry. This explanation of truth also does not rely on the correctness of any accepted content $I = m$, for some mode of presentation m distinct from the first person concept.

This explanation of why the judgement *I feel hungry* is immune to error through misidentification is not intended to be a description of something going on in the mind of the ordinary thinker who comes to judge, on the basis of his experience of hunger, that he is hungry. No such explanation need be present to his mind. The explanation is in the first instance rather one which explains why the norms are as they are. It is an explanation of why there can be good reason for making a judgement *I feel hungry* in this way, and why there is no vulnerability to misidentification when the judgement is so made.

Example Two: here the judgement is *I'm in front of a desk*, made in normal circumstances, on the rational basis of a visual experience as of being in front of a desk.

In this example, all of the following hold:

(a) The judgement is true iff the thinker is in front of a desk (by the fundamental reference rule for *I*).

(b) A subject has a spatial or material property iff the subject's body has that property (by a plausible constitutive account of what it is for a subject to have such properties).

(c) The subject's body is the body from which he perceives, the body over which he has action control (by the constitutive account of what makes something the subject's body).

(d) In ordinary circumstances, a perceptual experience, from the point of view of one's perceptual apparatus, as of one's own body being in front of a desk makes rational the judgement that that body is in front of a desk.

Hence, the visual experience makes rational the judgement *I'm in front of a desk*.

In this explanation of the rationality of the judgement, (c) is indeed an identity, but it is a constitutive and a priori truth. There is also reliance on, or better perhaps a presupposition of, the content *I am the person with this body*. But the holding of that too is something characteristic of normal conditions (a form of the proposition holds for any normal person in relation to his body in normal circumstances). There is no reliance on empirical propositions, which may or may not hold for arbitrary humans subjects in normal circumstances, such as *I am that person in the photograph*, or *I am the author of such-and-such book* or *I am the owner of the ringing cellphone*.

The explanation of the correctness of the judgement *I'm in front of a desk*, when it comes to be made in this way, does not involve any such empirical identities. It relies only on (a) through (c) in this explanation, together with the fact that in normal circumstances, an experience as of being in front of a desk is sufficient for point of view enjoyed in the experience really being one that is in front of a desk. Why there is an entitlement to take such perceptual experiences at face value is a debated matter; that there is such an entitlement is all we need for the present point.

On the account I am offering, in the explanation of the rationality of a thinker's judgment *My left arm is straight*, when made on the basis of proprioceptive experience of one's arm being straight, there would be analogues of each of (a) and (d) above, and of the same principles (b) and (c). The treatment of Example Two instantiates a model applicable in a wide range of cases.

One can conceive of a more austere formulation of the explanation in Example Two. *I'm in front of a desk* could be judged truly, and known in a way immune to error through misidentification, even if someone is not experiencing his body at all, and had only a moving point of view on the world, without experiencing it as the point of view from within a body. In such a case, we would not need to make reference to the body and material properties in (b) and (c). We would need only the point, of constitutive status, that a thinker's first person spatial predication is true iff the thinking subject has a point of view on the world, a point of view of which the relevant spatial predicate holds.

It is noteworthy that the treatment in these two examples does not rely on any premise to the effect that a subject referred to by the first person must be essentially or fundamentally embodied. The derivations rely only on the premise that when a subject is embodied, certain equivalences hold between first person spatial or material predications and predications of the subject's body. The derivations are thus not as deeply committed to embodiment as is Evans's position in the chapter on Self-Identification in *The Varieties of Reference*. The derivations are consistent with a wider view of the possibilities for subjects of consciousness, a wider view that still respects the metaphysical principles given in Chapter III above, on which subjects must have an integrating apparatus on which their identities are dependent.

2. Can We Dispense with First Person Notions and Concepts?

A rival approach to these issues holds that we can explain the immunity phenomena without appeal to the nature of the first person concept. This rival approach is motivated by the thesis that there is no distinctive first person concept, so a fortiori the first person concept cannot explain anything. This competing thesis need not be claiming that there are not distinctive features of mental states picked out using the first person pronoun. The thesis is rather that none of these distinctive features require a theory that appeals to a first person concept. The features can, according to the rival account, all be explained in some other way. Such a competing approach to immunity to misidentification and the thesis that there is no need in our theory for a first person concept have been endorsed in a resourceful and challenging series of papers by John Perry (see especially 2002a and 2002b). I turn to a consideration of Perry's account.

Perry suggests that ways of knowing that are immune to misidentification are just a special case of what he calls 'normally R-informative ways of knowing'. He writes, 'A perceptual state S is a normally self-informative way of knowing that one is ϕ if the fact that a person is in state S normally carries the information that the person in state S is ϕ and normally does not carry the information that any other person is ϕ' (2002a: 204). This is certainly an account that does not draw on a theory of a first person concept or notion. But it does not apply in all cases. It is not a sufficient condition of a perceptual state's being a normally self-informative way of knowing *I'm* ϕ. Consider a judgement with the content *I am in central neural state N*, where N is the central neural state a normal human being is in when his or her legs are crossed, and N is identified in neurophysiological terms. Take S as the proprioceptive experience of having one's legs crossed. S normally carries the information that the person in state S is in central neural state N, and it normally does not carry the information that any other person is in central neural state N. But being in S is not a normally self-informative way of knowing that one is in neural state N. You are not in a position to know that you are in a neurophysiologically identified state simply by having the proprioceptive experience of your legs being crossed.

Would it be an adequate revision to amend Perry's proposal to a more qualified version which states only that in the cases in which being in S is a way of coming to know *I'm* ϕ, then his condition on carrying information is met? That revision faces two problems. First, it leaves unexplained why some states S are ways of coming to have self-knowledge, while others are not. That is an epistemic fact about *de se* contents that needs explanation. If it is left unexplained, we will not have explained all the *de se* epistemic facts without appeal to the nature of the first person concept. Second, the proposal appeals to the condition that S is a way of coming to know *I'm* ϕ, but this restriction will be insufficient unless we also add that this way is itself immune to error through misidentification with respect to the first person. The experience of looking in a mirror will be a way of coming to know *I'm* ϕ for a range of concepts ϕ, but these will not be cases of knowledge which is immune to error through identification with respect to the first person. But if we add the restriction that S as a way of coming to know *I'm* φ is immune to error through misidentification, that will be circular as part of an attempt to explain the grounds of immunity to error through misidentification.

An alternative revision would be to insist that the perceptual state *S* must be such that when one is in it, that very state presents oneself as φ. Again, that may be true and also avoid the counterexample, but it does so by placing either or both of the *de se* intentional content and first person concept inside the scope of 'presents'. That is, it seems to be using the *de se* and/or the first person concept in precisely the way the approach was intended to explain away, rather than simply employ.

The example of the experience of crossing one's legs and the neural state N at a minimum illustrates the need, in explaining cases of immunity to misidentification, to respect a close connection between three things. They are the concept of the property self-ascribed, the first person concept, and the way that is in question of coming to know self-ascriptions of the property under the given concept of the property. The right kind of connection between these three is lacking in the case of the concept of the neurophysiological property. Treatments of immunity to misidentification that rely on a relation of acquaintance very properly introduce the idea that an acquaintance relation comes with a channel of information (Recanati 2012: 34ff., and references therein). When the relation of identity is said to be a relation of acquaintance par excellence, we can certainly agree with that, in the sense that there are many informational channels in which a subject stands to her own states, physical and mental, present and past. The informational channel presents the state under a distinctive kind of mode of presentation. Nonetheless, not every property a subject possesses at a given time is one that stands in an informational channel, with associated mode of presentation, to that subject at that time (or soon after). The neurophysiological state N, identified under a mode of presentation drawn from neurophysiology, is one such state.

What unifies all the cases of immunity to error through misidentification with respect to the first person? The range of examples of such immunity includes: judgements based on external perception of one's body and its relation to things and events around it; judgements based on internal perception (proprioception) of such properties as bending at the knees; judgements based on action-awareness of events, mental and physical; judgements that are rational reactions to events occurring passively in consciousness, as in 'It occurred to me that he might have missed the plane'; judgements based on propositional and/or autobiographical memory. What distinguishes precisely those judgements that are immune to misidentification with respect to the first person cannot be merely a matter of reliability of method for supplying information about the subject. The example of the experience of crossing one's legs and the neural state N already shows such an account would be too wide. It cannot be a matter of endorsing some mental state with a *de se* representational content. That is present in many cases of immunity, but certainly not in all. It is not present when a self-ascription is rationally made on the basis of a passively occurring thinking (see further Chapter VI). What seem to me to unify all the cases of immunity to misidentification relative to the first person is rather that in each case, there is an explanation, involving the nature of the first person concept, its relation to the predicative concept involved, and the ways of coming to judge that are present in the case, together with the nature of entitlement, an explanation of why there will be no error of misidentification. The explanation is somewhat different in each kind of case. But in all cases, the explanation draws at some point on the nature of the first person concept, as individuated by its fundamental reference rule.

I would offer a similar account of what unifies all the cases in which present tense judgements are immune to error through misidentification with respect to the *now* component of the judgement's content. The explanations of the immunity all draw on the fact that the concept *now* is individuated by its fundamental reference rule, which states that in any thinking in it which it occurs, it refers to the time of that thinking.

The approach to immunity to misidentification that does not appeal to a first person concept, and to what individuates it, is not an approach that comes out of the blue, as an isolated proposal. The proposal (and its analogue for the present tense) is of most interest when it is offered as an instance of the more general thesis already noted, the thesis that there are no phenomena distinctive of ordinary uses of the first person for which we need in a philosophical theory to postulate a special *de se* notion or concept. Here I continue to use 'notion' for nonconceptual content (for ways things, events, properties are given in nonconceptual intentional contents). In the remainder of this chapter, I discuss a series of proposals for explaining the first person phenomena without appealing to a first person concept or notion, and to what individuates it. Once again, the person who has done most to develop the more general thesis is John Perry (2002a). Although I will be disagreeing with his account, I have certainly learned from reflecting on his rich discussions. Some of these proposals are explicitly in his writings, others are proposals it is natural to extract from his explanations.

There are three salient questions we need to address in assessing the more general thesis that we do not need the *de se* intentional content or the first person concept in explaining first person phenomena.

(1) Is it possible to give an account of a subject's file on himself that does not appeal to a first person concept?

(2) Can we dispense with a first person notion or concept in basic cases of action and perception?

(3) Is it possible to give a treatment that adequately describes the role of the first person concept or notion in imagination without postulating a distinctive *de se* notion and concept?

Perry himself has given an affirmative answer to these three questions (2002a, 2002b), supported in the case of his answer to question (1) by Recanati (2012). I take the questions in turn.

(1) As I argued in Chapter II, and as Perry has independently argued, there are purposes for which we need to postulate, for each subject, a mental file that the subject has on himself, his self-file. When a subject comes to believe that he is the F, the mental files that he already has on himself becomes linked with the file that is labeled with the concept or notion *the F*. My own view is that we should regard each subject's self-file as labeled with the first person concept or notion *me*. That is a conception of mental files and their labels that embraces, rather than dispenses with, the first person concepts or notions. It is, in the terminology used back in Chapter II, Section 2, a conception of mental files that is complementary to, rather than reductive of, the level of senses and notions.

A different approach to self-files, an approach that does dispense with any first person concept or notion, might say this: for each subject *x*, what makes something *x*'s self-file is that it is the file which contains information on *x* gained by means that are normally informative about *x*. I have formulated this as a constitutive thesis, about what makes something a self-file, because that is what a philosophical thesis should be claiming. If a position says only something about what properties *de facto* a self-file has, it is not addressing the constitutive question. In the terminology I used in Chapter II, Section 2, the approach just suggested is an instance of the more radical treatment of the relation between mental files and sense, rather than one that regards sense and mental files as complementary components of a theory.

It should be common ground between these two approaches to the first person concept and mental files that each individual has several self-files, even individuals who are not subject to some kind of internal dissociations. As we noted in Chapter II, a subject will have a phenomenological file on himself, a file whose contents specify how he seems to himself to be. Some of these seemings may be overruled by judgement—he may judge some of these seemings to be illusory—so we must distinguish the phenomenological file from the file whose contents specify what he accepts about himself. The issue between the rival approaches is not over the multiplicity of self-files for a given person, but of whether we need to use a first person notion or concept in a constitutive account of them.

My objection to the proposal is that, for a given subject x, there is no such thing as *the* file which contains information on x gained by means that are normally informative about x. When files are labeled either by concepts or by notions, there is more than one such file. Consider the file with the label *the person who normally has this body*, where *this body* is a mode of presentation of a body given by a subject's current proprioception, and by his current visual and tactile perception of his body. For a particular person x, this file does in fact contain information on x gained by means that are normally informative about x. But this file and the self-file can become unlinked in any of the following four ways.

(i) For a subject with no proprioception, and no other perception of his own body (in a sensory deprivation tank, for instance, with his proprioception blocked), there is nothing for a perceptual-demonstrative *this body* to refer to. But this subject's use of *I* still refers in these circumstances. As Anscombe (1975) says, the subject may think to himself *I will make sure I don't get into this situation again*. The predicate or concept *not perceiving anything now* will, at the time the subject is in this deprived state, enter the subject's self-file. But this subject will have no file labeled with the concept *the person who normally has this body*. The self-file and the file labeled with *the person who normally has this body* have different conditions of existence; so they are distinct. Both files meet the condition that in actual circumstances, they contain information on the subject that is gained by means that is normally informative about the subject.

(ii) In Dennett's examples, already mentioned, in his paper 'Where Am I?', a subject can very reasonably wonder, 'Am I the person who normally has this body?' (1978). In some of the possible worlds Dennett describes, the answer to this question is negative. The subject's brain may be hooked up by radio links to perceptual and proprioceptive input from a body that is not normally his own.

(iii) For those familiar with the film *The Matrix*: the principal character Neo initially does not realize that he is in a software-induced illusory world. He seems to have a body in that illusory world, but these seemings are not genuine perceptions of his own actual body. As used by Neo when in the illusory world, the concept *the person who normally has this body* fails to denote, for *this body* so used fails to denote. But Neo's use of *I* continues to refer in the illusory world (as we can imagine Descartes insisting), when for instance he thinks 'It looks to me as if I am approaching a payphone'. When Neo comes to discover his situation, he will not even attempt to form a file labeled *the person who normally has this body* when he is having experiences as of the illusory software-induced world. But he will continue to have first person beliefs and to have a self-file. When he discovers that his initial experiences were illusory, he discovers that there is no such person as the person who normally had the body he seemed to experience. He does not discover that he did not then exist. He did exist then.

(iv) In an imagined language in an example developed by Anscombe (1975), a person truly utters 'A is F' iff 'A' is the letter written on the inside of his wrist and the person with 'A' written there is F. Some of the points I have been making are entirely analogous to the one Anscombe makes when she insists, rightly in my view, that in her example of the 'A'-users, 'A' does not mean the same as the first person pronoun. For each person x in Anscombe's imagined community, x's 'A'-file will contain information on x gained by means that are normally informative about x. It does not follow that a subject's 'A'-file is his self-file.

Would it help the proposal to revise it to say: for each subject x, x's self-file is the file which contains information on x gained by means that are normally self-informative (that is, y-informative for any subject y) for normal members of x's species? This would not cover all the examples. Perceptual experience is normally self-informative for normal members of the subject's species in examples (i), (ii) and (iv) above, so those counterexamples still apply. Even in *The Matrix* example, we can alter it so that Neo is the first human to be subject to the illusions of the software world. So perceptual experience is then still normally self-informative for normal members of his species—it is just not self-informative for him. His use of the first person still refers when he is in the illusory world in the example thus modified; his use of *this body* still fails to refer; and when he comes to discover his situation, he will have no file associated with the concept *the person who normally has this body*. He will still have a self-file.

An alternative proposal that purports to offer a self-file without a first person concept or notion is this: for each person named NN, the file labeled with the name NN can be his self-file. John Perry writes, 'there is only one person I will ever be identical with, myself. I never have to unlink my self-buffer from my John Perry notion. It can be a self-notion; it can just be my self-buffer. Accumulating information in one's self-buffer for life is valid, unlike accumulating in one's here buffer longer than one stays in one place' (2002a: 212). This proposal could not apply to all cases, because a person can have a self-file without having any proper name at all. But even for subjects who do have proper names, it does not work. It may in some sense be 'valid' for John Perry to put information about himself into his 'John Perry' file, but it will not in all cases be epistemically justified for him to do so, and in some cases it may be irrational. As we know from other cases that Perry has discussed, if Perry is suffering from amnesia, he may not know whether he is John Perry. In such case, he will rationally place some information in his self-file or self-buffer without placing the same information in his 'John Perry' file. The fact that he will only ever be identical with John Perry does not mean that his self-file can be his 'John Perry' file.

Question (2) is whether we can dispense with a self notion or concept in basic cases of perception and action. Perry writes, 'When one sees dirty hands in a certain way, it is the perceiver's hands that are dirty. When one washes hands in a certain way, it is the agent's hands that get clean. And when a perception of the first sort causes an action of the second sort in a more-or-less direct way, the subject of the perception is the agent of the action. We don't really need a self-notion to handle any of this. We will need one when we start to get information about ourselves in ways that are not normally self-informative' (2002a: 208–9). Earlier in the same paper, he writes, 'The identity between the perceiver and the agent is (normally) guaranteed outside of thought, by the "architectural" relations between the eyes and arms. One need not keep track of it in thought' (2002a: 208).

By contrast, I think we should attribute a *de se* content to both perception and action even in such basic cases, for several reasons. First, in the example Perry gives, the content of the perceptual experience is partly *de se* and first personal. In that experience, the hands the subject sees are also experienced as his own. *Those hands are mine* is part of the representational content of his total conscious state. This sense of ownership of the hands is part of the explanation of why he moves them.[1]

A first person notion can also enter the content of experience even when the subject is not perceiving any part of his own body. You can experience a ball as coming through the air towards you even if you have no sensation in any part of your body, and do not perceive any part of your body.

Second, to attribute *de se* contents in these basic cases of perception and action is not at all to imply that the subject needs to keep track of the object picked out by the *de se* component of the intentional content of the event. On the contrary, precisely in part because the first person is not a perception-based or a sensation-based demonstrative, but is rather an experience-independent indexical notion in its own right, there is no question of keeping track of what is thought about or represented as oneself. Keeping track of something is fundamentally a perceptually based capacity that does not need to be exercised when one perceives (and may also know) that one's hands are dirty, and that one is washing one's hands oneself. The architectural relations Perry mentions are, I agree, important. They contribute to making possible various properties and relations of states and events with *de se* contents. The existence of these acknowledged architectural relations does not imply that the states and events do not have *de se* contents.

---

[1] For more on the sense of ownership and the first person, see my article 'Perception and the First Person' (2015, Section 3, 'Experienced Ownership'). This presents a view of the first person and ownership distinct from both of two significant proposals in the literature, those of M. Martin (1995) and F. de Vignemont (2007).

Perry is very clear that when a subject also thinks of himself using 'an objective notion', as when Perry thinks 'I am John Perry', and so knows from reading his air ticket when his flight takes off, the subject must link his more objective notion—his 'John Perry' notion in this example—with some first personal notion. But it is problematic what this linking can be if we do not acknowledge a distinctive first person notion or concept in the more basic cases. Where c is the more objective notion, this linking cannot consist merely in the subject x coming to think of x that it is c. That purely *de re* condition is much too weak to ensure a linking with the first person. But if what I have said earlier under (1) above about self-files is correct, then we also cannot explain the linking of the more objective notion with the first person simply by saying that some representation of being identical with c enters the file the subject x has which contains information obtained in ways that are normally x-informative. That is not sufficient for being the subject's self-file, hence not sufficient to explain what is going on when Perry knows 'I am John Perry'. I suggest that the way out of this is to acknowledge *de se* intentional content that enters the content of a huge range of perceptions, action awareness, and intentions; that contributes also to the individuation of a first person concept; that noncircularly labels a self-file; and whose conceptual analogue is employed in the content *I am c* when our subject does come to link an objective notion c with his self-file.

(3) Imagination famously, even notoriously, has a close relation with the first person (see Williams 1973; and Peacocke 1985). How are we to describe the situation, very pertinently mentioned by Perry, of imagining being in one's daughter's situation as she prepares to make a difficult shot towards the end of a basketball game (2002b: 256–7)? Perry acutely notes that when imagining this situation, he need not be imagining John Perry to be the shooter.

The correct description of the imagining is unproblematic when we employ the *de se* notion. Any imagining is imagining, from the first person point of view, some conscious state or event. In the imagining with which Perry is concerned, *de se* intentional content enters the content of the imagined experience, as it would enter the content of the corresponding real experience. The hoop is imagined as at a certain distance and direction from oneself (*de se*); a guarding player is imagined as located between oneself (*de se*) and the hoop; and so forth. In the situation as Perry imagines it, the reference of the *de se* component is not

Perry. It need not be anyone, for the imagining is of a certain kind of situation, and it need not always have specific individuals as components.

Perry himself, aiming to give a description of this imagining without using a *de se* notion or concept, writes this: 'An actual situation corresponding to my imagining would be one in which *this* imagining and the remembered shooting were done by the same person' (2002b: 257); and 'What connects the imagined proposition to me is not that I am a constituent of it, but that my imagining is a constituent of it' (2002b: 257). I question this analysis. The state of affairs Perry is imagining, when he imagines being in his daughter's situation, is not one in which there needs to be any imagining going on at all. In the imagined state of affairs, all that needs to be going on is perception of a certain kind of situation. There can indeed be imaginings about imaginings, a sophisticated thing, and not something that is necessarily involved in imagining being in the situation of making the difficult basketball shot. Putting an imagining into the imagined state of affairs is not the right way to capture the distinctive first person point of view involved in imagining being in the situation of the basketball player. To capture the first person point of view, we need to use *de se* notions in specifying the content of the imagining.

I conclude for these reasons that self-files, and the phenomena they help to explain, cannot be properly characterized without using the *de se* notion and the *de se* concept. I do not mean to imply that sense is never to be explained in terms of relations to a mental file. The idea that the thought expressed by someone who uses a proper name involves a sense whose reference is, constitutively, the dominant source of the information in that file, has many attractions, and is not excluded by anything here. My point is only that the first person concept is not such a sense.

Another important alternative approach that does not use a distinctive notion of a first person mode of presentation has been developed by Robert Stalnaker (2008). The relation of the account I have been developing to Stalnaker's centred-world approach is an important issue. For the case of belief states, Stalnaker gives this account:

A belief state will be represented by a pair consisting of a centered world (representing the believer and time and world in which the believer is in the belief state) and a set of centered worlds (representing the ways the world might be, according to that believer, the time that, for all he believes, it might be, and the person that, for all he believes, he might be). Call the world that is the first term of this pair "the *base* (centered) *world*". The centered worlds in the set that is the second terms are the *belief worlds*. The role of the centers is to link the believer, and time of belief, to the possible worlds that are the way that the believer takes the world to be at that time, and to represent where, in those worlds, he takes himself to be. (2008: 54)

Stalnaker writes that his aim is to 'sketch an account of self-locating belief that I hope will begin to make sense of a notion of informational content that is not detachable from the situation of a subject, or from a context in which the content is ascribed' (2008: 47–8). On one under-standing of Stalnaker's point here, there is clearly one respect in which I agree with his overarching point. Quite generally, each notion or concept is, on the account I have been offering, individuated by the relations in which an entity is required to stand to the notion or concept to be its reference, when it features in the content of some mental event or state. For indexical notions and concepts, these will be contextual relations of the experiences or attitudes containing the indexical notion or concept. Since the *de se* notion and the first person concept are indexical, this entirely general point applies to them. So I am committed to agreeing with Stalnaker's general observation that an account of content in this area involves a certain kind of non-detachability from context.

Suppose, in the spirit of Stalnaker's approach, we aim to represent an actual perceptual token experience e, occurring at t to a subject s, as having a certain content. Let us suppose that this experience e has what I would call a *de se* and present tense content. Then, adapting Stalnaker's proposal in a straightforward way to the case of experience, there is a relation of experiencing between the subject s, the experience e, and an ordered pair consisting of a base centred world and a set of centred worlds, for which this holds:

experiences $(s, e, < <s, t, @>, \{<x, t', w>: <x, t, w'>$ is a way the world might be, according to experience e, at the time it might be according to e, for the subject the experience might have according to $e\}>)$.

Here @ is the actual world.

A question arises: why is the first term of the first ordered triplet $<s, t, @>$ the same as the subject of the experience? One might say that this is just stipulatively written into the notation. But we need to say something more. Not all perceptual experiences have a *de se* content. The perceptual experiences of the creatures, imagined in Chapter II, Section 3, at Degree 0 of involvement of a self-conception in the subject's conception of the world have no *de se* content. What is the underlying distinction between those experiences that do have such content and those that do not? It seems to me that in cases in which the content of perceptual experience is legitimately represented, on the Stalnaker treatment, in a way involving a world centred on the subject, that is so because it is a case in which the intentional content of the experience contains a notion that, *de jure*, refers to the subject who is enjoying the experience. Centred-world content is appropriately attributed in virtue of the experience's having a nonconceptual *de se* intentional content. This is not, however, to say that Stalnaker cannot capture the distinction between the two kinds of case. The ways the world might be, according to a perceptual experience of a subject at Degree 0, do not involve any conditions on the subject who is enjoying the experience. By contrast, the ways the world might be according to a perceptual experience of a subject at Degree 1 or 2 will involve conditions on the subject of the experience—that that subject is in front of a table, or in sunlight, and so forth.

Stalnaker's account seems to me to have the required expressive power, and to be a substantial advance over previous centred-world accounts. If his aim is to show how best to capture first person content in the most plausible kind of possible worlds approach, as far as I can see nothing in this book contradicts his position.

The issue on which there may be a divergence is the further philosophical question of whether centred-world content, when appropriately attributed for first person cases, is present in virtue of some further condition holding. My position is that it is so present in virtue of some further condition, the presence in the intentional content of a *de se* notion or first person concept individuated by its fundamental reference rule. Saying that centred-content is present in virtue of some further condition's holding would be vacuous unless that further condition can be shown to do some explanatory work. My position in this book is that it does contribute to the explanation of phenomena that would not otherwise be fully explained. We have had several examples.

First, we offered an explanation, back in Chapter III, Section 2, of why there is no such thing as attending to something given purely as oneself. That explanation made essential use of the fact that for something to be given as oneself is for it to be given in a way individuated by this condition: that it refers, *de jure*, to the subject of the experience in question.

Second, the notions and modes of presentation underlying the cases in which it is appropriate to attribute centred-world states can also be used in explaining the reason-giving and entitlement relations in which centred-world states stand. Why does a subject's pain give a reason for her to judge *I'm in pain*? A centred-world theorist might be tempted to write such a transition in as a primitive entitlement, that of moving from pain experience to judgement with centred-world content. But there seems to be a simple explanation of why the entitlement exists. The fundamental reference rule for the first person concept entails that a judgement (made by the subject) *I'm in pain* is true iff that subject is in pain. Since the same subject who makes the judgement is experiencing the pain, the experience is one that ensures, for relatively a priori reasons, that the truth condition of the judgement *I'm in pain* is fulfilled. This seems to me more explanatory than just accepting a primitive relation of entitlement as holding between a subject's being in a pain state and that subject's making the judgement *I'm in pain*. There is an entitlement relation in that case, but not, for instance, between the subject having the property of being in London and judging *I'm in London*; nor (not even if our subject is Descartes) between being in pain and judging *Descartes is in pain*. It seems to me that the nature of the first person concept is an essential resource upon which we should draw in explaining these differences.

Third, the same seems to me to apply to the explanation of a range of cases of immunity to error through misidentification that turn essentially on the fundamental reference rule for the concepts involved, as illustrated earlier in this chapter. In trying to explain some of these epistemic phenomena by appeal to a substantive theory of notions and concepts, I have been trying to do something for these first person cases that it seems to me we need to do for a wider class of epistemic and cognitive phenomena, and certainly not only for first person cases. I doubt we can achieve such explanations without appeal to the conditions in virtue of which the constituents of intentional content have the references they do.

VI

Descartes Defended

The general position on subjects and self-representation for which I have been arguing provides resources that support the soundness and the epistemic interest of Descartes' *Cogito*. The general position can also help to make intelligible some grounds that might tempt a thinker to some further Cartesian theses, even if such temptations should be resisted.

I will not be undertaking the quixotic enterprise of defending the full range of Cartesian doctrines on these matters, such as the utter independence of the mental from the physical, or the primary foundational role of the *Cogito* in some proposed reconstruction of human knowledge. But I do believe that the soundness and epistemic interest of the *Cogito* follows from a good conception of consciousness, of the subject of consciousness, and of the nature of first person content. At several points, Descartes uses arguments or considerations that seem to me best defended by drawing on the conceptions of these matters that I have outlined in earlier chapters.

Descartes' *Cogito* is not how we ordinarily know of our own existence. That actual knowledge is massively overdetermined. As we discussed in earlier chapters, your ordinary perceptions, memories and action awarenesses have a *de se* content. You are entitled to take these conscious states at face value in a wide range of cases. In taking these perceptual and other representational states at face value, you are entitled to take for granted the existence of the objects of their singular intentional contents, including their *de se* content. In everyday circumstances, you conceive of yourself as the thing given in the *de se* way in your perceptions, memories and action awarenesses. So, for example, when you have a perceptual representational state with the nonconceptual *de se* content *i am f*, you will be entitled to judge the corresponding conceptual content *I am F*. My limited claim is only that the Cartesian *Cogito* can give you knowledge of your existence in circumstances in which, for one reason or another, you are not taking at face value the content of your states of perception, memory and action awareness—just as Descartes was not taking them at face value.

1. The Soundness of the *Cogito*

We need a little stage setting, and some reactivation of our memories of what Descartes actually said. Here are some of the passages in which Descartes formulates the *Cogito*. In the *Discourse on the Method*, he writes

> But immediately I noticed that while I was trying to thus to think everything false, it was necessary that I, who was thinking this, was something. And observing that this truth *'I am thinking, therefore I exist'* was so firm and sure that all the most extravagant suppositions of the sceptics were incapable of shaking it, I decided that I could accept it without scruple as the first principle of philosophy I was seeking. (1985: 127)

And a little later in the *Discourse*,

> I saw on the contrary that from the mere fact that I thought of doubting the truth of other things, it followed quite evidently and certainly that I existed. . . . (1985: 127)

In the Second Meditation, he writes

> and let him [a deceiver of supreme power and cunning] deceive me as much as he can, he will never bring it about that I am nothing so long as I think that I am something. So after considering everything very thoroughly, I must finally conclude that this proposition, *I am, I exist* is necessarily true whenever it is put forward by me or conceived in my mind. (1984: 17)

I am going to be taking the canonical form of the *Cogito* to involve three stages. First, Descartes engages in

(1)   a particular conscious thinking;

second, he moves from this conscious event to the judgement

(2)   I am thinking;

third, from (2) he infers

(3)   I exist.

In the transition from (1) to (2), we have a transition from a conscious thinking to a self-ascription of thinking, made for the reason that he is thinking. This first step in the transition (1)–(3) should not be identified with any kind of inference.

In taking (1)–(3) as the canonical form, I am rejecting any view under which the content of the consciousness that forms the basis for the *Cogito* must itself have a first-personal content. As far as the form (1)–(3) is concerned, the initial thinking of which the thinker is aware could have any content at all. It need not be a first person content.

The form (1)–(3) respects the idea of Descartes and his commentators that he could equally have formulated his argument in terms of other conscious properties such as doubting, willing, imagining, experiencing, and the like, including having a sensation with no representational content at all. (For further discussion, see Williams (1978: 79–81).) Descartes could equally have started from an event of

(4) his conscious imagining (his conscious doubting, willing, experiencing, sensing . . .)

From this conscious event, he moves to the judgement

(5) I imagine (doubt, will, experience, sense . . .);

and then on to the same original conclusion

(6) I exist.

The fact that Descartes said his conclusion could equally have been reached along the lines of (4)–(6) tells against any view that attempts to give as the canonical formulation of his thought a judgement of something self-referential such as 'I am in this very thought thinking that I exist'. While a thinking that is a judgement can refer to itself and still be a judgement, an imagining or a willing or a doubting cannot be a judgement that something is the case (in particular, that I exist). So such self-referential readings cannot accommodate the very natural extension of Descartes' reasoning to these other conscious mental states.

The *Cogito* as conceived in (1)–(3) is apparently sound even when the thinking an awareness of which is described in (1) is something a schizophrenic subject reports as an 'inserted thought', something experienced as inserted by the agency of another. Line (2) does not imply that the thinker engaged in the *Cogito* reasoning is experienced as the agent of the thinking which forms its starting point, nor even that the thinker actually is that agent.

So much by way of stage setting. Of the transitions made in (1)–(3), we can ask the question of their soundness. This is a question about the world, the question of whether the transitions lead to true judgements. We can ask too the question of whether the thinker is entitled to make the judgements, and in such a way that these transitions result in knowledge, as Descartes thought. We can also ask not merely whether the transitions are ones the thinker is entitled to make, but whether they also possess Cartesian certainty. I take the issue of soundness first.

Lichtenberg famously wrote 'We are acquainted only with the existence of our sensations, imaginations and thoughts. "Thinking is going on" is what one should say, just as one says "Lightning is occurring". Saying "Cogito" is too much, as soon as one translates it as "I am thinking"' (1971: 412, §76).

Lichtenberg's objection is unsound if the position I developed in Chapter 3 above is correct. The metaphysical interdependence of conscious events with the subjects of those events implies that there cannot be conscious thinking without a thinker. What it is for the event to be conscious requires it to have a subject.

Still, it may be objected, even if every conscious mental event must have a subject, what ensures, when anyone tries to apply the *Cogito* to himself, that that subject doing the thinking is the same as the subject referred to in its last line, the subject to whose existence he concludes? To this the answer is that only the subject whose thinking it is can be aware of the thinking in the distinctive way that stage (1) of the *Cogito* involves. Another person might be aware of your thinking by examining a real-time scan of your brain. That person is not thereby aware of your thinking in the special way in which only the subject whose thinking it is can be aware of it. Now suppose someone aware of the thinking in that special way judges 'I am thinking', and does so rationally because of that awareness. By the nature of the first person concept, he refers to the agent of his judgement 'I am thinking', viz., himself. So in the circumstances he certainly judges truly. In these circumstances, the agent of the judgement 'I'm thinking' is the subject of the conscious thinking that is his reason for making the judgement. 'I exist' then in turn follows from 'I'm thinking'. That is so, because for any content of the form a is F, where F is a concept of a conscious state, the truth of the content requires that a refers.

It would be a fair comment that if one is thinking explicitly about the metaphysics of consciousness and its relations to subjects of consciousness, and endorsing the metaphysics I have offered, then reaching (3) via

(2) is unnecessarily circuitous. On the metaphysics I have offered, the existence of a conscious event already involves the existence of a subject having conscious properties. If one is arguing from that metaphysical conception, the subject's existence is not really epistemically posterior to the subject's thinking. Nonetheless, it is still of interest to consider how the metaphysics can vindicate the style of thought and reasoning Descartes actually offered. In Descartes' own thought, there is clearly a step from (2) to (3).

If we return to consider Descartes' own thought, a logician might observe that the step from (2) to (3) is not valid in a pure free logic, unsupplemented by any other principles. (For an overview of free logic, see Lambert and van Fraassen (1972, Parts III–V).) But there are two reasons that free logic, which in general has many good claims for its use, does not undermine the particular step from (2) to (3). First, the more plausible free logics allow the inference from $A(t)$ to $\exists x\, A(x)$ when $A()$ is an atomic predicate. In the case in which $A()$ is an atomic predicate, it is hard to conceive of what could be the case in the world if $A(t)$ can be true without there being anything that is the reference of t. But the predicates 'am thinking', 'am imagining', 'am experiencing', and the other Cartesian examples are all atomic predicates in the relevant respect. In short, in a translation of Descartes' own words in his Reply to the Second Set of Objections, 'it isn't possible to think without existing' (1984: 100). Second, we are conceiving the example in such a way that (2) is a judgement, made by the thinker in rational reaction to the occurrence of the thinking specified in (1). Since the first person concept, in any judgement in which it occurs, refers to the producer of the judgement, and it is part of the specification of the example that there is a producer of the judgement made at line (2), the first person as it occurs in the content judged there must refer. (This reasoning would also of course apply to a judgement 'I am walking', made in rational response to an experience as of one's walking oneself; if the judgement is a mental action made by a subject, then the first person as occurring in that content refers. But in a case in which the subject is rationally doubting his perceptual states, the transition from an experience as of his own walking to the judgement 'I am walking' is not one to which he is entitled.) For these two reasons, the attractions of free logic elsewhere do not, it seems to me, undermine the transitions from (2) to (3) and from (5) to (6).

Kant gives a different criticism of this part of Descartes' reasoning. In *The Critique of Pure Reason*, Kant writes 'But I cannot say "Everything that thinks, exists"; for then the property of thinking would make all beings possessing it into necessary beings' (1998: B422, 453, fn). This is a modal fallacy. Kant fails to distinguish the true proposition that necessarily, anything that thinks also exists, that is, using the standard binary notation,

Necessarily, $\forall x$ (Tx, Ex)

from the different, and false, proposition that anything that thinks also necessarily exists, that is

$\forall x$ (Tx, necessarily (Ex)).

Descartes' writing commits him only to the first, true, proposition, and not to the second, false one.

That concludes the argument, drawing on the metaphysics of consciousness and subjects, and the nature of the first person concept, that the *Cogito* as conceived in (1)–(3) is sound, that is, yields true judgements given its starting point. But there are still some major issues about the metaphysics involved in this validation that I will pursue further. Some of the issues can be introduced by considering the points in Bernard Williams' justly famous discussion of the *Cogito* in his book on Descartes (1978: Chapter 3). Williams argues that Lichtenberg's subjectless, impersonal formulations cannot account for the distinction between the case in which

It's thought that *p* and it's thought that *q*

is understood in such a way that it implies that

It's thought that: *p and q*

and the case in which it is not so understood (1978: 96ff.). He introduces a 'here' to indicate the case in which the most recently displayed condition does hold, and in those cases Williams writes

It's thought here that *p* and it's thought here that *q*.

After some discussion, Williams concludes that this 'here' effectively reintroduces reference to a subject. Williams also mentions an objection that he says he will not pursue, the objection that there may be some way of construing 'It's thought here that *p*' that is weaker than something of the form 'A thinks that p' (1978: 99–100). On the metaphysical response to Lichtenberg's objection, and on the metaphysics of conscious events I have been offering here, there is nothing weaker. There is nothing weaker because by the very nature of conscious mental events, they have subjects.

We can put the point in the form of a dilemma for the formulations containing 'here'. Consider the first and second occurrences of 'here' in Williams's 'It's thought here that p and it's thought here that q'. Either the first occurrence is to be understood in such a way that it implies that it is thought in a certain subject that p, and the second occurrence is to be understood in such a way that it implies that it is thought in the same subject that q; or else these implications do not hold. In the former case, the two uses of 'here' are not weaker than something of the form 'A thinks that p and A thinks that q' after all. In the latter case, in which the conjunction is not implied, the condition will be insufficient for capturing the truth of 'It's thought that p and q', in which case the 'here' formulation fails in its intended purpose. Either way, we will not have a means of capturing 'It's thought that p and q' that avoid commitment to subjects who are thinking.

But, as Frege once put it, I think I hear an objection. This most recent dismissal of a particular fomulation of Lichtenberg's position may be correct, but there is certainly a further issue to be addressed. There are some other cases in which there is an operator O for which the transition from

Op and Oq

to

O (p and q)

also fails, and yet in which we have a strong impulse to reject the view that there is some more fundamental entity or object at which p holds and at which q holds. Perhaps the best example is that of modality, where the operator O can be taken to be 'it is possible that . . .', and a simple counterexample to the most recently displayed transition will be some instance in which we substitute $\sim p$ for q. From the fact that it is possible that p and it is possible that $\sim p$ it does not follow that it is possible that p *and* $\sim p$. So we face an important question: does the failure of the transition in modal cases mean that we have some model for explaining the failure of the transition Williams discusses, but without postulating subjects of consciousness? Many would be reluctant to see in the modal case any vindication of modal realism about possible worlds. So why, it may be asked, should the failure of the transition in Lichtenberg's case be any vindication of an ontology of subjects of consciousness? This is a new Lichtenbergian challenge, Lichtenberg's revenge.

The argument of Lichtenberg's revenge can be generalized. The various considerations of the relevant parts of Williams's argument involve considerations of expressive power. That applies to the argument about conjunction considered in the preceding two paragraphs, and it applies also when Williams (1978: 97) raises the issue of embedded Lichtenbergian formulations, such as

It is thought: it is not doubted whether q.

Williams argues, as it seems to me soundly, that we must be able to express the distinction between the case in which, using the 'here' and 'somewhere' formulations again, this is to be taken to mean

It is thought: it is not doubted anywhere whether q

And the case in which it is taken to mean

It is thought: it is not doubted here whether q.

Now this sort of consideration, the defender of Lichtenberg's revenge may say, is entirely analogous to some familiar arguments about expressive power in modal and temporal languages. There are, for instance, legitimate, and true, modal propositions that cannot be expressed using only a language with modal operators, but for which we need an 'actually' ('A') operator, and various generalizations thereof. A very simple example is

There could be something which does not actually exist.

This has to be formalized

$\Diamond \exists x {\sim} A(exists(x))$.

That is a truth, unlike the false

$\Diamond \exists x {\sim} exists(x)$.

More elaborate examples require indexed 'actually'-like operators linked to one another, or Vlach's linked inverted dagger and dagger operators (Vlach 1973; Peacocke 1978). Now, the defender of Lichtenberg's revenge may continue, does the need for such operators, argued from considerations of expressive power, really suffice to establish a realism about possible worlds analogous to a realism about subjects of consciousness? There would be a widespread reluctance to say so. But if we are so reluctant, then we had better have some stronger argument than expressive power in the proposed case against Descartes. From the standpoint of this Lichtenbergian protest, Williams' later invocation of a parallel between places and subject of consciousness (1978: 99) will appear to be begging the question at this stage of the argument. A realistic ontology of places is much less problematic than modal realism, and the legitimacy of any parallel with places must be earned by a more detailed consideration of the metaphysics of the cases of places and subjects of consciousness. It cannot be established simply from the above considerations of expressive power.

I respond to Lichtenberg's revenge by appealing to the fundamental differences between the ontology of possible worlds that one invokes to explain why the modal inference fails and the ontology of subjects one invokes to explain why the Williams transition fails. Possible worlds are entirely constituted by what is the case at them. Intuitively, they are constructed entities, constructed from sets of compossible propositions. This broad statement involves many oversimplifications, but in one way or another it is, in my view, underwritten by plausible substantive accounts of modality. In the 'principle-based' account of modality I advocate, a possible world is considered to be a set of propositions generated by an assignment of extensions to concepts, where the assignment must be admissible. That is, it must respect constraints on what makes concepts the concepts they are, and what makes objects and properties the objects and properties they are. This was the treatment I offered in *Being Known* (1999: Chapter 4). Other approaches to modality also take possible worlds as sets of propositions while not operating with that framework. Prominent examples are found in the work of Robert Adams (1974); Robert Stalnaker (2003); and Nathan Salmon (2005). But in all these cases, there is no more to a world than the set of propositions that hold at it. The various theories may differ on what determines a set as genuinely compossible, but they agree that there is no more to the world than the relevant set of propositions that hold at it. (Some might say that two worlds may differ only in what holds at worlds accessible from them, and not in what holds within the worlds themselves. I am sceptical of this, but even if it is so, it shows only that a world must be individuated not only by what holds at it, but also by its place in a system of worlds on which there is an accessibility relation. This is still a far cry from modal realism.) All such views differ from David Lewis's modal realism, according to which a possible world is a huge material thing of the same kind as the actual physical universe, which is not a set of propositions. The conception of possible worlds as constructed entities is, however, enough to allow an explanation of the difference between 'There could be something that does not actually exist' and 'There could be something that does not exist', without resort to Lewisian modal realism. (For a treatment of possibilia that fits with a principle-based approach to modality, see Peacocke (2002).) So on the approach to possible worlds as constructed entities, the modal distinctions cited in Lichtenberg's revenge are well taken. But, contrary to the position of Lichtenberg's revenge, there remains a fundamental disanalogy between possible worlds and subjects of consciousness.

The crucial point of disanalogy is that subjects of consciousness are not, on the view I have been developing, constituted by what properties they possess, or what 'holds at them'. How could a conception of subjects as constructed entities be developed? If the materials of the construction are experience-types, and types of other conscious states, events, and processes, we face the problem that there could be two subjects with the same types of conscious states, events, and processes over the course of their whole lives. The constructivist about subjects might try to avoid this by saying that two such subjects would be enjoying different mental states because at some points they would concern different objects, some states concerning the one subject himself, other states concerning the other subject. They would enjoy such states, but to appeal to that difference of object-involving content would be circular. It would be using distinctness of subjects in a construction that is aiming to explain distinctness of subjects. Alternatively, the constructivist might attempt to appeal to token conscious mental events and processes as the basic building materials of a proposed construction of subjects. But if what makes a token conscious mental event or process conscious in the first place is its contribution to what it is like for a certain subject, then these token occurrences are not ontologically prior to subjects themselves. On the contrary, they presuppose the existence of subjects. For reasons such as this, we should be fundamentally realists about subjects of consciousness. There are no comparable pressures to be modal realists.

It can be helpful in reflecting on the space of conceivable philosophical positions in this territory by considering what parallels do, and what parallels do not, holds between the cases of times, worlds, and subjects of consciousness. Some of the relevantly different significant conceivable positions are actually occupied by Arthur Prior, by me, and by a theorist envisaged by Kit Fine. Prior introduced a language he called 'Egocentric' (2003b). In this language, we say that such expressions as 'standing', 'drinking', 'sitting' are the case with respect to individuals. As Prior writes,

'Standing' is the case with *a*

is equivalent to

'I am standing' is true when said by *a* (2003b: 225).

Prior's own stated motivation for inventing Egocentric was to 'bring out both the similarities and the differences' between 'the machinery of tenses' and 'that of personal pronouns' (2003b: 225). He described Egocentric as a language 'in which properties *are* located in individuals in the same way as events are located in times by means of tenses' (2003b: 225). However, while Prior thought tense logic to be of fundamental metaphysical significance, he did not believe the same to hold of Egocentric. He wrote,

> I cannot *understand* 'instants', and the earlier-later than relation that is supposed to hold between them, except as constructions out of tensed facts. Tense logic is for me, if I may use the phrase, *metaphysically fundamental*, and not just an artificially torn-off fragment of the first-order theory of the earlier-later relation. Egocentric logic is a different matter; I find it hard to believe that individuals really are just propositions of a certain sort, or just 'points of view', or that the real world of individuals is just a logical construction out of such points of view. (2003b: 232, see also 219–20)

So Prior groups modality and tense together in respect of their metaphysics. Prior is neither a realist about times nor about possible worlds. Against that, I would group selves and times together in respect of their metaphysics, and contrast both of them with the right metaphysics of modality.

Fine formulates—though he explicitly refrains from endorsing—the view that Prior's language Egocentric *is* of metaphysical significance. Fine is interested in 'first-personal realism', which for him is a form of aspectual realism, and he suggests that such a realist 'should not accept the reality of selves' (2005: 312). Fine is of course very well aware that the properties that hold of a time are not essential to it. It may in fact be sunny now, but this present time could exist without being a time at which it's sunny. In this respect, times are unlike possible worlds. Selves also do not have their properties essentially: you and I could have had different properties from birth, and even earlier.

Fine's first-personal realist has to make some sense of identities such as 'I am Kit Fine', as thought or uttered by Kit Fine, in a way consistent with not accepting the reality of selves. Fine suggests that, for the first-personal realist, this apparent identity should be regarded as 'restricting egocentric reality to the experience of experiences that only KF can have' (2005: 318). The background supposition here is that for each subject, there are token experiences that only that subject can have. The realist about subjects, whose position I endorse, could of course agree that there are such experiences, but would suggest that token conscious events, and even consciousness itself, cannot be elucidated without already incurring a commitment to subjects or selves who enjoy the experiences. Whatever genuine phenomena underlie the motivation for the first-personal realism Fine formulates, they should be accommodated at the level of modes of presentation of events, properties and objects, and not by distinctions in reality itself. Nonetheless, Fine's characterization of what he at one point calls 'First-Personalism' is certainly of great interest when we come to consider the taxonomy of conceivable positions in this area, part of which can then be diagrammed thus:

Non-constructionist, realist view of:	Prior	Fine's 'first-personalist'	Peacocke
Possible Worlds	No	n/a	No
Times	No	n/a	Yes
Selves	Yes	No	Yes

To summarize the point we have now reached in this discussion: there are indeed operators for which the Williams-like inference fails, but that fact cannot support Lichtenberg. Subjects of consciousness are not entities constructible from materials that do not already involve subjects of consciousness. When the Williams-like inferences fail and do so without commitment to non-constructed entities (as in the modal case, on my view), they cannot give a model for the case of subjects of consciousness. So Lichtenberg's revenge fails. Descartes remains vindicated against Lichtenberg's objection.

This is not to say that Lichtenberg's brief discussion may not have been driven by some important insights. One can conceive of various points that might have been motivating Lichtenberg, or someone tempted by his position. One salient possible motivation might be an appreciation that in many cases, a subject's reason for making a psychological self-ascription *I am* ψ is not a state or event with a representational content *I am* ψ. In a wide range of cases, including self-ascriptions of conscious occurrent mental states or events, those states and events themselves give reason for the self-ascription. Thus an imagining of some state of affairs can itself give a thinker reason for self-ascribing an imagining. There need be no prior state with the content *I am imagining so-and-so* that gives reason for making the self-ascription of the imagining. The same applies to self-ascriptions of perceptual experiences, of some memories, and of some emotions. These are all cases of what I called 'representationally independent' uses of the first person in *Being Known* (1999: Chapter 6). If part of what elicits sympathy for Lichtenberg's position is that there are these representationally independent uses of the first person, then that is an aspect of a Lichtenbergian position with which I agree. But it does not follow that the *Cogito* is some kind of fallacy. What is right in such motivating thoughts is entirely consistent with the metaphysical interdependence of mental events and the subjects who enjoy them. Only if one had a mistaken account of the conditions under which a first person content could be known, or a mistaken account of the nature of the ontology of subjects, or both, could an appreciation of representational independence be thought to undermine the *Cogito*.

2. What Can the Perspective of Consciousness Supply?

Williams makes a further comment on Descartes' *Cogito* in this passage:

The thought-event formulation we have been examining requires the notion of objectively existing thought-events, and in supposing that it can start out merely from the idea of thoughts as experienced, and from that achieve the third-personal perspective which is necessary if this notion is to apply, it shares a basic error with Descartes. There is nothing in the pure Cartesian reflection to give us that perspective. . . . Descartes thinks that he can proceed from that [the perspective of consciousness – CP] to the existence of what is, from the third-personal perspective, a substantial fact, the existence of a thinker. The objection I have been discussing (viz. Lichtenberg's – CP) tries to find a fact which is less substantial; but that too will have to be capable of being regarded from the third-personal perspective if it is to be an objective fact, and the mere perspective of consciousness no more gives us a way of getting to that kind of objective fact, than it gives us a way of getting to Descartes's more substantial fact. This is not a verificationist point . . . it is a question about the coherence of the conception, of what it is one is invited to conceive. (1978: 100)

What is the reasoning here? Suppose for the sake of argument we grant Williams's thesis that any objective fact must be capable of being regarded from a third personal perspective. That is a thesis about the metaphysics of the mental, a claim about the relations between being an objective fact and the third-personal perspective. We should distinguish between

(1) Metaphysical principles that hold of some domain of entities; and
(2) The conditions for a subject to think about, or to otherwise mentally represent, elements of that domain.

The conditions for thought in (2) do not in general require knowledge or beliefs about the metaphysical principles of kind (1). Williams seems to write as if they do. He writes in the above passage of 'the third-personal perspective which is necessary if this notion [the notion of a thought-event – CP] is to apply', but we should distinguish what is necessary if a notion is to apply from what has to feature in a perspective on a domain. There are many examples in which thought about some domain exists without the subject knowing or even so much as thinking about or representing the metaphysical principles that hold of that domain.

One straightforward example is perception of physical objects and events, and of their properties and relations. Animals and very young children enjoy perceptual states and events whose correctness conditions concern objects and events in the physical world, and concern their properties and relations. It is a metaphysical truth that these physical items and properties are in general mind-independent, and in particular exist independently of perception of the objects and their properties; but this fact is not something that needs to be known by or represented by the perceiver. Reflection on the correct metaphysics of what one is perceiving or thinking about is something much more sophisticated than such primitive spatial perception. It does not need to be present for perception with objective content to occur. This point has been made in several recent writings on perception.[1]

Perception is only one of many such cases. To take an example at the other end of one ontological spectrum, consider the meaning (the sense) of linguistic expressions. Thinkers sometimes know that a particular expression has a particular meaning. There will be some account (no doubt controversial) of the nature of the meaning of a particular expression, an account of the metaphysics, the nature, of that particular meaning. But that account does not need to be part of the conscious knowledge or thought of a subject who simply knows that a particular expression has that meaning. The metaphysical account of the nature of that particular meaning does not have to be part of 'the mere perspective of consciousness', as Williams puts it.

The general phenomenon here is that of relation-based thought or mental representation (Peacocke 2010a). Sometimes a subject can think about something in virtue of standing in a certain relation to it, and that relation does not at all require that the subject have a correct conception of what is involved in that thing's being what it is. If the thinker has any conception of such matters at all, she may even be radically mistaken, entirely consistently with still thinking about that object or state. We have long accepted this point as applied to physical particulars, properties and relations. It applies equally to the mental too—even more saliently, because it is clear that a thinker stands in special relations to her own mental states and events, relations that allow her to think of them in distinctive ways.

We must indeed have an account of thought that makes it possible to conceive of mental events and of subjects as accessible from the third person perspective. If Descartes had a general conception of thought and of the mental that would make it impossible, his account is objectionable. But there is no such commitment simply in holding that a subject can make a possibly knowledge-generating transition from thinking (in Descartes' broad sense) to the conclusion that he exists.

Once we have distinguished metaphysical principles from conditions for mental representation, it is still of interest to pursue the issue

---

[1] See Peacocke (2001: last paragraph); and the extended discussion in Burge (2010).

Williams raises, that of the relation between the correct metaphysics of mental states and events, on the one hand, and what is available to the point of view of consciousness on the other. Is he right that the idea of other subjects of experience, and of mental events 'elsewhere', and the correlative idea of one's own experiences being thinkable about by some other subject, is not something available merely from the point of view of consciousness? Williams writes that 'sticking solely to the point of view of consciousness' (1978: 100), 'events either happen for it, or they do not happen, and there is no way of conceiving of such events happening, but happening (so to speak) elsewhere' (1978: 101). It seems to me that there is a true starting point in this line of thought. When a mental event—a perception, a pain, or even an action—is experienced from the inside, if it is experienced as owned by anyone, it is ordinarily, in non-pathological cases, experienced as the subject's own. The same applies to imagining an event from the inside: imagining an event in an ordinary, non-patho-logical way, is imagining it from the first person point of view in the imagined situation (Peacocke 1985). This gives a clear sense in which these conscious events, considered from the inside, do not by themselves involve any conception of mental events that are not the subject's own.

A state of affairs that is of a psychological kind may, however, be represented as of that kind in a subject's consciousness, without its being given from the inside. One can see others as acting, and can see others as perceiving, as when you see someone as looking at you. Such seeings do belong to the point of view of consciousness. So even from the point of view of consciousness, there is a way of conceiving of such events happening, but happening to others, or 'elsewhere'. Since acting and seeing are things that only subjects can do, they must be properties of subjects, but in this case they are subjects other than oneself. Indeed one also experiences some other agents and perceivers as subjects, a real phenomenology much discussed by Sartre (1943). Our conception of subjects other than ourselves is drawn upon in such familiar states of consciousness. These states have correctness conditions that require other subjects to be a certain way—looking at things, or acting in a certain fashion.

Do these simple observations show that Williams is wrong? I think there are still Williams-like claims about what is available to the per-spective of consciousness that hold, and which vindicate Williams's fundamental insight.

First, as I suggested in earlier work, a thinker's conception of another conscious subject is a conception of *something else of the same kind as me* (2008: Chapter 5). On this understanding what it is to have the conception of another subject, that conception does, in making essential use of the first person (in the accusative form *me*), draw on the point of view of consciousness. But it also uses the more theoretical notion of sameness of kind. Now the notion of sameness of kind is not something given solely by the point of view of consciousness. It is not an observational notion or concept, on any reasonable understanding of observationality.

Though not sufficient for supplying the materials for the general concept of a subject of consciousness, the point of view of consciousness is still necessary under this elaboration of thought about another conscious subject. The presence of the more theoretical notion *of the same kind as* should no more make us deny that the point of view of consciousness is involved in grasp of other subjects than the presence of a general notion such as *same shape as* in the elucidation of observational concepts should deny that grasp thereof is founded in perceptual experience.

Under this account of grasp of other subjects, I have to work out what kind of thing I am. I am a perceiver, enjoy sensations, and act mentally and physically. The relations in which I have to stand to my environment, my body, and my actions (mental and physical) to be the kind of thing I am are relations that it makes sense to suppose other things—and thereby other subjects—may also stand to their environments, their bodies, and their actions. Even for a subject who does not see events as actions, and who does not see others as perceiving things, the non-perceptual idea that there can be something standing to other events and a body as he himself stands to other events and to a body is something accessible in thought. So I am inclined to think that what Williams calls 'the pure point of view of consciousness' (1978: 100), when considered properly and reflected upon from its own standpoint, contains at least an indispensable resource for elaborating the idea of other subjects of consciousness. It provides a starting point for discovering which other things in the perceived world are subjects of consciousness, beside myself.

On this account, we have a vindication of Williams's claim about what cannot be extracted from the point of view of consciousness in respect of a conception of multiple subjects of consciousness. Although we can see other persons as acting and perceiving subjects, this is possible only because we have the conception of subjects just outlined (or at least some restriction of that conception, perhaps a restriction to members of our own species). A perception of someone else as acting or perceiving is possible for a thinker only because he the thinker has grasped the idea of other things of the same kind as himself, and hence has the idea of them as perceivers and agents. This indeed is an essential bridge if the notions of perceptual experience and of action are themselves first personal (on which, see Chapter IX, Section 3).

Here then we have a strong contrast with observational spatial concepts. Each such observational concept is individuated by its relations to kinds of perception with a certain type of nonconceptual representational content, a content whose presence in a perception makes reasonable application of the concept. A perception with the nonconceptual content that a presented object is oval can make rational the judgement that the object so given falls under the concept *oval*. But there is nothing in the perceptual application of the concept (as opposed to nonperceptual applications) that requires grasp of some highly general relation of sameness of shape, in the way in which a notion of sameness of kind is plausibly involved when one perceives someone else as a subject who acts and perceives. This difference between the two kinds of case supports Williams's claim.

A second, closely related, point offers further support for Williams. Even though we sometimes experience someone or something else as a subject of consciousness, it is not true, let alone a priori, that everything that is a subject must be perceivable by us as a subject. Our general idea of a subject of consciousness is, in the nature of the case, as general as the idea of consciousness itself. Consciousness may exist in organisms and species wholly unlike us, organisms that act and perceive, but who do not look to us as if they are agents or perceivers. The positive account of our general conception of subjecthood in terms of a sameness relation is capable of respecting and explaining this point. It gives the notion of subjecthood a potential extension ranging far beyond what is or can be given in consciousness as a subject. In fact on this account, prima facie being a subject has nothing, fundamentally, to do with being perceivable as a subject by us.

Let us return to the *Cogito*. The account I have offered of the soundness of the *Cogito* differs from those neo-Humean accounts that say they find something sound in it. On Parfit's moderate reductionist view of subjects of consciousness, as he explicitly notes, the *Cogito* is sound, but only because of the way we talk. In *Reasons and Persons*, Parfit writes, 'We do in fact ascribe thoughts to thinkers. Because we talk in this way, Descartes could truly claim, "I think, therefore I am"' (1987: 226). Earlier in the same book, Parfit writes, 'A Reductionist can admit that, in this sense, a person is what has experiences, or the subject of experiences. This is true because of the way in which we talk' (1987: 223). Parfit diverges from Lichtenberg only in adding that observation about the way we talk to a fundamentally subject-free view.

On the view I am advocating, Descartes' *Cogito* is sound not merely because of the way we talk. The conclusion of the *Cogito* concerns a subject whose existence is not reducible to something else. I argued that it is not, on my view, even correct to make the weaker claim that the licensed conclusion is merely that some subject or other is thinking, and not necessarily me. The sound conclusion that can be reached by the *Cogito* goes beyond this because the *Cogito* employs distinctive ways of thinking of conscious states, including thinking itself, that can be employed in thinking about a mental state or event only by the subject of that state or event, and in virtue of being the subject of the state or event.

In *Reasons and Persons*, Derek Parfit does address Williams' response to the Lichtenberg objection, and writes after his own discussion that 'Lichtenberg's objection to Descartes thus survives' (1987: 226). Parfit's strategy is to agree that some kind of relativization is needed in response to Williams's argument, but that the relativization required does not attribute mental states and events to irreducible subjects of experience. Parfit offers, instead of relativization to a subject, these formulations:

In the particular life that contains the thinking of the thought that is expressed by the utterance of this sentence, it is thought: . . .

or

In the particular life that is now directly causally dependent on body A, it is thought: . . . (1987: 226)

As Parfit notes, this will require a subject-free elucidation of the notion of a life.

I argued that subjects are already involved in what makes an event conscious. Identity of subject over time cannot be reduced to subject-free relations and entities. If that is correct, then the kind of intermediate relativization Parfit suggests will not solve the problem.

I would make the same point if a reductionist about subjects aims to use relativization to brains or other causal bases of a subject. Two subjects may in exceptional cases be associated with the same brain. Some conceivable split-brain cases could be like that (even if actual split-brain cases are not). In such conceivable cases, we would need to use the notion of a subject in characterizing the relativization, on pain of insufficiency in solving Williams' problem, since in these cases, a relativization to brains would not meet the purpose. I conjecture that any form of relativization that actually suffices involves subjects directly or indirectly in a way that the reductionist cannot accommodate.

3. Entitlement, the Second *Cogito*, and Anscombe

I turn now to the issues of entitlement and certainty. Are the transitions in (1)–(3) ones to which Descartes was entitled, and can they yield any kind of certainty? Not everything ensured by the metaphysics of a subject matter and by the nature of the concept employed in a thought is thereby known to those who think about the subject matter. So these are certainly questions that go beyond those already addressed.

Two further premises would suffice to explain why the transitions in the *Cogito* do not merely lead to true judgements, but also lead to knowledge. We have several times noted that the concept *thinks* has an individuative tie to the first person in the present tense. Any plausible account of the nature of that concept entails that to possess it involves taking one's own conscious thinking as conclusive reason for self-applying the concept of thinking in the present tense. This first person character of the concept can be accommodated on several different theories of concepts in general. On conceptual role theories, it can be written in as part of the specification of the role of the concept, the role which, if those theories are true, individuates the concept. On theories that say that concepts are individuated by their fundamental reference rules, the fundamental reference rule can be formulated so as to imply that someone's consciously thinking at a given time suffices by itself for that person to fall under the concept at that time. Whichever of these approaches to concepts, or some other, is adopted, there will also be the task of elucidating predications of other objects, at other times, too.

The other premise that contributes to the status of the *Cogito* as knowledge-yielding is the principle that if someone judges a content on grounds that are, as a matter of the nature of one or more concepts in the content, conclusive grounds for judging the content, then the content so judged is knowledge. This is a principle we accept in other cases, for concepts at some distance from the psychological and the first person. I refer the reader to earlier discussions.[2]

I will not discuss here the very strong indubitability that Descartes claimed for the *Cogito*, for it would take us too far off track. I just note that there are more modest notions of rational first level certainty on which one can be rationally certain of some transition if a thinker's willingness to make the transition is built into the very identity of the concepts involved. This is plausible both for the step from (1) to (2) and for the step from (2) to (3) in the *Cogito* as I have formulated it. For such rational first level certainty, these claims about the connection between concept identity and certainty do not themselves need to be known by the thinker in question, let alone indubitable. They need only to be true.

I call this kind of certainty rational first level certainty because it may well fall short of absolute indubitability. A philosophical thinker might come to doubt that a concept really has the status of having the willingness to make a certain transition built into its identity. A thinker may also doubt the connection of this property with rational certainty. So I am not sure absolute indubitability can be secured from the resources I am deploying; nor is it obviously desirable that it should be.

There is another reason absolute indubitability is not ensured by the resources I have been deploying. It has to do with the temporal references in the *Cogito*. At the start of this chapter, we represented Descartes' *Cogito* as involving these transitions. Descartes starts from

(1)   a particular conscious thinking;

he moves from this conscious event to the judgement

---

[2] See especially the epistemological principle linking knowledge of a content with those sufficient conditions for judgement of a content which are specified in possession conditions for concepts contained in the content: see Peacocke (1992: 157ff.). A version of this principle, and also its rationale, survives the change from possession-condition theories of concepts to concepts as individuated by fundamental reference rules.

(2)   I am thinking;

and then from (2) he infers

(3)   I exist.

Now in general, it is a mistake to think that deductive argument involves reliance on propositions about the correctness of memories of what one was thinking when carrying out the deduction. The point has been forcefully made by Burge (1993). But when the propositions involved in some deduction contain indexicals, there is a substantive question about preservation of reference of the terms of the propositions of the deduction. This provides an opportunity for the evil demon to get to work. Both (2) and (3) in the *Cogito* are present tense propositions. In an actual inferential transition in thinking, in real time, (2) and (3) refer to different times. They refer respectively to the time at which (2) is thought and to the time at which (3) is thought. If Descartes loses any entitlement to think that he existed a moment ago, he loses any entitlement to think that what is true of him now was also true of him a moment ago. If it is absolute indubitability that Descartes seeks, there is then a problem for him here. If we try to resolve the problem by taking the time at which (3) is thought as the reference of the present tense component throughout the deduction, the earlier thinkings simply do not concern that time. If we take the time at which (2) is thought as the reference of the present tense component throughout, it is not clear that the knowledgeable earlier thinkings have any bearing on what holds at the later time at which (3) is thought, if the evil demon, with his powers to deceive memory, is a real possibility. Ordinary everyday inference in normal circumstances does rely on a background that an evil demon of unlimited powers would undermine.

I am, then, not supplying everything Descartes wanted on the epistemic side in his imagined confrontation with the evil demon. All the same, if we accept the positive accounts I have been offering, we can in ordinary circumstances move from the consciousness of thinking to rational, knowledgeable self-ascription of thinking, to a self-ascription that has what I called first level certainty. This still constitutes a limited defence of Descartes against Lichtenberg. The defence rests on an array of principles from different parts of philosophy. It relies essentially on principles of metaphysics, in its treatment of conscious mental events and their relations to subjects, as outlined earlier in Chapter III. It relies essentially on principles about the nature of concepts. It relies essentially on principles linking the individuation of concepts to entitlement and to knowledge. All these contribute to the explanation. I doubt that we could defend a version of the *Cogito* without them. But they are also principles we need elsewhere. They have not been constructed *ad hoc* simply to validate the *Cogito*.

This defence is limited in other respects too. The defence obviously does not show that the thinker is an immaterial, immortal object. In fact I argued in Chapter III that subjects, as conceived in this very defence of the *Cogito* as represented in (1)–(3) must be something material. On the other hand, the argument equally does not establish that the subject who is known to be thinking must be a Strawsonian person.

Descartes defended as 'evident' another claim that goes beyond 'Cogito ergo sum'. In the *Meditations*, Descartes follows his statement of the *Cogito* with something I have sometimes heard called 'the second *Cogito*'. He writes,

> Is it not one and the same 'I' who is now doubting almost everything, who nonetheless understands some things, who affirms that this one thing is true, denies everything else, desires to know more, is unwilling to be deceived, imagines many things even involuntarily, and is aware of many things which apparently come from the senses? Are not all these things just as true as the fact that I exist, even if I am asleep all the time, and even if he who created me is doing all he can to deceive me? Which of all these activities is distinct from my thinking? Which of them can be said to be separate from myself? The fact that it is I who am doubting and understanding and willing is so evident that I see no way of making it any clearer. But it is also the case that the 'I' who imagines is the same 'I'. For even if, as I have supposed, none of the objects of my imagination are real, the power of imagination is something which really exists and is part of my thinking. Lastly, it is also the same 'I' who has sensory perceptions, or is aware of bodily things as it were through the senses. For example, I am now seeing light, hearing a noise, feeling heat. But I am asleep, so all this is false. Yet I certainly *seem* to see, to hear, and to be warmed. This cannot be false; what is called 'having a sensory perception' is strictly just this, and in this restricted sense of the term it is simply thinking. (1984: 19)

Here Descartes seems to be saying that his knowledge that it is he, one and the same subject, who affirms, and also denies, and also desires, and also seems to see, is as secure as the knowledge that he exists. He says it is 'evident', and even if he who created him is doing all he can to deceive Descartes, he will not succeed in deceiving Descartes about this. Can this second *Cogito* also be validated by the metaphysics and epistemology of conscious subjects that I have presented?

Suppose we have a subject *s* who is:
imagining something at *t*
willing something at *t*
seeming to experience something at *t*.

Back in Chapter III I also endorsed this principle stating what co-consciousness of states and events consists in:

(CC) Co-consciousness of mental events *a* and *b* occurring at the same time *t* consists in *a* and *b* being events in the awareness of the same subject, as elements of that subject's single total, unified state of consciousness.

If (CC) is correct, then the imagining, the willing and the seeming-experiencing of our subject *s* at *t* are all co-conscious. By parallel reasoning to that which we used in the discussion of the original *Cogito*, our subject can now move from a complex conscious state in which his imagining and willing and seeming to experience are co-conscious, to a rational and knowledgeable judgement 'I'm imagining and I'm willing and I'm seeming to experience'. So our subject is indeed in a position to know that it is one and the same thing, himself, that imagines and wills and seems to experience.

I offer this as a defence of Descartes' second *Cogito*. Again, the defence relies extensively on theses in the metaphysics of the subject, including (CC), and the nature of concepts together with their link with epistemology.

The position I have been defending is one on which the use of the first person concept *I* in thought has guaranteed reference. Elizabeth Anscombe has argued that one species of guaranteed reference will force us to take the reference of the first person as a Cartesian Ego. What she means by 'guaranteed reference' is specified in this passage: 'The object an "I"-user means by it must exist so long as he is using "I", nor can he take the wrong object to be the object he means by "I"' (1975: 57). Under the assumption that the first person concept refers, and has guaranteed reference in Anscombe's sense, Anscombe argues that 'it seems to follow that what "I" stands for is a Cartesian Ego' (1975: 57). Her argument is that under such a conception of guaranteed reference, the reference would have to 'remain in view so long as something was being taken to be *I* (1975: 57). And, 'Even so there is an assumption that something else does not surreptitiously take its place' (1975: 57). At the end of this section of her discussion, Anscombe writes, 'Thus we discover that *if* "I" is a referring expression, then Descartes was right about what the referent was. His position has, however, the intolerable difficulty of requiring an identification of the same referent in different "I"-thoughts' (1975: 58).

Anscombe's reasoning has been widely, and in my view fairly, criticized as assimilating the first person to some kind of perceptual or experience-based demonstrative. There is no justification for such assimilation. Nevertheless, her argument still raises questions that my position needs to address. If we are committed to guaranteed reference, how can the reference not be a Cartesian Ego? And Anscombe's question, of how we know it is the same reference in different 'I'-thoughts still needs an answer, whether or not the reference is something Cartesian.

What the *Cogito* arguments establish is the existence of a subject. I argued in the chapter on the metaphysics of subjects that subjects must be materially realized. It does not follow that whenever a thinker is in a position to deploy the reasoning in the *Cogito*, he as a subject must be presented to himself in his material aspect. He need not be, consistently with the *Cogito* still being valid, and consistently also with his being a material, as well as a thinking, thing.

For present tense mental self-ascriptions made on the basis of the consciousness of the mental states in question, the treatment of the Second *Cogito* is intended precisely to explain how the thinker can know that it is one and the same thing that has all his current conscious properties. That argument involves no commitment at all to the immateriality of the subject. It involves the metaphysics of subjects and co-consciousness, and the relation of consciousness to entitlement and knowledge. As far as I can see, all those commitments can be fulfilled if subjects and their conscious states and events are materially realized.

What of the question—Anscombe's question—of identifying the same object as the reference of the first person in 'I'-thoughts at different times, as opposed to different 'I'-thoughts at a given time? There is at least one alleged problem in this area that is spurious. Suppose a given subject s at an earlier time t_1 has an 'I'-thought. By the fundamental rule of reference for 'I', 'I' in this thought refers to the thinker of that thought, viz. s himself. Suppose also that at a later time t_2 the same thinker s has an

'I'-thought. By the same reasoning, 'I' in this later thought also refers to *s* himself. So there is, on the present account, no possibility that the earlier and later 'I'-thoughts of a given subject *s* refer to different things. It would be an ill-founded concern to think that there is some open possibility here that needs to be excluded. If it is the same thinker having the thought at two different times, the reference of 'I' at the two times must be the same, given the fundamental rule of reference for the first person concept and for its linguistic expression.[3] There might be a doubt if one had a perceptual or experiential model of the first person concept; but such models are incorrect, and are certainly not what is being proposed in this book. So I suggest that one can take the first person to refer to a subject, there can be guaranteed reference of a subject's uses of the first person, without incurring insoluble problems of identification of the reference in different uses of 'I'—and without commitment to Cartesian, immaterial Egos either.

I said at the start of this chapter that there are some further Cartesian theses which the position I have been developing makes more understandable than they would be otherwise. The theses themselves both have a somewhat antiquated feel to them, but the reasons one can see a thinker might be led to hold them need not be antiquated at all.

The first Cartesian thesis is that the subject of consciousness is not a material thing at all. Suppose it is true, as I argued in an earlier session, that a conscious subject can exist without representing itself as located in the objective world, the case of what I called Degree 0 of involvement of self-representation in the subject's conception of an objective world. One can see why the possibility of such cases could tempt someone to say the subject is not a material thing at all. The temptation should of course be resisted. A transition from 'not represented as located' to 'correctly represented as not located' is fallacious, involving an illegitimate repositioning of the negation operator. I also argued in Chapter III that the identity of subjects requires material realization. Nonetheless, at least one thought that leads one into immaterialist temptation is correct, and constitutes a philosophically significant point about subjecthood.

---

[3] So here I am endorsing an argument Evans gives in *The Varieties of Reference* (1982: 214). It is striking that in giving the argument, Evans uses just a form of self-reference rule for the first person, rather than the complex account of self-reference involving embodiment that he develops further in the chapter on self-identification.

Something similar applies to claims of indivisibility of the subject of consciousness, a claim found also in Thomas Reid (1785: Essay III 'Of Memory', Chapter 4, pp. 317–18). Since the subject need not be represented in the subject's own thought or experience as located in space at all, a fortiori the subject need not be represented as an extended thing. (And even when it is, the representation is open to sceptical doubt.) Hence the subject need not be thought of or represented in a way that would make it appear that divisibility is a possibility. In precise parallel with the preceding paragraph, it does not follow that a subject could not divide. It also does not follow that a subject's physical realization is not an extended thing, for it is. But these points about the non-necessity of the subject's locating itself in space do help to explain how the door is opened to deep illusions about the conscious subject.

VII

Paralogisms and First Person Illusions

The conceptions of the first person and of the self developed in the preceding chapters bear upon Kant's discussion of Descartes and other 'rational psychologists' in the *Critique of Pure Reason*. By considering the relevance of these conceptions to the contributions made by these two great philosophers, we can understand better the nexus of relations between the first person concept, the self, and their epistemology and metaphysics. Kant accuses rational psychologists, amongst whom he cites Descartes as a representative, of a mistaken conception of this nexus of relations. I will be arguing that plausible theses in the philosophy of mind and the theory of intentional content imply that not all the problems lie on Descartes' side of the argument.

1. The Issues

Kant's treatment of rational psychology in the section entitled 'The Paralogisms of Pure Reason' in the *Critique of Pure Reason* is philosophical writing of such brilliance and depth, admired by successive generations of philosophers, that several disclaimers about my aims are required right at the outset. I have no dispute with Kant's critique of the idea that the subject of consciousness must be a simple, non-complex entity. Kant's writing on that topic looks extraordinarily prescient, even in an age of cognitive science. More than two centuries later it could hardly be bettered in so short a compass. Nor do I think that any of the other characteristic metaphysical doctrines of Descartes and the rational psychologists are true. Those doctrines hold that the subject of consciousness is immaterial and non-spatial, and not only persists over time, but also never ceases to exist. My dispute with Kant is not about many of his conclusions. The disagreement concerns rather some crucial points in his reasoning, and his corresponding diagnoses of Cartesian thought.

Kant's section on the Paralogisms has also been the focus of some important critical commentary in recent years, and I will at some points draw on some of this work in comparing his position with one that seems to me more defensible.[1] Kant's treatment of the Paralogisms involves the intertwining of many strands in his thought, and a full textual discussion would merit a book-length examination.

The conceptions on which I want to draw in developing my argument can be specified by four theses, all of which have been defended earlier in this book. The first thesis is one for which I argued in Chapter IV (and see also Campbell 1994). It concerns the individuation of the first person concept, and it is itself twofold. The first part of the thesis states that

What makes something the reference of the concept *I* in any particular event of thinking is that it is the agent, the producer, of that thinking.

The second part of the thesis states that the displayed condition is not merely a constitutive condition for something's being the reference of *I* in a particular thinking. The second part holds that the displayed condition, the fundamental reference rule for the first person concept, is also what makes something, what individuates, the first person concept. This second part of the thesis can be seen as an instance of a broadly Fregean claim. It is an application of the idea that what individuates a sense is the fundamental condition for something to be the reference of the sense (Dummett 1981; Peacocke 2008).

The second thesis in the theory of intentional content applies to first person, or *de se*, contents more generally, and is one for which I made a case in Chapter II:

For a mental state or event to have a *de se* content is simply for it to have a content that, *de jure*, concerns the subject who enjoys that state or event.

This applies both to conceptual and to nonconceptual contents. Again, it is plausible that this is what makes *de se* content the content it is, both in the conceptual and in the nonconceptual instances. In the special case in

---

[1] In the past thirteen years, see especially Ameriks (2000), and the references therein to literature to that date, and more recently Longuenesse (2008) and Proops (2010).

which the mental event is a mental action of making a judgement with a first person content, there is no conflict between this second thesis and the first thesis. In the case of a mental action that is the judging of a first person content, the agent making the judgement is identical with the conscious subject who enjoys the action awareness of making the judgement.

The third thesis, one in the philosophy of mind, is also one for which we argued in Chapters II and IV:

A subject who possesses the first person concept has a mental file on himself, a file for the first person concept. When all is functioning properly, the present tense contents of this file are updated noninferentially, as time passes, to the appropriately corresponding past tense contents. So, for instance, if on one day the subject's file contains something with the content *Today I am in Princeton*, then the next day the file will contain something with the content *Yesterday I was in Princeton*, without any personal-level inference on the subject's part.

The last of the four theses concerns the metaphysics of subjects. It states what I argued for in Chapter III, that

The identity of a conscious subject over time is constitutively dependent on the identity of an integrating apparatus that integrates the precursors of perceptions, sensations, thoughts and emotions.

This is not a conception on which identity of subject is dependent on a subject's having a body. The conception does, however, involve the identity of a material entity, the integrating apparatus.

So much by way of very brief statement of the contemporary position on which I will be drawing. Now we can turn to the application to Kant's critique of Descartes and the other rational psychologists. When Descartes presents his arguments about what he is, and his essential properties, it is overwhelmingly plausible that he is using the first person in its ordinary sense. Descartes' arguments simply employ the first person pronoun, or first person case, in natural language (Latin or French), without any stipulation of a special sense. The sense expressed by these uses of the first person is the way of thinking of himself employed in Descartes' ordinary first person thoughts. We are meant to assess his arguments as sound or otherwise taking them to involve this normal sense. When you adapt Descartes's arguments to your own case, as when you think through the *Cogito* and refer to yourself, you will be using the ordinary first person way of thinking that you employ in your other first person thoughts.

Kant himself relies on a series of highly substantive theses in the philosophy of mind, the philosophy of thought, and the theory of meaning and intentional content in his critique of a Cartesian-style position. Here is a selection of these theses:

The rational psychologist is making a mistake that involves a failure to appreciate the importance of the point that 'not the least intuition is bound up with' first person representations (A350).[2] A genuine and non-empty singular concept of an object that can be given (or at least an object that is a substance) must be based on an intuition of that object (B412-3).

There is a positive account to be given of the role of the first person in the rational psychologist's premise 'I think', an account that involves the idea that the I in 'I think' is 'rather purely intellectual, because it belongs to thinking in general' (B423). Kant says that if he has called 'I think' an empirical proposition, that is because 'without any empirical representation, which provides the material for thinking, the act I think would not take place, and the empirical is only the condition of the application, or use, of the pure intellectual faculty' (B423).

'rational psychology has its origin in a mere misunderstanding. The unity of consciousness, which grounds the categories, is here taken for an intuition of the subject as object' (B421).

The rational psychologist's reasoning as captured in the First Paralogism 'passes off the constant logical subject of thinking as the cognition of a real subject of inherence' (A350). 'Meanwhile, one can quite well allow the proposition **The soul is substance** to be valid, if only one admits [. . .] it signifies a substance only in the idea but not in reality' (A350-1).

The apparent awareness of we have of our own identity over time should be given a construal that does not involve awareness of the genuine identity of anything over time (A362-4). 'The identity of the consciousness of Myself in different times is therefore only a formal condition of my thoughts and their connection, but it does not prove at all the numerical identity of my subject' (A363).

What exactly these claims mean, and what they are targeted against, we will consider below. My general position is that while some of these points involve incisive and original insights, which is why Kant's discussion has been so admired, what is right in these points cannot be soundly applied against significant parts of Descartes' reasoning. Others amongst the displayed Kantian claims I will be arguing to be untrue. Any case

---

[2] All translations from Kant are from the Guyer and Wood edition (Kant 1998).

against Descartes' metaphysics of the mind needs to be differently organized, and in part differently based. I divide the relevant issues into three clusters.

(i) Kant's complaints about the Cartesian use of the first person concept

The first cluster of questions concerns some plausible claims that Kant makes about the first person concept. Does what is right in Kant's points about the first person concept as it occurs in certain premises used by the rational psychologist really undermine the early stages of Descartes' argument? Kant seems to suggest that an appreciation of his points about the relevant occurrences of the first person concept, when taken together with other theses held by the rational psychologist, will show that the rational psychologist's position involves the violation of constraints on significance, or at least the violation of constraints required for a singular concept to refer to a 'substance'. What, if anything, is the connection between what is right in Kant's points about the first person, in its relevant uses, and the alleged violation of a principle of significance? Is Kant's target the transitions made in Descartes' thought from certain states of consciousness, or is it something else?

(ii) Kant's Positive Account

The second cluster of questions centres on Kant's positive account or conception of how the 'I' in 'I think' operates. What is Kant's own positive account, and with which parts of Descartes' position is that positive account incompatible?

(iii) 'A Merely Logical Subject'

The third cluster of questions concerns Kant's frequently expressed idea that there is in first person ascriptions of conscious states a 'merely logical subject'.[3] Kant's idea is that the rational psychologist is mistaking this 'merely logical subject' for something more substantial. What is a 'merely logical subject'? How does this notion relate to the concerns in the question clusters (i) and (ii)? Is it really true that there are uses of the first person that are correctly described as involving 'merely logical

---

[3]   A350; A363 (which speaks of the 'the logical identity of the I'); and B413 (which speaks of 'a merely logically qualitative unity of self-consciousness in general').

subjects', and produce illusions of reference to something more substantial? If we question the idea of a 'merely logical subject', is there any good reason for a subject not to take her apparent awareness of her own identity over time at face value?

2. Some Replies to Kant's Objections

I will be arguing that an account of the first person and the self that endorses the conception captured in the four theses stated in Section 1 suggests answers to some of the questions raised in these clusters (i)–(iii). They are answers that diverge from Kant's own position.

(i) Kant's complaints about the Cartesian transitions involving the first person concept

In developing his case against rational psychology, Kant makes the point that there is a use of the first person which does not involve its reference being given in an intuition: 'For the I is, to be sure, in all thoughts; but not the least intuition is bound up with this representation, which would distinguish it from other objects of intuition. Therefore one can, to be sure, perceive that this representation continually recurs with every thought, but not that it is a standing and abiding intuition, in which thoughts (as variable) would change' (A350). That the first person 'representation' about which Kant is saying this is something he takes to be genuine, and not something illusory postulated by the rational psychologist, is evident in several other passages. In the following passage, from the B edition, he emphasizes that this representation is used in describing what the thinker can really become conscious of, and again it does not involve any intuition of the subject: 'this identity of the subject, of which I can become conscious in every representation, does not concern the intuition of it, through which it is given as object' (B408). Later in the second edition he writes of 'the empirical but in regard to all kinds of intuition indeterminate proposition "I think"' (B421).

Kant emphasizes the absence of any intuition associated with this use of the first person, because the rational psychologist is concerned to establish the existence of purely mental, non-material substances. For Kant, any genuine thought about substance must involve an intuition of the substance. He writes of 'the category of substance, which always presupposes a given intuition' (B422). He repeatedly asserts this link between substance and intuition. 'The concept of substance is always related to intuitions, which in me cannot be other than sensible' (B408). We must 'ground the persistence of a given object on experience if we would apply to that object the empirically usable concept of a substance' (A349). 'Thus if that concept, by means of the term "substance", is to indicate an object that can be given, and if it is to become a cognition, then it must be grounded on a persisting intuition as the indispensable condition of the objective reality of a concept, namely, that through which alone an object is given' (B412-3). So the argument seems to be: the use of the first person in the rational psychologist's premise 'I think' does not have the required connection with an intuition that it would have to have if the rational psychologist's reasoning is to establish what he wants it to establish. Kant summarizes his discussion of the Paralogisms in the second edition discussion: 'From all this one sees that rational psychology has its origin in a mere misunderstanding. The unity of consciousness, which grounds the categories, is here taken for an intuition of the subject as object, and the category of substance is applied to it' (B421-2). No doubt Kant did not think that absolutely every significant singular term has to refer to something given in intuition, and has to be understood by means of that intuition. It does, however, seem clear from these passages that he thinks there is some general class, including all substances of the sort in which Cartesian egos would need to be included, must conform to such a connection with intuition. Kant's view seems to be that Cartesian subjects fail a substantive requirement concerning intuition.

Kant's starting point in this reasoning, that there is no intuition 'bound up with' the first person seems to me entirely correct. It is supported by everything in a good account of the first person concept. No demonstrative, either of the form 'that' or 'that F', in perception or sensation or any other form of consciousness, is equivalent to a notion or concept of something as oneself. Even when a perceptual experience has a genuine first person content—as in the example of seeing something as coming towards oneself—there does not need to be an intuition of oneself in the experience which gives it that first person content. Kant's premise seems to be true and important. It is in part a Humean insight. The point is completely independent of Kant's phenomenal/noumenal distinction, and of other contentious theses in his theoretical thought. That is, dialectically, part of the strength of this premise and of Kant's starting point.

The explanation of the truth of this point about the absence of any intuition 'bound up with' the first person lies in the difference between the fundamental reference rule for any demonstrative and the fundamental reference rule for the first person (in both its conceptual and its nonconceptual forms). Any intuition based demonstrative picks out the object experienced, either perceived or sensed. That is, it refers to the object standing in a certain relation to what Kant would call the intuition. The first person by contrast always refers *de jure* to the subject of the experience or conscious event in question. These are utterly different conditions. The condition for the first person to refer does not even require an intuition of what is in fact the subject, for the first person may feature in the content of an experience in which the subject is not given in any intuition. The first person may also feature in an intuition-free thinking. This difference between any intuition-based demonstrative and the nature of the first person is brought out clearly by the first two theses above of the contemporary conception.

I pause the argument briefly to note that this account of what is arguably defensible in Kant's thought makes the point one that is quite specific to the first person concept, rather than something applicable to any singular concept that can feature in subject position in the content of a thought. In his highly illuminating article 'Kant's First Paralogism', Ian Proops (2010) gives a construal of Kant's treatment of that paralogism. On his construal, the rational psychologist rightly points out that the first person concept cannot feature in predicative position. Proops' point is that nothing follows from this about whether the subject referred to by the first person concept is something whose existence depends on the existence of other things. As Proops notes, a singular concept picking out something whose existence is obviously dependent upon the existence of other things, such as your right fist (Proops' example), is equally incapable of featuring in predicative position (2010: 475–7). I think that Proops is certainly identifying one strand in Kant's thought here. But this particular strand is not something unique to the first person, as the example of the fist shows. We need to cite something distinctive of the first person, amongst singular notions of persisting entities, if we are to contribute to an explanation of why there should be a special tendency to illusions about the self. The non-equivalence of *I* with any demonstrative concept of the form *that F*, where this demonstrative is some perceptual or sensorily based singular concept, is certainly a feature of much more restricted application. The feature integrates well with some of Kant's adumbrations and analysis. In particular, if the *F* that occurs in a perceptual demonstrative is something true of material extended things, then if *I* were equivalent to such a demonstrative *that F*, then the subject would even be given as something material and extended; and in fact the subject is not so given.[4] In the first edition's treatment of the First Paralogism, the absence of any 'intuition bound up with' the first person is certainly playing a role in the argument (A350). By contrast, there would, of course, be an intuition bound up with the perceptual demonstrative 'this right fist'.

To return to the main argument: I have argued that Kant is recognizing an important point about the distinctive nature of the first person concept *I*, viz. that its fundamental reference rule does not mention or require any relation of the reference of the concept, on a particular occasion, to any experience enjoyed by the thinker. This elaboration of the point on which I want to agree with Kant about the first person does, however, undermine part of the use Kant wants to make of the very same point. The explanation just given of what seems right in his point is entirely at the level of modes of presentation, at the level of intentional content rather than the level of reference. The explanation is quite neutral on the nature of the ontology of subjects. It does not advert to the metaphysics of subjects at all, but only to distinctions drawn between ways in which something can be represented.

It is, then, entirely consistent with acceptance of Kant's point about the first person to insist that in a thinking of 'I think', the first person concept does refer. It just does not refer by means of a relation to some particular intuition. It would even be consistent with such a position to hold that, if the first person is to refer, it must be to something that could be an object of intuition (though Kant would not agree, in this particular case). Such a constraint is not at odds with the explanation at the level of modes of presentation.

---

[4] Of course, from the true premise that the subject is not so given in first person thought we should not move to the false conclusion that the subject is not in fact material and extended—the fallacy of moving from 'not being given as having property P' to 'not having property P'. I do not in fact think that Descartes made any such fallacious inference. His arguments for the distinctness of mind and body involve other, further premises.

There are other genuinely indexical concepts that refer on particular occasions of their use, but do not do so via a relation to a perceptual intuition. If we prescind from Kant's own very special and complex views about time, the present tense concept *now* is plausibly a salient example. The present tense concept can feature in thoughts ('I wonder what is happening in Congress now') without there existing any perceptual intuition of which it is true that it is an intuition of the time referred to by *now* in the thought in question, and is an intuition whereby *now* as used on this occasion gains its reference. Perceptual experience represents events as occurring in the present, and one's thinkings are experienced as occurring in the present, but none of this means that the present is itself given in a perceptual intuition. Also, the way the present is given in experience is not something that makes the present time something that is available as an object of attention. A detailed discussion of time in experience is a topic for some other occasion, but still it should be clear a broad parallelism is present. The fundamental reference rule for *now* is that in any mental event in whose content it occurs, *now* in that event refers to the time of occurrence of that event. Since any event occurs in time, its present tense component will refer to a particular time, even if there is no such thing as a perceptual intuition of a time. If it is equally in the nature of mental events that each such event must be enjoyed by a subject, then equally in any mental event with a first person content *I*, that use of *I* will refer, under the fundamental reference rule we have been discussing, and it will refer to the subject of that event.

We can now ask a pivotal question about Kant's intended target in the argument of the Paralogisms. When Kant makes what we have endorsed as the sound point that 'no intuition is bound up with' the first person as it occurs in the rational psychologist's reasoning, what is his target? Is his argument aimed

(a) against the transitions that lead the rational psychologist to his conclusion *I think*, as inadequate to ground knowledge about the thing that is the reference of *I*? This we can call 'the inadequate-grounds interpretation'. Or is his argument aimed

(b) to establish that the rational psychologist is presupposing an incorrect theory of the nature of the first person concept? This is the 'misunderstood-concept interpretation'. Or is his argument

(c)   that if the rational psychologist's general metaphysics of the subject is to be correct, the first person concept together with its reference would have to have various properties that the rational psychologist's reasoning has in no way established that they have? This is the 'missing properties' argument.

Kant might of course have had more than one of these aims simultaneously. But I will argue that the first two of these interpretations take as their target something to which a rational psychologist such as Descartes has a good defence, while the third interpretation, when considered in more detail in the light of Kant's text, has problems as an interpretation of Kant's intentions.

The inadequate-grounds interpretation, (a), has Kant as insisting that the transitions that, for example, Descartes makes from thinkings or experiencings or imaginings or willings to *I think* are fallacious. But there is a strong case to be made that such transitions, taken simply at face value, are not fallacious. That they are not fallacious is what I argued in the preceding chapter. What makes it the case that some event or state is a conscious event is that there is something it is like subjectively for the subject of that event (Nagel 1974; and Chapter 3 above). If that is correct, then a transition in thought from enjoyment of a conscious state to self-ascription of a state, of the conscious kind it is, will always yield a true judgement. If the conscious kind is thought of in a way that has constitutive links to self-ascription when the subject enjoys the conscious state or event, then there is a good case to be made that the transition not only yields a true judgement, but one to which the thinker is entitled, and which can be knowledge. There is not required to be any intuition of the subject in the conscious state from which the transition to *I think* is made. Even if *per accidens* there is an intuition of the subject in the initial conscious state, that is not what makes the transition truth-yielding, entitled, and knowledge-yielding.

These points do not rest on or presuppose any questionable Cartesian metaphysics of subjects of consciousness. They stand independently of any such metaphysics. Nor do they presuppose some bleached-out or *ersatz* notion of reference for the concept *I* as it features in the conclusion *I think*. Whatever is wrong with a Cartesian metaphysics of subjects, it is not these transitions.

The misunderstood-concept interpretation, (b), has Kant protesting that the rational psychologist is presupposing an incorrect theory of the nature of the first person concept. I suspect this interpretation does an injustice to both Descartes and Kant. Of course neither Descartes nor Kant, to the best of my knowledge, formulated explicit semantic theses about the first person concept. A fortiori, neither connected semantic theses with the epistemology and metaphysics of subject. (Much as one may wish to the contrary: the question of what Kant might have said had he had Frege's sense/reference apparatus to hand is as intriguing here as it is in other areas too.) The reason this interpretation (b) seems to be an injustice is that some of the most striking points that each of these philosophers makes about the first person is vindicated under the supposition of correctness of the first thesis in the philosophy of mind we mentioned at the outset: that what makes something the reference of the concept *I* in any particular event of thinking is that it is the agent, the producer, of the thinking. As I said in in the preceding chapter, this reference rule contributes essentially to the validation, both semantic and epistemic, of the *Cogito* transitions in Descartes. If Descartes had thought some intuition had to be associated with the first person for it to gain reference, he would never have accorded to the *Cogito* the status he actually gave it. Nor could the *Cogito* have turned back the doubt for him. Equally, there are comments in Kant that would seem to be best explained by his having some tacit appreciation of the above reference rule for *I*, or at least the independence of any correct rule from intuitions of the thing that is its reference. Kant acutely observes that 'even if we supposed' 'secure observation' of a soul (whatever that might involve), that would not establish the persistence of what is referred to by the first person, precisely because 'not the least observation is bound up with this representation, which would distinguish it from other objects of intuition' (all quotes from A350). More generally, Kant comments: 'I would not say by this that the *I* in this proposition [viz, *I think*—CP] is an empirical representation; for it is rather purely intellectual, for it belongs to thinking in general' (B426). If Kant had held that an intuition of an object were required for *I* to refer to the object, he would after all be holding that the *I* in *I think* is an empirical representation, which is precisely what he is denying.

Kant does repeatedly emphasize in his discussion of the Paralogisms that one cannot obtain from a concept alone 'the usual conclusions of the rationalistic doctrine of the soul' (A350-1); 'here as elsewhere we can have little hope of broadening our insight through mere concepts' (A361). His point here concerns what conclusions can be drawn from various phenomena involving the first person concept, not that Descartes or other rational psychologists have mistaken the nature or fundamental identity of that concept.

The missing-properties interpretation, (c), has Kant saying that the rational psychologist has failed to establish that the first person concept and its reference has certain properties they would have to have if the rational psychologist's conclusions are to be true. Certainly anyone who agrees that subjects do not exist forever, and are not immaterial, is committed to saying that Descartes' arguments must be unsound somewhere. His arguments must either have false premises, or rely on invalid transitions. Now in the *Meditations*, the stage of Descartes' reasoning at which he concludes that he is purely a thinking thing, and not an extended thing, is to be found in Meditation VI. His reasoning there is complex and articulated. It involves the notion of a clear and distinct idea; it involves a conception of the natures of things; it involves the notion of a 'complete' thing; and his argument involves his own supposed capacity to conceive of thought without extension. There is a particularly good discussion of the structure of Descartes' argument at this point in Margaret Wilson's book (1978, Chapter VI, esp. p.197 ff.). So one might have expected Kant to address Descartes' reasoning involving these various notions and claims about what he can conceive in his section on the Paralogisms. In fact he does not. Rather, what Kant does is to imply that Descartes had already gone astray in his conception of conscious mental events and states, and of their relation to what contents we can know that contain the first person concept in their content. The implication is that he is under some illusion about the role of the first person and its relation to consciousness, and about what conscious states can justify.

Here are some of Kant's statements. One of his formulations is that the rational psychologist has confused a 'formal condition' of the identity of his thoughts with the numerical identity of a subject (A363). 'I relate each and every one of my successive determinations to the numerically identical Self in all time, i.e. in the form of the inner intuition of my self. On this basis the personality of the soul must be regarded not as inferred but rather as a completely identical proposition of self-consciousness in time, and that is also the cause of its being valid a priori. For it really says no more than that in the whole time in which I am conscious of myself, I am conscious of this time as belonging to the unity of my Self' (A362). Most striking, in discussing the concept of personality, conceived of as applying to subjects who are aware of their identity over time, he writes that: 'we can never boast of it [the concept of personality—CP] as an extension of our self-knowledge through pure reason, which dazzles us with the uninterrupted continuous duration of the subject drawn from the mere concept of the identical self, since this concept revolves in a circle around itself and brings us no farther in regard to even one single question about synthetic cognition' (A366). At the start of the B edition discussion of the Paralogisms, he emphasizes, clearly intending his remarks in opposition to the rational psychologist, 'I cognize myself not by being conscious of myself as thinking' (B406). It is, on Kant's view, the philosophical scrutiny of consciousness, its nature, and its relations that reveals the errors in the rational psychologist's thought. Presumably that is why he thinks there is no need to go into the theory of clear and distinct ideas, complete natures, and the rest, in the case of Descartes. 'Thus through the analysis of the consciousness of myself in thinking in general not the least is won in regard to the cognition of myself as object' (B409). Kant's summary diagnosis of the errors of rational psychology mentions a mistake about consciousness, and not anything about the (highly problematic) argumentative apparatus of Meditation VI. In his summary, Kant writes, 'From all this one sees that rational psychology has its origin in a mere misunderstanding. The unity of consciousness, which grounds the categories, is here taken for an intuition of the subject as object, and the category of substance is applied to it. But this unity is only the unity of *thinking*, through which no object is given; and thus the category of substance, which always presupposes a given *intuition*, cannot be applied to it, and hence this subject cannot be cognized at all' (B421-2).

If Kant's arguments are indeed confined to the domain of the consciousness/thought relations, where does this leave him if we accept the positions in the philosophy of mind, thought, and metaphysics that I mentioned at the outset? As far as the first paralogism is concerned (I will return to the third), it looks as if an option has been overlooked. It is possible to maintain that the *Cogito* transitions are sound, that they yield knowledge, and that it is simply open to further investigation what other kind of properties are possessed by the entity to which the ordinary first person in the *I think* refers. It is consistent with the soundness and knowledge-yielding status of *Cogito* transitions that the first person refers to something, perhaps must refer to something, that could be an object of intuition. There is no obvious requirement that if *I* is to refer to something that could be an object of intuition, it must be an object of intuition in the very mental states or events that are the starting point of a *Cogito* transition. Under this overlooked option, there is no reason for saying that *I* is not being treated as fully referential in *I think* when that conclusion is reached by a *Cogito* transition. Attempts in the spirit of Lichtenberg to say that what is supported by the starting point of a *Cogito* transition can be explained in subject-free terms have proved difficult to sustain, as we argued in the preceding chapter. Though I have no brief for the full Cartesian metaphysics of the subject, it is not clear to me that Descartes has made any mistake within the sphere of consciousness/ thought relations when he concludes that one can have knowledge of an entity in making a *Cogito*-like transition in thought.

This objection to an element of Kant's line of thought, like the other objections I will raise, does nothing to support a rational psychologist's conception of an ontology of purely mental subjects that never go out of existence. As I said, the objection in this case is to Kant's reasoning, not to his conclusion. Moreover, it is hard not to sympathize with Kant's view that a Cartesian conception of egos violates some form of a prin- ciple of significance. No possible experience has been associated, even indirectly, with the distinction between one Cartesian ego persisting and its replacement by another with the relevantly same mental states. I certainly agree with Kant on the conditional that if the reference of the first person were something of the sort Descartes thought it to be, then there would be a problem in the theory of significance raised both by the nature of that thing and of what is involved in its identity over time. Such appeals to a principle of significance operate, however, at the level of reference and objects. It is an objection to the Cartesian concep- tion of a certain kind of object, Cartesian egos. The objection does not fundamentally have to be formulated at the level of sense, at the level of the first person concept; though it will of course have ramifications for the truth conditions and understanding of first person thoughts.

(ii) Kant's Positive Account

The second cluster of questions asks whether Kant's own positive account of the 'I' in 'I think', or the underlying motivations for it, are incompatible with Descartes' position. The first task here is to say exactly what Kant's positive account is. On this, Béatrice Longuenesse (2008) has some important suggestions. Her view is that according to Kant, 'In referring his thoughts to "I", the thinker (perceiver, imaginer) is doing nothing more than committing himself to the unity and consistency of his thoughts, and committing himself to obtaining a unified standpoint that could be shared by all' (2008: 17). Following her description of the role of 'I' in relation to these unifying functions, Longuenesse writes that 'There is nothing more to be known of "I" in the context of this argument' (2008: 17); and 'It is thus apparent that the function of "I" in this argument is quite different from what it was in Descartes' *cogito* argument' (2008: 17). '"I" in "I think" does not refer to a permanent *object* whose properties *change*. "I" is just the term to which we refer our thoughts in order to think of them as unified by one standpoint and bound by rules that commit us ("me") to bring about unity and consistency under a unifying standpoint' (2008: 22) '. . . of course what we refer to by "I" has to be one and the same through the whole time of our experience. And of course this identity is prior to and different from the identity of any object identifiable and reidentifiable *in* time, although it may readily be mistaken for such an identity' (2008: 23). Of such a statement as that the reference of 'I' in 'I think' is a mind distinct from a body, on this reading of Kant, 'when we make this kind of statement we make a category mistake. For we compare the certainty of the pre-categorial existence contained in "I think" and the certainty of the *actuality* of objects given, identified, and reidentified in space and time' (2008: 25).

There is considerable textual support for some aspects of this reading, even beyond the passages Longuenesse cites. One such passage is a note Kant made about 'I think' in his own copy of the first edition of the *Critique of Pure Reason*: '[This] is a proposition a priori, is a mere category of the subject, intellectual representation without anywhere or at any time, hence not empirical. Whether the category of reality lies in it, whether objective inferences are to be drawn from it' (1998: 413 note *a*). The reading gives further significance to such passages as A346/B404: 'consciousness in itself is not even a representation distinguishing a particular object', and to the idea of what Kant calls *modi* of self-consciousness, which he describes in the second edition as 'mere functions, which provide thought with no object at all' (B407). There is further support in these passages: 'I would not say by this that the *I* [in "I think"—CP] in this proposition is an empirical representation; for it is rather purely intellectual, because it belongs to thinking in general'; 'I think of myself, in behalf of a possible experience . . .' (B426).

The first set of points I want to make about this interpretation is that, under this reading of Kant, the 'I' in 'I think' must still have a very close connection with the ordinary first person concept, for three reasons.

First, to engage with such a rationalist as Descartes, these Kantian points will be relevant to Descartes' reasoning only if they employ the same first person concept as Descartes was employing in reasoning. But it was the ordinary first person that Descartes was employing. This is consistent with Longuenesse's main points if we regard Kant as making a contribution to a constitutive account of what is involved in grasp of the first person. That account can be developed consistently with the first person being governed by the fundamental reference rule I have been defending. The Kantian account aims to say something philosophically informative about grasp of the same first person concept mentioned in the fundamental reference rule.[5]

Second, it is very plausible that the constraints of consistency and unity that Longuenesse very properly emphasizes must involve consistency and unity of predications about objects in the world. These predications will include both contents that are not about oneself, and also some that are about oneself (including one's spatial, temporal, and causal properties and relations). Having consistent and unified predications about the wrong thing would not be enough. How is the reference that is the target of these consistency and unity requirements determined when the contents involve the first person? The plausible answer is that the reference must be the thinker who is thinking the 'I' in 'I think'. But that rule is precisely the rule that individuates the normal first person concept, on the account I have been defending earlier in this work, and summarized at the start of this Chapter.

---

[5] When Longuenesse writes, elaborating Kant, '"I" in "I think" does not refer to a permanent *object* whose properties *change*' (2008: 22), we have to agree with the proposition thereby attributed to Kant, because 'I' does not refer to a permanent object. But it does refer to an impermanent object whose properties change. That is something we are committed to by our ordinary views, in combination with the thesis that both Kant and Descartes are using 'I' with its ordinary sense. This observation does not, however, damage the point that there are consistency and unity constraints on the first person concept that contribute to its having the sense (and thereby the reference) it does.

Third, Longuenesse emphasizes that '"I think" is a *universal* form of thought, which can be attributed to *any* thinker; on the other hand, this universal form is necessary for *particular, empirically determined perceivers and thinkers* to come up with thoughts about the world that *are independent of their own particular standpoint in the world*' (2008: 17). I agree. This interplay between the general requirements that apply to an arbitrary thinker in the world, and those that apply to each one of us thinkers individually, is entirely consistent with taking the constraints with which Kant is concerned in the 'I' in 'I think' as applying to its normal sense when used by any one of us. The first person concept as employed by any one thinker is an instance of a general type instances of which are employed by other thinkers. This is the type labeled the '[self]' type in the kind of neo-Fregean terminology account I would favour myself (1981). The constraints of unity and consistency can be formulated for an arbitrary thinker, for anyone who is employing an instance of the [self] type; the constraints are then given for arbitrary instances of that type. That is consistent with use of any instance of the type, so constrained, being the ordinary first person concept as used by a particular thinker.

It would, however, be a mistake to think that Kant's points about 'I' apply only at the level of the type of concept. On the contrary, it is clear that in many passages, Kant is talking about his own uses of 'I'; and it is clear that anyone else is meant to appreciate that the same points apply to his own uses (involving that instance of the [self] type available to him). This point applies to many of the passages quoted or cited above. As we saw, Longuenesse wrote '"I" in "I think" does not refer to a permanent *object* whose properties *change*' (2008: 22). But if Kant's points apply at the level of instances of the first person type, those are instances that do refer—not indeed to a permanent object, but certainly to an object that changes. What is true is that in thinking of something in the first person way, one is not thereby thinking of it as an object identified in a particular way in relation to space, nor as something temporally reidentified in a certain way, nor as an object given in an intuition. These are all points at the level of sense, not of reference. As far as I can see, accepting these points and acknowledging their philosophical importance is consistent with the soundness and knowledge-yielding character of *Cogito*-like transitions, when taken at face value. The points elaborate constraints on what is involved in grasping the first person that features in the *Cogito*-like transitions. The constraints do not undermine those transitions, taken at face value. In particular, they do not undermine that part of Descartes' discussion that is confined to the nexus of consciousness/judgment relations involving the first person, as opposed to the further metaphysics of Meditation VI, and Descartes' views about the nature of the reference of the first person.

(iii) 'A Merely Logical Subject'

The third cluster of questions concerns Kant's idea that the rational psychologist mistakes what is a 'merely logical subject' for something more substantial, a mistake that involves confusing the unity of experience with an experience of unity. The first paralogism, he writes, 'passes off the constant logical subject of thinking as the cognition of a real subject of inherence' (A350). Kant's view seems to be that all conscious states have a certain common form; this form is captured by the characterization 'I think . . .'; 'consciousness in itself is not even a representation distinguishing a particular object' (A346/B404), but the 'I' in 'I think' is still a logical subject, and the fact that the 'I think' can accompany all my representations may, according to Kant, lead to the mistaken thesis that from all this, with no other premises, one can conclude that some entity stands in a relation to all one's own conscious states.

I agree that there is a phenomenology of all of what Kant would call one's 'representations' being one's own. This is a feature of consciousness, of its form if you will. Nonetheless, Kant's argument as summarized in the preceding paragraph is open to objection if the points I made on the second cluster of questions are correct. If 'I' in 'I think' does not have a reference at all, then of course mental states with an intentional content 'I think . . .' cannot be a source of knowledge about the normal reference of 'I' in 'I think', since it has no such normal reference. But if it does have its normal reference, the possibility is reopened that such mental states can, on occasion, be a source of knowledge about the thing that is its reference. That it does have a normal reference in Descartes' thought is implied by what I have been arguing. If Descartes' *I* has its normal sense, it must also have its normal reference, however mistaken Descartes may have been about the properties of that normal reference.

If a thinker, including a rational psychologist, is clear-sighted about how the reference rule for *I* works, then is it quite unfair to accuse him of mistaking the unity of experience for an experience of unity. The clear-sighted thinker will not hold that an experience of unity (as opposed to unity of experience) is in any way necessarily involved in a correct, referential use of *I*. Neither the rational psychologist, nor we, in judging 'All these experiences are mine', need to be committed to thinking that, in making this attribution of common ownership of the experiences to a single subject, there needs to be an experience or intuition of that subject. According to the fundamental reference rule, a thinking 'All these experiences are mine' is true iff all the experiences in question belong to the subject doing the thinking. The experiences can all seem to be the thinker's, and the thinker can be entitled to take this seeming as correct, without the thinker needing to have an intuition of himself. In its seeming to the thinker that all the experiences are his, he enjoys a seeming with a primitive first person content. The correctness condition for that content is as given in the second thesis at the outset of this chapter, that all the experiences do in fact belong to the subject enjoying that seeming. (Of course we also have to give an account of the entitlement to take the seeming at face value.) If Descartes did ever say that he has an experiential (Kantian-style) intuition of himself that is involved in such self-ascriptive uses of the first person, it is not something he ever needed to say. An easy acceptance of the stylish formulation 'unity of experience, not experience of unity' should not lead us into thinking that this was a mistake Descartes had to make.

In his discussion of the third paralogism in the first edition, Kant makes a further point. He rightly and forcefully observes that its seeming to oneself that one was thus-and-so in the past does not suffice to make it the case that one was thus-and-so in the past (A362-5). His discussion is cast in terms of consciousness of the identity of oneself at different times.

Now it cannot follow from Kant's true observation that there is a seems/is distinction in this area that there is no such thing as genuine awareness of one's identity over time. To argue from that premise alone would be to apply the fallacious argument from illusion to the case of apparent awareness of identity over time.

The third thesis I repeated in outlining a conception at the outset of this chapter serves further to illustrate why a fallacy would be involved. A temporally sensitive mechanism that noninferentially updates a subject's file on itself, a file of the sort described in that thesis, can generate knowledge-sustaining awareness of identity over time. The mechanism will not be infallible, any more than perception needs to be infallible. But when the temporal updating mechanism is working properly, it can give a subject genuine awareness of its identity over time, an awareness that it did or was thus-and-so in the past, just as perception can give genuine awareness of physical objects and events. The operation of the updating mechanism also does not at all require that the subject that is aware that it was thus-and-so in the past have a current intuition of itself.

An adequate defence of the claim that such memories give genuine awareness of identity must involve an account of the kind of thing of whose identity over time the thinker is aware (even though of course a thinker may be unaware of his or her own kind in making ascriptions of individual identity over time). It is very plausible that Descartes, given the metaphysics of Meditation VI, has no good account of the matter. On the particular account I have been developing, the identity of the subject over time involves identity of integrating apparatus. The view that identity of subject in the most fundamental case involves identity of embodied subject also has an account, a different one, of the matter. Insofar as Kant's point was merely that the rational psychologist has no good account of the kind of entity the awareness of identity is awareness of, I am in agreement. But again, this is a point having to do with the level of reference, and the nature of the entities referred to, rather than one turning on the nature of the intentional content of mental states. It does not rule out genuine, knowledge-sustaining awareness of one's own identity with the person who was so-and-so in the past.

At this stage in the discussion, we reach a point at which I find myself in agreement with John McDowell in his book *Mind and World* (1994). Although a quick review of the literature will rapidly show that McDowell and I differ on the nature of subjects of consciousness, and differ on the correct account of the nature of the first person concept, we are nevertheless in agreement on a further point. McDowell writes that 'we make room for supposing that the continuity of "I think" involves a substantial persistence, without implying that the continuant in question is a Cartesian ego', once we discard a certain assumption (1994: 101). The assumption is 'that when we provide for the content of this idea of persistence, we must confine ourselves within the flow of "consciousness"' (1994: 101). If 'confining ourselves to the flow of "consciousness"' means confinement to what is common to both genuine and illusory experiences as of the identity of the subject over time, then I agree.[6] In good cases, there is no more obstacle to saying that a subject is genuinely aware of his having been so-and-so in the past than there is to saying that perceptual experience is, in good cases, of an external material object. If I have understood him aright, McDowell and I agree that there can be genuine awareness of one's own identity over time.

This general approach to Kant's treatment of the third paralogism is not at all a complete dismissal of his thought. What it suggests rather is that Kant's insights should be put in a conditional form, and regarded as part of a *reductio* argument against the Cartesian conception. If the first person refers to something like a Cartesian ego, then grasp of the (alleged) distinction between one continuing ego and the replacement of one by another similar ego is something that would not show up in the thinker's psychology. In those circumstances, we could not properly make the distinction between mere apparent awareness of one's own identity over time and illusions of identity. The argument could be elaborated within the non-verificationist framework I developed in 'The Limits of Intelligibility' (1988). The truth of this conditional formulation of Kant's insight is, however, entirely consistent with the distinction between apparent and genuine awareness of identity being applicable when subjects are something other than Cartesian egos. Further, on this construal of what is valuable in Kant's discussion of the third paralogism, the argument does not turn on any kind of misinterpretation of the first person concept, nor on misunderstanding of the consciousness/judgement nexus for first person contents. It turns rather on the consequences of the Cartesian metaphysics of the self for the intelligibility of certain distinctions in memory and awareness.

We can contrast this treatment of the Paralogisms with that of Peter Strawson in *The Bounds of Sense* (1966: 163–9). Strawson's position and my own agree that the 'I' in the Kantian 'I think' does in fact refer, and refers to an entity for which there are empirical conditions of identity. For Strawson, that entity is a person conceived of as fundamentally

---

[6] If I have understood him correctly, the quoted formulation from McDowell superficially seems to endorse a 'highest common factor' conception of consciousness, a conception he strongly rejects for perceptual experience in its role of ordinary justification of perceptual knowledge. On that rejection, see for instance McDowell (1994: 113) and the references on that page. But his point about awareness of identity over time could be reformulated without such apparent endorsement of something he rejects elsewhere.

embodied. He writes of 'the fact that our ordinary concept of *personal identity* does carry with it empirically applicable criteria for the numerical identity through time of a subject of experience (a man or human being) and that these criteria, though not the same as those for bodily identity, involve an essential reference to the human body' (1966: 164). '... the notions of singularity and identity of souls or consciousnesses are conceptually dependent upon, conceptually derivative from, the notions of singularity and identity of men or people. The rule for deriving the criteria we need from the criteria we have is very simple. It is: *one* person, *one* consciousness; *same* person, *same* consciousness' (1966: 168–9). On an account endorsing the contemporary theses displayed above, the entity is a subject whose identity over time turns on the identity of an integrating apparatus. This produces several divergences from Strawson's position. In one direction, the integrating apparatus may or may not be embedded in a body which is the body of the subject in question (see further below). In the other direction, we can apparently, in certain conceivable split brain cases, make sense of there existing two subjects in the same body. In such cases there will, functionally, be two pieces of integrating apparatus. In those cases, Strawson's rule '*same* person, *same* consciousness' is incorrect if there is meant to be only one consciousness per body at a given time. I acknowledge that this position has a commitment to, and an obligation to justify, the proposition that the nature and identity of an integrating apparatus over time can be explained independently of embodiment.

Strawson usually formulates the conceptual issues in terms of language rather than thought. For the most part, this makes no substantive difference. Strawson regards part of Kant's crucial insight as the recognition that when someone 'ascribes a current or directly remembered state of consciousness to himself, no use whatever of any criteria of personal identity is required to justify use of the pronoun "I" to refer' to the subject of that experience (1966: 165). That is, such ascriptions are, as we have come to say, immune to errors of misidentification. I agree that they are so immune, and that there is some more or less explicit recognition of the point in Kant. The immunity does, however, need some explanation. There are explanations of the immunity, explanations that go hand-in-hand with the contemporary conception outlined above: I offered some such explanations back in Chapter V. A crucial part of such explanations is the account of the soundness of the transition, noninferentially, from a conscious event or state enjoyed by a subject to the subject's self-ascription of an event or state of the relevant kind. The account emphasizes that a subject who moves from a mental state or event to the judgement that he is enjoying a state of event of the relevant kind will not, for reasons in the nature of the case, thereby be led to a false judgement on the contemporary conception outlined above. That explanation does not, apparently, require that subjects are fundamentally Strawsonian persons. Nor does it require that they be subjects whose experience is in part as of a route through an objective spatial world.

Strawson also says, and I agree, that in the criterionless self-ascription of mental states, 'reference to the empirically identifiable subject' is 'not in practice lost' (1966: 165). On my account, a public utterance of 'I have an experience as of a lawn in front of me' will be produced by a subject, and this subject's identity depends on the identity of an integrating apparatus whose persistence and identity over time is an empirical matter. The experience itself makes rational the self-ascription, when thought of under psychological concepts of experience. The experience could not exist without a subject, and its subject must be the subject for whom the ascription is thus made rational. For Strawson, such an utterance of 'I' can still refer to a subject 'because—perhaps—it issues publicly from the mouth of a man who is recognizable as the person he is by the application of empirical criteria of personal identity' (1966: 165). This indeed explains how the term refers, but it does not yet explain the immunity to error through misidentification.

Strawson could, of course, endorse the explanation of immunity to error through misidentification that I offered. It would then need much further argument that the subject for whom such self-ascriptions are thus made rational must also be fundamentally embodied, rather than meeting the weaker condition of having an identity dependent upon a continuing integrating apparatus. Strawson does give part of an argument for that view. He argues that subjects with a unified consciousness must have experiences that are unified, in being (in part) experiences having a certain relation to a path through an objective world. His argument is of great interest, given our present concerns, for it would question the adequacy of a contemporary conception based on the theses displayed above. I turn now to consider Strawson's argument.

3. Strawson's Neo-Kantian Conception of Subjects

Nothing in the four contemporary theses displayed at the start of this paper implies that there are not also further true theses that equally constrain the properties and relations of conscious subjects. Nothing that has been argued so far rules out the possibility that further investigation of the nature of conscious subjects may not reveal that there are plausible principles implying that conscious subjects must in some central cases be embodied, and must have perceptions that involve a route through the spatio-temporal world. In *The Bounds of Sense*, Strawson argues precisely that there are such principles.

We can distinguish various strengths of a proposed requirement on conscious subjects concerning either embodiment or experienced spatio-temporal history. In the case of embodiment, the requirement might be:

(B1)   that the subject actually possess a body;

(B2)   that the subject once had a body;

(B3)   that it must be for the subject as if it has a body; or

(B4)   that it must be for the subject as if it at least once had a body.

There is a similar range of possible proposals for a requirement of experienced spatio-temporal history. The requirement might be

(S-T1)   that the subject has throughout its history a location the subject either perceives, or is capable of perceiving, as its own;

(S-T2)   that the subject in an initial segment of its history had such a perceived or perceptible location;

(S-T3)   that throughout the subject's history it is for the subject as if it has such a perceived or perceptible location; or

(S-T4)   it is for the subject as if in some initial stage of its history it had such a perceived or perceptible location.

My own view is that not even the weakest of these proposed requirements is correct, either for embodiment, or for spatio-temporal location and history. There is in my view no conceptual or metaphysical obstacle to the possibility of a subject having only a sequence of monaural sound experiences, of a sort that do not represent objective events. This possibility is arguably that of Strawson's own sound world in *Individuals*

(1959). Again, the subject may have a sequence of visual experiences with only what I called sensational properties in *Sense and Content* (Peacocke 1983), or olfactory experiences, or any combination of the preceding, non-representational experiences.

In *The Bounds of Sense*, Strawson sets out to expound a Kantian argument intended to prove the opposite. He considers 'the thesis that for a series of diverse experiences to belong to a single consciousness it is necessary that they should be so connected as to constitute a temporally extended experience of a unified objective world' (1966: 97). This formulation seems to be of the form (S-T1) of the spatio-temporal view. Strawson writes 'of a unified objective world', not '*as* of a unified objective world'. The requirement is also stated for the whole sequence of experiences, not just for some initial segment thereof. Strawson, rightly in my view, takes this thesis to be in conflict with the view that there could be a subject of consciousness whose experiences consist solely of 'a succession of items such that there was no distinction to be drawn between the order and arrangement of the objects (and of their particular features and characteristics) and the order and arrangement of the subject's experiences of awareness of them' (1966: 98–99). 'Such objects might be of the sort which the earlier sense-datum theorists spoke of—red, round patches, brown oblongs, flashes, whistles, tickling sensations, smells' (1966: 99).

Strawson's argument in support of his thesis can be divided into the following steps. I label them 'Points', because they are set out here in not exactly the order in which he expounds them, to bring out the direction in which the argument is proceeding:

Point (1): 'Unity of the consciousness to which a series of experiences belong implies, then, the *possibility* of self-ascription of experiences on the part of a subject of those experiences' (1966: 98).

Point (2): Nothing but 'a form of words' is added to the hypothesis of a 'succession of essentially disconnected impressions' by saying that they all belong to a single subject, or that a unitary consciousness is aware of them all (1966: 100).

The remainder of Strawson's argument argues for a necessary condition for a series of experiences to belong to a single subject.

Point (3):   There is a necessary condition for a series of experiences to belong to a single subject, a condition without which 'even the basis of the idea of the referring of such experiences to an identical subject of a series of them by such a subject would be altogether lacking' (1966: 101).

The argument for the necessary condition proceeds from a claim about the nature of experience:

Point (4):   'There can be no experience at all which does not involve the recognition of particular items *as* being of such and such general kind. It seems that it must be possible, even in the most fleeting and purely subjective of impressions, to distinguish a component of recognition, or judgement, which is not simply identical with, or wholly absorbed by, the particular item which is recognized, which forms the topic of the judgement' (1966: 100).

Strawson immediately goes on to say there is an apparent difficulty here:

Point (5):   'Yet at the same time we seem forced to concede that there are particular subjective experiences (e.g. a momentary tickling sensation) of which the objects (accusatives) have no existence independently of the awareness of them' (1966: 101).

Strawson says the tension he sees between Points (4) and (5) can (actually, he writes 'must') be regarded by Kant, or a Kantian, as resolved by this observation:

Point (6):   'the recognitional component, necessary to experience, can be present in experience only because of the *possibility* of referring different experiences to one identical subject of them all. Recognition implies the *potential* acknowledgment of the experience into which recognition necessarily enters as one's own, as sharing with others this relation to the identical self' (1966: 101).

Point (7):   The potentiality of such an acknowledgment implies that 'some at least of the concepts under which particular experienced items are recognized as falling should be such that the experiences themselves contain the basis' (1966: 101) for a seems/is distinction; and 'collectively, the distinction *between* the subjective order and arrangement of a series of such experiences on the one hand and the objective order and arrangement of the items of which they are experiences on the other' (1966: 101).

I am not at all sure, well over forty years after first reading it, that I understand the conception of the subject matter that generates this bold and fascinating argument. But I do think the argument as formulated here is vulnerable to the following objections.

(a) There is a fundamental distinction between giving a theory of the relation

experience *e* is owned by subject *s*

and giving a theory of the different relation

the subject *s* is capable of self-ascribing experience *e* in thought.

Having an experience *e* is one thing; having the mental capacities to be able to self-ascribe *e* is another. Prima face, many animals and young children have the former and lack the latter. Some passages from Strawson show him using now a thesis about ownership of experiences, now a thesis about using some form of first person representation and self-ascribing experiences. At the start of the argument, he is apparently writing about first relation, that of ownership: 'First, we ask: how can we attach a sense to the notion of the single consciousness to which the successive "experiences" are supposed to belong?' (1966: 100). Yet the argument later mentions what's 'in fact self-ascribed': 'Not all the members of such a series [of "experiences which belong to a unitary consciousness"—CP] are in fact self-ascribed: a man may be more prone to forget himself in contemplation of the world . . . than he is to be conscious of, or to think of, himself as perceiving' (1966: 104). If it is the relation of ownership itself that is in question, no 'in fact' qualification necessary. For self-ascription, the qualification surely is required. The starting point of the argument concerns the unity of the consciousness to which a series of successive experiences belongs. Any move from this to consideration of self-ascription needs justification.

Strawson almost certainly thought there is a connection between the two relations, a connection that can be formulated in two propositions. First, he likely thought that a subject enjoys a token experience only if the subject can self-ascribe it. Thus, 'The notion of a single consciousness to which different experiences belong is linked to the notion of self-consciousness, of the ascription of an experience or state of consciousness to oneself' (1966: 98). It is not only the animals and young children that make this problematic. The passage also seems to imply that consciousness requires a certain kind of self-consciousness (a form that is sometimes called reflective self-consciousness). The second connecting proposition that Strawson likely accepted is that a subject can self-ascribe an experience only if he enjoys a sequence of interconnected experiences of an objective world—though this of course would have to be the conclusion of the argument, not its premise.

Even if we restrict our attention to the case of subjects who have the concepts required to self-ascribe experiences, we need to draw a further distinction. The fact that, for such subjects, when s owns e, it is possible for s to self-ascribe e does not imply that that fact is what *makes* e one of s's experiences. For there may be some philosophical explanation of why that possibility always holds that traces the possibility to a quite different constitutive origin. That seems to me to be the case here. e as a conscious event is in an element of its subject's total subjective state. Thereby e can make rational for the subject various judgements, including a judgement of it, demonstratively given, to the effect 'That's mine', or 'I am having that experience of such-and-such kind'. It is entirely consistent with this non-Strawsonian, non-Kantian direction of constitutive explanation that whenever there is ownership of a conscious event, there is the possibility of self-ascription. But this 'whenever' claim is true not because ownership consists in the possibility of such self-ascription. Rather, it is ownership that grounds the possibility of the self-ascription. In short, in the order of philosophical explanation, Strawson has not established that an 'ascription-first' view of these matters is correct, rather than an 'ownership-first' view.

An ownership-first view can be correct, and is a rival to such neo-Kantian views as Strawson's, only if there is a background account of the nature and identity over time of the subjects who are said to enjoy the experiences. But that is precisely what is offered by the contemporary conception, outlined in the theses displayed at the start of this Chapter. That conception offers an account of conscious subjects capable of representing themselves that involves identity of integrating apparatus and the possession of files on themselves that does not involve the neo-Kantian materials.

(b) Points (4) through (6) of the argument raise other issues. Strawson says that in even the most fleeting of impressions there is a 'component of recognition, or judgement' (1966: 100). Judgement has conceptualized content. Not every subject who has experiences or impressions has to possess mental states with conceptualized content. Even for a subject who possesses concepts, the occurrence of a mental event need not engage or involve the subject's concepts. Once we distinguish judgement from awareness, then even when a subject has a rich conceptual repertoire and conceptualizes his mental events under various kinds, there is no incompatibility between this conception of awareness and the fact that for pains, for instance, there is no distinction between the experience of the pain and the pain event itself. There certainly would be a problem if awareness were to consist in judgement; but it does not. So the 'yet' that starts off the quotation in Point (5) ('Yet at the same time we seem forced to concede . . .') does not seem to be well motivated; there is no apparent need to see the acknowledgment of such subjective sensations as any kind of concession.

Why is the possibility of self-ascription thought to solve a problem that is alleged to exist for sensations, but which is apparently not thought to exist for objective perceptions of the spatio-temporal world? One can imagine an argument that is motivated as follows. If one fails properly to distinguish awareness and judgement, and one thinks, as apparently Strawson (or at least Strawson's Kant) does, that all awareness has to involve judgement, then it may indeed seem that in sensation we have collapsed the item/recognition distinction. Such a combination of views may lead one to think that a sensation being of a certain kind cannot come apart from the subject's thinking that it is. By contrast, it may be said, for objective perception, since it is always possible that some objective state of affairs exists without experience as of it, and conversely, there is no such (alleged) danger of the so-called item/recognition distinction collapsing. Then, this argument may continue, genuine recognition in the sensation case is secured because the possibility of self-ascription means that this is a subjective item. Presumably on this view that means that we can thereby have recognition of kinds without the kind of seems/is distinction that is present for experiences with objective content. The ascription of purely subjective experiences to a subject is not vacuous, on this view, only because the subject is an independent entity that traces a path through the spatio-temporal world.

I confess to being utterly unclear how the argument of this reading is meant to work. Recognition needs to be recognition of the subjective item as of a particular kind—as a pain, as a particular kind of smell or sound, and so forth. Consider the self-ascription to which appeal is made in this version of the argument: does that self-ascription specify the kind of the experience, or is it not? If the kind of the experience is not included, the argument has not provided for what is involved in recognition.

If the kind is included, how has the specific kind of the subjective experience been secured merely by the possibility of self-ascription of a particular experience? Isn't self-ascription of an experience of a specific kind, and ascription as that specific kind, possible, and made rational, by the experience's already being of the kind in question? Then it seems that the experience's being of the kind it is is causally and explanatorily prior to the possibility of proper self-ascription. Without that basis, it is not clear how a specific kind is available for self-ascription on the Strawsonian conception.

Perhaps the argument is meant to be that a conception of the experience and its properties as causally and explanatorily prior, as in the ownership-first view, is some kind of illusion. We say that the experience makes reasonable the self-ascription, but this is, it may be said, a way of speaking that should not be confused with constitutive or metaphysical priority in this area. The problem is that we have been given no real reason for taking these appearances as illusory. If we combine the conception of subjects outlined in the contemporary conception with an insistence on the awareness/judgement distinction, there will indeed always be the possibility of self-ascription of a sensation as being of a particular kind, when the sensation occurs to a conceptually competent subject. There is no obvious obstacle to the naïve view that the kind of the sensation, at an appropriate level of kind, contributes to the rational explanation of the subject's self-ascription of a sensation of that kind.

There is a parallelism here between this criticism and the earlier criticism of Strawson's discussion of the way links are not 'in practice' severed with a bodily subject in 'criterionless' mental self-ascription (in language). In both cases, Strawson's argument aims to succeed in securing an embodied subject, as, respectively, owner or ascribee of the mental state; but in both cases, the rationality and entitlement to the transition involved in each case seems to be left unelucidated in his account.

(c) Point (2) of Strawson's argument, taken in the context of his reasoning, suggests that there is some vacuity in saying 'all the experiences have the same owner' when the experiences are purely subjective, and that the vacuity disappears when some at least of the series are perceptions of an objective world, through which the subject traces a route. But having a continuous spatio-temporal route and point of view on an objective world is neither sufficient nor necessary for identity of subject over time or for identity of owner of the experiences. We can conceive of inserting a new brain, of a new subject, into one identical continuing body that traces a continuous path in space. This possibility shows that even if the perceptions of the new subject trace a continuous series of points of view with experiences of the previous subject on that route, that continuity is not sufficient for identity of subject over time. A further condition is needed: continuity of integrating apparatus over time.

This further condition is not vacuous. Moreover, this further condition can also hold without the condition of an experienced spatio-temporal route condition being met. The condition of an experienced spatio-temporal route is not met in Strawson's own sound world in *Individuals*, but the relevant auditory experiences could all be enjoyed by a subject with continuity of integrating apparatus over time.

I am inclined to think that what objective perceptions add to the purely subjective ones is not by itself enough to make sameness of subject intelligible if it were not so already. And when we add what is enough for identity of subject, viz. identity of integrating apparatus, then tracing a continuous spatio-temporal route through an objective world is not obviously required. Indeed it is not met in some cases even when there are objective perceptions. Such is the case of Daniel Dennett's subject in his paper 'Where Am I?' (1978), in which a subject whose physical integrating apparatus is in Houston may control, and perceive from, different bodies at different times. The location of the body controlled by this subject does not need to possess spatio-temporal continuity over time. It may jump around as the subject controls different bodies at different times.

We can also add that if some split-brain cases are possible in which there are two conscious subjects in the same body at the same time, then it is possible that two subjects have exactly the same genuinely perceived spatio-temporal path through the world, yet remain distinct subjects. The two subjects could share a visual perceptual apparatus in such cases. A spatio-temporal path through the world does not fix identity of the subject of experience either at a given time, or over time.

There is, I agree, an important psychological and representational distinction between a subject whose experiences are interconnected because they are of an objective world, and a subject whose experiences are not so interconnected. The former subject, but not the latter, is able to locate itself as an element in the objective order of things and events. On my view, that is a difference between a subject that has an applicable conception of itself as having a location in the world, and a subject who does not have such a conception. That is a distinction in respect of the conception available to two subjects who differ in that respect. It is not a distinction in point of existence of the two subjects (see Chapter II, Section 3).

(d) Strawson's argument relies upon an alleged experience/concepts connection: 'Certainly concepts, recognition . . . would be necessary to a consciousness with any experience at all' (1966: 99). There is by now a fairly extensive literature detailing what would be involved in a notion of non-conceptual content of experience.[7] Perhaps Strawson's arguments should not be taken as required to dispute the possibility of nonconceptual content. Perhaps much or all of what he says should be translated to the level of nonconceptual content. There is a legitimate notion of nonconceptual recognition of shape, of nonconceptual correctness conditions, and, on my own views, a nonconceptual version of subject-representation that refers to a subject of consciousness. But I do not see how any such translation of Strawson's argument rules out the possibility of a subject of consciousness with a sequence of purely sound, visual-sensational, or olfactory experiences. The account of subjects with updateable subject-files on themselves helps to explain how such subjects could represent themselves as having been in certain states earlier, without having any conception of themselves as occupying spatial locations.

These points are all arguments that the conclusion of Strawson's argument is too strong. If the conclusion is too strong, then there is no point in trying to construct different arguments to the same conclusion (the reasoning is too strong however the conclusion is reached). It does not at all follow that there are not successor arguments to Strawson's that draw in interesting ways on the materials he deployed, to related, though to different, conclusions. It would take us too far afield to develop

---

[7] Examples of my own efforts are in Peacocke (1992: Chapter 3); and Peacocke (2001). See also the important contributions in Burge (2003, 2010).

successor arguments here. But I note that consideration of what is involved in having experiences that do have objective spatio-temporal content, and consideration of the nature of subjective properties and their relation to the public world may each have interesting interconnections and consequences for self-representation in an objective world. The light cast by neo-Kantian arguments may come not from a Strawsonian conclusion, but from what they illuminate in adjacent areas.

I also note a final point of agreement with Strawson, though it has a twist. Strawson writes, at the end of his section 'Unity and Objectivity' in *The Bounds of Sense*,

memory is involved in experience, recognition, consciousness of identity of self through diversity of experience. But it is far too deeply and essentially involved to be capable of being safely handled as if it were a separable and detachable factor which can, say, be conveniently invoked to link up temporally successive or separated episodes into an experiential sequence. If experience is impossible without memory, memory is also impossible without experience. From whatever obscure levels they emerge they emerge together. (1966: 111–12)

The non-Strawsonian view of subjects I have endorsed is committed to agreement with Strawson on his point in the final sentence of this most recent quotation. Part of what makes something a continuing and self-representing subject is its capacity for primitive self-representation in memory of its own earlier properties and relations. Self-representing subjecthood and memory really are essentially interdependent on the account I have been offering, and both involve the operation of the subject's file on itself. Neither self-representing subjecthood nor memory is something more primitive than the other: and so neither is available for reductive explication of the other. The twist in this point of agreement is, however, that on the treatment I propose, the way in which personal identity and memory emerge together, via identity of integrating apparatus and the subject's file on itself, is also a way that provides the materials for a non-Strawsonian, non-Kantian account of conscious subjects.

VIII

Perspectival
Self-Consciousness

Anyone who peruses writings on self-consciousness, whether from philosophy, psychology, sociology, or from the humanities in general, is likely to be bewildered by the variety of phenomena included under that heading. In this and the following chapters I aim to characterize three varieties of self-consciousness: the perspectival, the reflective, and the interpersonal. For some of these varieties, giving a characterization is a challenge in itself. Once we have a characterization of each variety, we will be in a position to explore the psychological and epistemological significance of each kind, their relations to one another, and their significance for some wider issues in metaphysics and the philosophy of mind. The full interest and significance of any one of these varieties of self-consciousness does not become apparent until one appreciates its relations to the other varieties. So the discussion of any one of these kinds of self-consciousness will not be complete until we have discussed all three of them.

These three varieties of self-consciousness may well not exhaust the extant varieties, and may well not even exhaust the varieties of self-consciousness that are of theoretical interest. I fix on the trio of the reflective, the perspectival, and the interpersonal for their foundational significance, and for their centrality to various classical philosophical and psychological issues.

Earlier I distinguished three kinds of conscious subjects. First, there are subjects, who although they enjoy conscious states, do not self-represent at all: those are the cases of subject at Degree 0 in Chapter II. Second, there are subjects who do self-represent, but who do so only in mental states with contents that contain a non-conceptual form of the first person. Much animal awareness may be like that. Third, there are subjects of consciousness who employ the genuine first person concept, something that features in the content of judgements that can be made for reasons.

In this and the following two chapters, I will be concerned with some more sophisticated forms of self-consciousness many instances of which are certainly found within this third general kind of conceptualized first person consciousness. Some subjects who employ the first person concept do so in ways that go beyond what is minimally required for use of the first person concept in physical and mental ascriptions. The various forms of self-consciousness that can be displayed at the conceptual level involve a wider conception of oneself in the physical and mental worlds than is minimally required for grasp of the first person concept. It is also arguable that certain forms of self-consciousness can be present even at the level of nonconceptual mental states with *de se* content. If they can, then similarly the capacities present in such self-conscious subjects go beyond what is minimally required for nonconceptual mental states with *de se* content.

It is important here to distinguish those issues that are merely terminological from those that are not. In *The Varieties of Reference*, Gareth Evans uses the word 'self-conscious' for the kind of thinking that employs the first person concept, but this, as he says is a mere label, and not a substantive thesis (1982: 206). In fact in the Appendix to his chapter 'Self-Identification', Evans introduces the notion of what he calls 'full self-consciousness', which involves appreciating that in your first person thinkings you are both subject and object of your thought. His discussion of these issues was sadly unfinished, and no settled view of full self-consciousness emerges from that chapter and its Appendix. But it certainly seems that he held that there is at least one notion of self-consciousness that goes beyond the plausible minimal conditions for the ascription of the first person concept. By contrast with the case of Evans, I suspect my divergence from Sebastian Rödl on some of these matters is more than terminological, despite some other important areas of agreement with Rödl. In his book *Self-Consciousness* (2007), Rödl identifies self-consciousness with the capacity for first person thought, and this is not announced as a stipulative matter. I in fact have no strong views about the use of the word 'self-consciousness' in English, or its cognates in other languages. My substantive claim is that however we use these words, we ought also to distinguish several varieties of self-consciousness, and that we should take it as a philosophical task to explain the nature of each of these varieties of self-consciousness.

Self-consciousness features as such in our everyday psychological thought, when we appreciate its involvement in such emotions and traits as pride, embarrassment, shame, and arrogance. Obama employed the notion in response to the question of whether living in the White House would spoil his young daughters. He replied, 'Right now, they're not self-conscious'.[1] In ethology, some variety of the notion is employed when it is debated whether passing some form of the mirror test is sufficient evidence for self-consciousness, an issue I will touch on soon. Self-consciousness and the states it makes possible are crucial to understanding Romantic thought and sensibilities. In philosophy, one or another form of the notion is central to the thought of such diverse thinkers as Kant, Hegel, Kierkegaard, Sartre, and Peter Strawson—to name but a few. Though I cannot discuss all such writing, I do hope to characterize the three target varieties of self-consciousness I will be discussing in such a way that one can trace some unified common threads through these various areas of thought and feeling. I begin with perspectival self-consciousness.

1. What is the Significance of the Mirror Test?

It is natural and illuminating to begin a discussion of perspectival self-consciousness by considering Gordon Gallup's famous mirror test (1970, 1979). The test involves placing on an animal's forehead a visible chalk mark when the animal is asleep or anaesthetized. In some cases, when presented with itself in a mirror after this marking, the animal is capable of locating the mark on its own forehead with its own limbs, and then wiping it off. In a series of beautiful experiments, Diana Reiss and Lori Marino have shown that dolphins also pass a suitably adapted version of the test (Reiss and Marino 2001; Reiss 2011). Does the presence of this ability establish that the animal has some form of self-consciousness?

---

[1] '"Those are some special girls, and everyone is rooting for them to make it through this intact," Craig Robinson, Mrs Obama's brother, said in an interview. The president echoed that sentiment. "Right now, they're not self-conscious. You know, they don't have an attitude," Mr Obama said on CBS News' (Swarns 2009).

And if so, what is the correct characterization of the self-consciousness so established?

We need to apply here the distinction between evidential conditions and constitutive conditions. It can, very reasonably, be objected that the ability to use a mirror in removing a mark from one's forehead can be explained without attributing to the animal recognition of itself in the mirror. Grasp of a correlation between what one is doing to oneself and what is seen in the mirror suffices. But that is not in fact the issue I want to pursue here. I want to raise a philosophical question about the case in which the animal does recognize itself in the mirror. So I am focusing on the case in which the animal has a representation with the content of a genuine identity 'That's me', where the 'That' expresses a perceptual-demonstrative mode of presentation individuated by the way an animal is given in the mirror. On what notion of self-consciousness does such self-recognition give a reason for attributing self-consciousness to the animal? How should we characterize that variety of self-consciousness? Whatever it is, does it also get a grip beyond the mirror cases?

When a subject learns something about what is on its forehead, or its other bodily features, by looking in a mirror, the subject comes to know something about himself in a way in which he could equally come to know something about some other object or other animal or person. The subject employs a way of coming to know a third person proposition or content. In these examples, that way involves taking at face value the content of his perceptual experience in respect of something thereby perceived. Because this is a third person way of coming to know, it is, broadly construed, also a way in which others can equally come to know about the subject. But the subject can employ this third person way of coming to know without having in advance a conception of other subjects of experience who are knowers.

In these mirror cases, the subject comes to know such a proposition as

That animal has a mark on its forehead

and uses an identity

That animal is me

to infer

I have a mark on my forehead.

So we can formulate what we can call the *mirror-motivated criterion* for this variety of self-consciousness. The mirror-motivated criterion states that an exercise of this form of self-consciousness consists in using knowledge of the form

That G is F

(or some other third personal mode of presentation in place of *That G*) gained by use of the mirror, together with the knowledge

That G is me

to infer

I am F.

In cases that meet this mirror-motivated criterion, the perception that gives the reason for making the judgement is not a subject-reflexive state in which the subject is represented as, for instance, himself having a mark on his forehead. Here we can apply the distinctions made in Chapter II above. Consider the perception of something as having a mark on its forehead. That perception is not one whose fundamental correctness condition requires, *de jure*, by virtue of the nature of the way the objects are given in perception, that the subject who is enjoying the experience have a mark on his forehead. That is why acceptance of the identity 'That G is me' is needed to reach from the perception knowledge or registration that represents oneself, as such, as having a mark on one's forehead. These are paradigm cases in which the way of coming to know something about oneself is subject to error through misidentification (Shoemaker 1968). I will return to the relation between Shoemaker-style immunity to error through misidentification and perspectival self-consciousness once we have an account of the latter.

It is not at all obvious that the kind of self-consciousness manifested by passing the mirror test is restricted to creatures who possess concepts. It is certainly an open question whether conceptual content, rather than nonconceptual content, should be attributed to chimpanzees, who pass the mirror test. Intuitively, the kind of self-consciousness required to pass the mirror test involves taking a third person perspective on oneself, while appreciating that it is oneself who is present in that third person perspective. That is something that could in principle be done at the nonconceptual level. The revisability, sensitivity to reasons, and rational reassessment that is distinctive of the conceptual level need not be present in the psychology of a creature who has a representation with the content *that's me* when seeing himself in the mirror.

There seems to be a general kind of self-consciousness of which the ability to recognize oneself in a mirror, and thereby gain knowledge of oneself, is a particular manifestation. It is this general kind or variety that I am labeling as perspectival self-consciousness. Is the mirror-motivated criterion a satisfactory way of capturing what is distinctive of this more general notion of perspectival self-consciousness? At a very crude and intuitive level, one wants to say that perspectival self-consciousness involves a certain appreciation. There is a distinctive third personal way in which it can be given that things other than oneself have properties and stand in various relations. Perspectival self-consciousness seems to involve the appreciation that one can oneself have those properties and stand in those relations too, as those properties and relations are given in that distinctive third personal way. A large part of the challenge is to explain what the 'distinctive way' is.

The idea of perspectival self-consciousness should not be collapsed into the simpler formulation that the perspectivally self-conscious subject appreciates that he is capable of having the same properties as other things or subjects. That simpler condition is met by someone who is capable of judging that he is spatially close to some object, and who is also capable of judging that other things are spatially close to various other objects. This falls far short of perspectival self-consciousness. The simpler condition is also met by someone who is both capable of judging that he himself is pain and capable of judging that others are in pain too. Such a subject may be merely capable of first personal thought, and will be conscious. But it is not in virtue merely of meeting the simpler condition that the subject is perspectivally self-conscious. So we really do need to take on the task of specifying the 'distinctive way' more clearly.

A major problem with the mirror-motivated criterion is that it treats only a very special case, a case that is not essential to perspectival self-consciousness. We have no difficulty in conceiving of a world in which there are no mirrors and no reflecting surfaces, no depictions, and no videos. In such a world, no subject can truly think an identity 'That G is me', where 'that G' expresses a perceptual demonstrative of the same general type that could be used in perceiving someone else's face. But it seems that there could be what we would classify as perspectivally self-conscious subjects in such a world without visual reflections. So what less restrictive criterion would these subjects meet?

When I was first thinking about these issues, I considered what I thought to be a merely hypothetical case of a world without reflecting surfaces merely as a conceptual possibility. It turns out that may in fact be actual, or have been actual, in the case of the Biami group in New Guinea: see Carpenter (1975). If Carpenter is right, many Biami people had never seen themselves in any reflecting surface. It is highly plausible that members of this adult social group were perspectivally self-conscious. Their reported fascination with their own image on first being shown a mirror is naturally construed as a case of people who knew there were third person perspectives on themselves, but each one of whom did not know how he or she in fact appeared.

It is also plausible that congenitally blind subjects can be perspectivally self-conscious. In both the world without reflecting surfaces, and in the world of the blind, there can intuitively be an appreciation that one features oneself in something given in a third person perspective. What then is the more general condition of which the mirror-motivated criterion is merely a special, and inessential, case?

2. A Wider Criterion for Perspectival Self-Consciousness

As a step towards formulating a more general condition for perspectival self-consciousness, I start by drawing a distinction. I continue to use the terminology under which a predicative concept is a mode of presentation of a property.

We can draw a distinction, amongst concepts, between those whose understanding-condition makes special reference to the thinker's own possession of the property picked out by the concept, and, by contrast, those concepts whose understanding-condition does not make any such special reference to the thinker's own possession of the property. Many thinkers hold that grasp of the concept *is in pain*, or grasp of the concept *has an experience of redness*, involves special reference to the thinker's willingness to apply these concepts to himself when he himself is, respectively, in pain or is enjoying an experience of redness. Those thinkers will place these concepts *is in pain* and *has an experience of red* in the first rather than the second of these categories. In such cases, the thinker's grasp of the concept, and its applicability in the world, gives a special place to his knowledge of what it is for he himself to fall under the concept (and so to have the property picked out).

In saying that the understanding-condition makes special reference to the first person application of the concept, I offer a formulation that is neutral between various substantive theories of concepts and of concept possession. As I said in earlier chapters, I myself hold that concepts are individuated by their fundamental reference rules, and that grasp of a concept is tacit knowledge of its fundamental reference rule. Under that approach, the fundamental reference rule for a concept like *pain* will mention the case in which the concept applies to oneself, and it will relate the correctness conditions of applications to others to that first person case. Under pure conceptual-role treatments of concepts, the special reference to first person application will be explicit in the formulation of the proposed concept-individuating conceptual role, which will treat first person present tense application in a separate clause. As far as I can see, the distinction between understanding-conditions that do, and understanding-conditions that do not, make special reference to first person applications of the concept will be available under any of the current contenders amongst theories of concepts and understanding.

Unlike the understanding-conditions for the concepts *pain* and *experience of red*, the understanding-condition for an observational shape concept does not make special reference to the first person present tense application of the concept. The understanding condition for an observational concept will indeed make special reference to the thinker's perception of something as having a certain shape; but it will not make reference to *his* having that shape. The same applies to concepts of mass, of temporal intervals and duration, concepts of number. In none of these cases will the understanding-condition make special reference to first person applications of the concept in question. I label concepts whose understanding-condition by contrast does make special reference to first person application *concepts anchored in the subject*.

I propose, as a first approximation, that a necessary condition for perspectival self-consciousness is the capacity to come to know propositions of the form *I'm* φ, for some range of concepts φ that are not anchored in the subject. When a subject meets this condition with respect to such a concept, I say the subject is perspectivally self-conscious with respect to that concept.

This necessary condition helps to capture the 'distinctive way' I mentioned earlier. On this account, what distinguishes a perspectivally self-conscious subject is that he is capable of knowing he falls under concepts for which his fundamental understanding is not given in terms of what it is for *him* to fall under them. It is natural to cast the point in terms of the perspective a thinker has to have on an object or property in order to think of it in a particular way. If we are allowed to do that, we can say: perspectival self-consciousness involves a subject thinking of himself as falling within whatever perspective on an object has to be employed in coming to know in a basic way that it is φ, where grasp of the concept φ is not given to him in terms of what it is for he himself to be φ. 'In a basic way' here means: in a way made immediately rational by the understanding-condition, or possession-condition, for φ.

This is a stronger condition than merely being capable of judging both of himself and of other things that they fall under a given concept. To meet the stronger condition, the subject must conceive of himself as placed in the world in such a way that he himself meets the same kind of condition for a concept φ, not anchored in the subject, to apply to himself as can be met by other objects to which the concept φ applies. Since the subject has to have a conception of himself that is not given simply by his grasping first person contents, and has intuitively to reorient his first person attributions in relation to his perspective on the world, I call this necessary condition for perspectival self-consciousness a contribution towards a *reorientation account*.

Though for simplicity of introduction of the ideas, I have stated the beginnings of the reorientation account at the conceptual level, analogous distinctions can be made at the nonconceptual level. For nonconceptual contents too, we have a distinction that is the analogue of the distinction between sense and reference. One and the same thing, or one and the same property, can be given in two ways in states with nonconceptual content. The animal without concepts may see a shape as a regular diamond rather than as a square. I will continue to write of notions as ways in which objects or properties are given in nonconceptual content. Then we can distinguish those notions that are anchored in a nonconceptual *de se* from those that are not. A nonconceptual notion that is an analogue of the concept *pain* will be so anchored, whereas notions of shape will not. I said that it is plausible that perspectival self-consciousness is possible even at the nonconceptual level. Under the reorientation account a necessary condition for perspectival self-consciousness at the nonconceptual level is that the subject is capable of coming to register nonconceptual contents of the form *i am f*, where as before *i* is the nonconceptual *de se*, and *f* is a notion not anchored in the subject. Here registration is a precursor at the nonconceptual level of knowledge at the conceptual level.

This necessary condition for perspectival self-consciousness concerning concepts or notions not anchored in the subject includes cases covered by the mirror-motivated account. It also applies more widely.

We take the claim of inclusion first. A subject who comes to know 'That's me' when seeing himself in the mirror, and thereby comes to learn new things about his body, will meet the necessary condition concerning concepts not anchored in the subject. The properties whose application to yourself which you come to know about by looking in the mirror—properties specifying your appearance, the state of your face, your girth, the state of your clothes and of your hair—are all thought about by you under concepts that are not anchored in the subject.

As we required, the necessary condition that is a step towards a reorientation account also applies more widely than the mirror-motivated account, because its requirements can be fulfilled in a world without mirrors and reflecting surfaces. The condition can also be met by congenitally blind subjects. Here is an example that illustrates both points. In the actual world, there are devices for making announcements on buses and in airports in which the public announcement made over the loudspeaker is delayed, sometimes by twenty seconds, after the event of the announcer speaking into the microphone. In such a case, an announcer may not realize that an announcement he is hearing over a loudspeaker was in fact made by himself. He may think, on hearing the announcement, *that person has an irritating accent*. If our subject eventually comes to appreciate that he is the announcer, he may come thereby to learn the unfortunate fact *I have an irritating accent*. Attaining such knowledge would be an exercise of perspectival self-consciousness, and it meets the necessary condition given in the reorientation account. The concept *has an irritating accent* is not anchored in the subject; the subject eventually realizes he is the person given in the third person perspective he employs in making the judgement about the accent he hears; and so forth.

Examples of exercises of perspectival self-consciousness need not involve current technology, or artefacts such as mirrors. They may involve something as humble as leaving a footprint in the sand. From a footprint of mine and a footprint of yours, adjacent in the sand, I may come to know that your foot is larger than mine. Even this is an application of a fundamentally third person method of judging relative size, together with an identification involving the first person (*that footprint is mine*). A blind person, by feeling both imprints in the sand, could also use this method.[2]

Even if someone is unaware of her current properties—as someone may be unaware of the pattern of her hair at a certain time, or, in a more extreme case, may be unaware of her height, like Alice at one point in Lewis Carroll's story—she may nevertheless be aware that she has some property in a certain range. This is still a variety of perspectival self-consciousness. One can know that one has some property or other within a certain range simply as a consequence, given one's background knowledge, of knowing that one is a material object. This unspecific perspectival self-consciousness is still actual, rather than being merely a state of potential self-consciousness. The subject has the capacity mentioned in the definition of perspectival self-consciousness without currently exercising it.

The examples I have given of concepts anchored in the subject have been concepts of psychological properties. A case can be made that some spatial concepts are also anchored in the subject. The relational concepts *x is to the left of y* and *x is to the right of y* are very plausibly anchored in the subject. A thinker's grasp of them primitively involves understanding of what it is for something to be to the left, or to the right of him. His understanding of other instances is that they involve the same spatial relation as is instantiated in these first person cases.

Is the capacity to know propositions of the form *I'm* φ for some concepts φ not anchored in the subject not merely a necessary, but also a sufficient, condition for perspectival self-consciousness? I do not think

---

[2] In Peacocke (2010b), I used different examples to make these points, examples concerning ways in which a subject could come to know his height. I have come to think that those examples are too close to the cases of spatial knowledge, discussed four paragraphs below, that are, for reasons explained there, not genuine manifestations of perspectival self-consciousness.

it is. Concepts such as *x is a certain distance from y*, *x is in front of y* are not anchored in the subject. Consider knowledgeable first person ascriptions of these made on the basis of perception, in contents such as *That chair is more than a foot from me*, or *I am in front of a house*. These judgements are not, intuitively, exercises of perspectival self-consciousness. They do not, intuitively, involve taking some form of third person perspective on oneself.

Why are these spatial cases not exercises of perspectival self-consciousness, even though the concepts self-ascribed in them are not anchored in the subject? I am inclined to think that these are not cases of perspectival self-consciousness because the rationality of making a specifically first person ascription in these cases is adequately explained by the conditions for something to be my body, and the fact that, for example, for *That chair is more than a foot from me* to be true is for it to be the case that *That chair is more than a foot from my body*. The condition for something to be my body is that it is the one from which I perceive, when all is functioning properly, it is the one that moves when I try to move, and so forth (see Shoemaker 1984). This condition and the equivalence of the relevant first person proposition with a proposition about my body suffice to explain the rationality of judging the first person content *That chair is more than a foot from me* when I perceive a chair to be more than a foot from my body. We are not concerned here with explaining the rationality of taking perception at face value, but only with the difference in the rationality of accepting different propositions in the light of perception, *modulo* the general default rationality of taking perception at face value. When the rationality of making such self-ascriptions can be so explained, the subject is exercising no more than a first person perspective on himself.

It is for this very reason that the ability to enjoy primitive spatial perceptions with contents concerning the layout of the subject's immediate environment involves only first person representation and consciousness. It does not in itself involve perspectival self-consciousness. It does not involve taking a third person perspective on oneself. This verdict seems to be in accord with intuition. More generally, given that any use of the first person concept refers to a subject, it should not be surprising that some epistemic features of first person contents trace back to features of the constitutive account of what it is for a subject to have a location and body in a spatial world.

So the full necessary and sufficient conditions for perspectival self-consciousness on the reorientation account I am offering are these: the subject must be capable of coming to know propositions of the form *I'm* φ where φ is not anchored in the subject, where the rationality of making these specifically first person judgements in the cases in which the subject comes to know them is not fully explained by what it is for something to be the subject's body, and by *my body/I* equivalences. No doubt a subject realized by a brain in a vat could in some sense enjoy perspectival self-conscious too, but this possibility seems parasitic on the conditions just given. For such a subject, it is as if he enjoys perspectival self-consciousness as described.

The notion of capacity in this characterization of perspectival self-consciousness is to be understood relatively broadly. Someone who has real reason to think there is an evil demon around, or real reason to think there are all sorts of misleading evidence nearby, may not be in a position to know the relevant propositions of the form *I'm* φ, even if he is perspectivally self-conscious. But he would be in a position to know them if he didn't have these real reasons for doubt, and in that sense has the capacity required in the criterion for perspectival self-consciousness.

I have formulated the criterion in terms of knowledge because my own view is that there is a close nexus between concepts and the conditions for certain kinds of knowledge (1999: Chapter 2). But theorists with different approaches to concepts, or to knowledge, could adapt these ideas to their own framework. One could, for instance, adapt the approach given here to warrant-based treatments. One could characterize perspectival self-consciousness in terms of a rational sensitivity to certain warrants for the relevant propositions of the form *I'm* φ. Perspectival self-consciousness would then be described as the capacity to be rationally sensitive to certain structured warrants for judging *I'm* φ, where φ is not anchored in the subject.

It is very plausible that judgements of the form *I'm* φ that are, under this reorientation account, exercises of perspectival self-consciousness are also vulnerable to Shoemaker-style error through misidentification relative to the first person constituent of their content. If I come to know *I have a Roman nose* by looking at a shadow of a nose, or come to know my height from a mark made on a wall, or come to know *I have a bad haircut* by looking at a photograph, these are clearly cases in which I could come to know, by these same methods, that someone has a

Roman nose, or has a certain height, or has a bad haircut, but be mistaken that it is I who have these properties. These cases also meet the finer-grained, more accurate, criterion for immunity to error through misidentification mentioned in Chapter V (Section 1). The various beliefs in these examples all rest on an identity belief involving the first person concept.

Why does perspectival self-consciousness as characterized by the reorientation account imply vulnerability to such errors of identification? I suggest that there are two ways in which immunity to error through misidentification can arise, and in the nature of the case neither of them is present in instances of perspectival self-consciousness as characterized in the reorientation account. In one kind of case, immunity to error through misidentification flows from the nature of the concept that is self-ascribed, that is, in the case in which the concept is anchored in the subject. The very account of what it is for something to fall under such a concept as *is in pain* will, if the subject applies the concept in a way suitably corresponding to the first person clause in the understanding-condition, ensure that it is the subject who falls under the concept.

The other kind of case is that in which the constitutive account of what it is for a predication *I'm* φ to be true, for a certain range of concepts φ, also ensures that when such a predication is made for certain reasons, the concept applied will be true of the thinker. That is the case illustrated by such spatial predications as *That chair is more than one foot from me*.

Now the very characterization of perspectival self-consciousness ensures that the self-ascriptions it involves are cases of neither of these two kinds. The first kind of case is ruled out by that part of the characterization that concerns concepts φ not anchored in the subject. The second kind of case is ruled out by the requirement that the way of coming to know *I'm* φ is not founded on *my body/I* equivalences. So, if there is no other source of immunity to error through misidentification, then every self-ascription that is an exercise of perspectival self-consciousness will be vulnerable to error through misidentification. The two kinds of case of immunity to error have their sources in the nature of the predicative concept and the nature of the subject concept involved in a judgement *I'm* φ.

Why, it may be asked, should we not simplify the criterion for perspectival self-consciousness by formulating it immediately in terms of vulnerability to error through misidentification? Can we not say that a perspectively self-conscious subject is one capable of coming to know contents of the form *I'm φ* in ways which are vulnerable to error through misidentification?

My principal reason for rejecting this suggestion concerns the explanatory force of the account I have been presenting. The account in terms of concepts anchored in the subject, and judgements made reasonable by the account of what it is for a subject to have a location and to have a particular body, is explanatory of some of the boundaries of immunity to error through misidentification. The account traces the phenomena to those sources, to the nature of those concepts. As I argued in Chapter V, we should seek explanations of epistemic phenomena, explanations that are sufficiently general to cover the range of cases in which the phenomena occur.

There are other cases of immunity to error through misidentification, outside the first person examples. *This book is blue* is immune to error through misidentification, relative to the constituent *This book*, when it is judged in ordinary circumstances on the basis of a perceptual experience of the book as blue, the same experience which makes available the perceptual demonstrative *This book*. These cases of immunity to error through misidentification have their explanation too, an explanation which traces back to the fundamental reference rules for the perceptual demonstrative *This book* and for the observational concept *is blue*. In offering an explanation of the boundaries of immunity to error through misidentification in the first person cases in terms of features of the first person concept and of the predicative concepts in question, we offer an explanation of the same structural character as applies in the explanation of such immunity in the cases beyond the first person. We meet the desideratum of explanatory generality.

I close this section with two comments relevant to assessing the role and significance of perspectival self-consciousness. First, prima facie perspectival self-consciousness can be present in subjects who neither exercise nor possess concepts of mental states and events, whether their own or others. The exercises of perspectival self-consciousness in the examples of coming to know I have a Roman nose, or a certain facial profile, or a certain size of foot as compared with someone else, do not require me to have concepts of perceptual experience. They require only a certain rational sensitivity to my experiences in coming to make judgements about the non-mental world.

The second comment concerns the fact that the examples of perspectival self-consciousness I have been using involve spatial and material properties and a subject's self-ascription thereof. One of our intuitive notions of self-consciousness runs far beyond these cases. We speak in everyday discourse of someone being self-conscious in respect of how he is thought about by another particular person, or by his friends, or by his colleagues, or in respect of how he is represented in the academic literature, or in the press, or on the web. As far as I can see, these are all phenomena that can be accommodated by the reorientation account, once we recognize that the concept φ involved in the self-ascription may be *thought of as irritable by his friends*, or *represented as competent in the press*. These concepts are not anchored in the subject. Knowledgeable self-ascriptions of them can be exercises of perspectival self-consciousness in the sense of the reorientation account. There is correspondingly a generalized notion of perspective in each of these more specialized varieties of perspectival self-consciousness: the perspective given by the view of the subject's friends, or of the representations of the press, and so forth.

3. The Reorientation Account and Other Minds

Perspectival self-consciousness with respect to a range of properties prepares the way for a subject's ability to think of himself as an object of others' awareness. It prepares the way, but it does not suffice for that ability. Perspectival self-consciousness is, on the characterization I have given, something more primitive than having a conception of oneself as the object of others' consciousnesses. Perspectival self-consciousness as defined does not involve the thinker's having the conception of many minds, of a range of other subjects of consciousness, at all. The methods you employ in coming to know *I'm* φ in an exercise of perspectival self-consciousness, where φ is a spatial or material concept, do not, to all appearances, involve or presuppose that you have a conception of other minds.

When, however, a thinker does have a conception of many minds, and is perspectivally self-conscious with respect to a concept, these two can be combined to make available a conception of herself as the object of others' perception that she falls under the concept. When you come to know the arrangement of your hair by looking in a mirror, then (modulo left-right reversal) you come to see yourself largely as others see you. If you also possess the conception of many minds, you can thereby be in a position to know this is how others see you. Use of a third person way of coming to know something about yourself can be an important step in attaining certain sorts of knowledge of how others see you.[3]

There are some claims in Sartre's writings that seem to contradict what I have said in the preceding two paragraphs. Sartre writes, for example, in a passage in which 'the Other' means another subject of consciousness: '. . . for how could I be an object if not for a subject? Thus for me the Other is first the being for whom I am an object; that is, the being through whom I gain my objectness. If I am to be able to conceive of even one of my properties in the objective mode then the Other is already given' (1956: 270).[4] Sartre's views in the general area of subject-hood and consciousness of oneself as a subject are of great interest, and deserve more attention than I can give them here. But Sartre's claim in the passage just quoted, if taken at face value, seems too strong. If we are concerned with a sense in which the only way I can be an object is to be an object for a subject, that sense presumably concerns being repre-sented, either in consciousness or thought, as an object. Under that reading, Sartre's rhetorical question—'How could I be an object if not for a subject?'—invites a straightforward answer. In perspectival self-consciousness, there is indeed a subject for which one is (represented as being) an object; but that subject is oneself.

Sartre could reply that in perspectival self-consciousness as I have characterized it, the thinker is merely thinking of himself as object, as falling under concepts not anchored in the subject. The thinker 'is not perceptually conscious of something both as himself and as object. Sartre's insistence on the distinction between what is thought and what is in perceptual consciousness is one of the best features of his writing, and it needs to be respected. Nonetheless, I do not think the reply just drafted for Sartre would be a defence for him. Consider Sartre's famous example of the person bending down to spy through a keyhole, who

---

[3] It is not the only way of attaining such knowledge. See the discussion of mirror-neuron related knowledge later in this section.

[4] The original French reference is Sartre (1943: Part III, Chapter One, Section IV, 'The Look', p. 317).

suddenly realizes that he is being seen by another person in this com-promising posture and purpose (1943: 298, 1956: 259). Though Sartre considers the example to be one in which, as he would say, I am an object, viz. one in which I am aware of someone else perceiving me, it is not really true that what is especially distinctive of this example is that I have a perceptual awareness of myself as object. What is distinctive is, rather, that I have a perceptual awareness of someone else perceiving me as an object (as well as perceiving me as being a subject).

It is indeed true that it is impossible for something to be given in consciousness in such a way that it is thereby both a presentation of something as an object—by which I mean, presented in such a way that it's potentially informative that it's me—and simultaneously a presenta-tion of something as me. This is arguably an insight that is common to Hume, Kant, Fichte, and Wittgenstein, an insight we discussed back in Chapter III, Section 2. But that agreed impossibility cannot be used in support of the present aspect of Sartre's position. The introduction of the Other into the phenomenology does not make something possible which would otherwise be impossible. It is still impossible after the introduction of the Other. The introduction of the Other gives us a case of a subject's conscious awareness of another perceiving him as an object. That remains distinct from perceiving himself, given as himself, also as an object.

The full realization by the subject looking through a keyhole that he is being seen by another person is available only to someone who is capable of thinking of his posture in a way that is not completely anchored in the subject. He has an observational way of thinking of a person bent down and looking through a keyhole. That observational concept is not anchored in the subject (which is not to say that his own knowledge that he falls under it is observational). This observational concept of this particular posture is constitutively prior to the conception of other subjects who may also apply this spatial concept and may perceive it to be instantiated. In the embarrassing case, another subject perceives it to be instantiated by oneself. Such spatial concepts make possible detailed and specific psychological predications of other subjects in respect of what they are seeing, when a thinker has the conception of other perceiving subjects. It seems to me that that is the order of philosophical and constitutive explanation, rather than the converse.

Other theses may be at stake in the passages from *Being and Nothing-ness* that I have been considering. At least two other readings are possible (and perhaps Sartre intended more than one). A second possible con-strual is that the passages in question propound the thesis that what may seem to be first person representation is not genuinely referential, refer-ring to a subject, until the Other is recognized. Sartre says that what I get from the Other is 'the abstract moment when the self is apprehended as an object'; and that 'I must obtain from the Other the recognition of my being' (1943: 281–2, 1956: 236–7). I do not reject this as a construal, but I do dispute the truth of the thesis. I argued earlier that for fundamental metaphysical reasons, there is no making sense of attribution of mental events and states except as possessed by a subject. Further, even in the case of some of those states that Sartre would describe as 'non-thetic consciousness', where he agrees there is consciousness of one's own consciousness, but says there is no reference to a subject, I would say that these consciousnesses include subject-reflexive events and states in the sense of Chapter II. These events and states have a rather primitive kind of *de se* content made possible by the character of subjects that have information on themselves. The first person in these conscious events and states still refers to the subject who has the consciousness in question. I do not think we have any account of the correctness conditions of the contents of such consciousnesses that does not involve reference; and the reference must be to subjects.[5]

A third possible construal of these passages is that the subject has no conception of himself *as a subject* until he has the capacity to perceive the Other as perceiving him. This is a thesis worthy of consideration in its own right. The first question for this third construal is: what does '*as subject*' mean in its formulation?

One answer would be that it means that the subject is employing a one-place concept ζ *is a subject*; the subject applies it to himself; and the substantive thesis is that a perception of the Other is what makes this possible. The problem with accepting this as a true thesis (again, as opposed to correct interpretation of Sartre) is that in thinking of some-one as the Other, one must already be thinking of him as a subject. For this, one must have some conception of being a subject. It is highly

---

[5] For additional considerations, see the discussion of Anscombe's views in Peacocke (2008: Chapter 3); and Chapter III above.

plausible—and indeed, a principle accepted by Sartre himself earlier in *Being and Nothingness*—that other subjects are conceived of as things of the same very general kind as oneself.[6] But that account of being a subject makes it immediately obvious, and makes it a priori, that I am a subject. My appreciation of that truth does not, on this account of grasp of the notion of subjecthood, need to proceed via perception of the Other.

A different answer to this question about the third interpretation is that thinking of oneself '*as subject*' means thinking of oneself as someone who is not merely employing the first person in thought, but thinking of oneself as employing the first person. This interpretation is invoking the entirely appropriate distinction between using the first person way of thinking, and thinking about that way of thinking, as the first person way of thinking.[7] As a thesis, it is open to the objection that various forms of reflective self-consciousness, the forms that involve thinking about one's own conscious mental states and events in ways made available by their being one's own conscious mental states and events, already involve attributing to oneself use of the first person way of thinking, as the first person way. It is far from apparent that the capacity for this self-attribution involves perception of the Other perceiving oneself. I discuss reflective self-consciousness in the next chapter.

I return now to perspectival self-consciousness in its own right. If indeed other subjects are conceived of as things of the same kind as oneself, then they will stand in the same sorts of relations to things, and to properties and relations instantiated in their environment, as the subject himself stands to things, and to properties and relations, instantiated in his own environment. Perceptual relations constitute an important subclass of such relations. So when a thinker comes to know of a concept, not anchored in the subject, that she falls under that concept, she will be employing a kind of method that will be available to other subjects of consciousness in coming to know about her. She will

---

[6] 'The Other is a thinking substance of the same essence as I am, a substance which will not disappear into primary and secondary qualities, and whose essential structure I find in myself' (Sartre 1943: 267, 1956: 223). This seems to me to be the same fundamentally first personal account of grasp of the general concept of subjecthood as I proposed in *Truly Understood*. I discovered this with mixed feelings.

[7] The distinction is crucial to explaining the communication of first person thoughts. See Peacocke (1981: 191–7). The distinction will be put to work in Chapter X in characterizing interpersonal self-consciousness.

also be in a position to appreciate that others can use that method to come to know about her. Again, this seems to me to be the direction of explanation of knowledge and understanding, rather than that asserted by Sartre in his treatment of his example.

Perspectival self-consciousness is thus a necessary condition for a wide range of familiar psychological phenomena that we describe in everyday discourse as involving some intuitive notion of self-consciousness. The psychological states of embarrassment, shame, and certain kinds of arrogance all involve the conception of others' awareness of oneself as having certain properties, where these properties are thought of, by the subject of these states, under concepts that are not anchored in the subject.[8] For those interested in a particular form of Romantic fantasy, as exemplified in one of Heinrich Heine's poems in his *Buch der Lieder*: to form the idea of a Doppelgänger of oneself requires one to have perspectival self-consciousness with respect to some of one's own properties. We can give the following continental-style formulation. One can be aware that one is an object of a certain kind for others only if: one has a conception of that kind that involves an appreciation of its instantiation by oneself as given in a perspective that is not purely first personal.

This combination of perspectival self-consciousness with a conception of oneself as an object of other's consciousness is a crucial element in articulating what is right in Kierkegaard's treatment of some of his discussions of the self as involving a certain kind of self-consciousness. There are insights here that are completely independent of Kierkegaard's religious inclinations. In *The Sickness unto Death*, Kierkegaard writes:

this self takes on a new quality and qualification by being a self directly before God. (1980: 79)

... what an infinite accent falls on the self by having God as the criterion! The criterion for the self is always: that before which it is a self, but this in turn is the definition of 'criterion'. (1980: 79)

Kierkegaard's conception of the self as being 'before' some other subject, another person or God, who evaluates it, involves the idea of a person, and his properties, being known about by another. One must feature in the other's, the evaluator's, perspective. For a subject to have this conception of herself as so evaluated, she must have the conception of at

---

[8] For further discussion of these states, see O'Brien (2012).

least some of her properties as available from the other's point of view. She must conceive of some of her properties in such a way that there are ways of knowing of them that are not only available to she herself. Perspectival self-consciousness in respect of the relevant range of properties, and its underlying grounds, make available this conception.

We should also draw a conceptual distinction between the case in which the other perceives one as having certain properties that are not psychological—one's spatial and material properties, for instance—and that in which the other perceives one as having properties that only a subject can have, such as acting and perceiving. Kierkegaard's discussion, and also our ordinary states of embarrassment and pride, both involve the second of these as well as the first. So does the conception of a genuine Doppelgänger. Since one is oneself a subject, so must one's double also be a subject.

What is the relation between what have become known as the mirror-neuron phenomena and perspectival self-consciousness? Humans have the ability to think of a bodily action in a way that has special ties to both action and perception. A subject may perceive a particular gesture in a certain way on a particular occasion. Having so perceived it, our subject does not need to engage in any conscious and personal level inference to act in that same way, to imitate it. Conversely, if a human subject makes a gesture on a particular occasion, he needs no conscious and personal level inference to recognize that an action of another human is of the same kind as he has just made.[9] We can call these special ways of representing actions 'bouncing ways', since they permit representations of perceived and produced actions to bounce back and forth without the need for conscious inference between the contents of action and the contents of perception. We can now pose the question: is it necessarily the case that anyone who is capable of employing these bouncing ways is also perspectivally self-conscious?

I answer this question in the affirmative, and offer this argument in support. Suppose a subject sees another's bodily movement as tracing out a certain shape in space. Perceiving something as tracing out, or as occupying, this shape does not in itself involve the ability to represent shape in one of the bouncing ways. This aspect of the perception just

---

[9] For an engaging introductory overview, see Iacoboni (2008).

involves spatial perception—although of course other features of the percept may involve much more than spatial perception. The concept of tracing out or occupying that particular shape, whether the shape is thought of demonstratively ('that shape', made available by the recent perception), or as recognitionally (V-shaped, oval-shaped, etc.), is not a concept anchored in the subject. An account of what individuates these shape concepts, whether demonstrative or recognitional, has no special clause treating the case in which the thinker herself is V-shaped, or oval-shaped, or has that (demonstratively given) shape, or is making that shape in some action. But when a subject is capable of employing these bouncing ways of representing actions, he will have a way of knowing a content of the form *I am making a gesture with a path of such-and-such shape*, where the gesture is thought of both under the spatial way of thinking, not anchored in the subject, and in the bouncing way. This means he has a way of coming to know that he is making a gesture tracing a certain kind of spatial path, where this last is, as we said, not anchored in the subject. So he meets the reorientation criterion for perspectival self-consciousness.

Consequently, as we also noted, this subject has a conception of his action-type which, when he has the conception of other subjects, makes available to him the thought that others will be able to perceive it as of a certain type (given under the bouncing way). I am therefore in agreement with those who see intrinsic connections between one type of self-consciousness, viz. the perspectival, and the mirror-neuron phenomena. No doubt there are several views falling under that general description. The particular form of connection that I am endorsing is the thesis that subjects who employ the bouncing ways of representing actions will enjoy perspectival self-consciousness with respect to their own actions when represented in these ways.

In this respect at least, I am in partial agreement with V. S. Ramachandran's remark that the mirror-neuron phenomena may be 'the dawn of self-awareness'.[10] This may not be the only route to perspectival self-consciousness,

---

[10] Quoted in Colapinto (2009: 87): 'So I made the suggestion that at some point in evolution this system [the mirror-neuron system—CP] turned back and allowed you to create an allocentric view of yourself. This is, I claim the dawn of self-awareness'. We also need to distinguish constitutive claims about the connection between allocentric views and perspectival self-consciousness from etiological claims of how such allocentric

and it is certainly not in principle the only route. But it may be an actually existing, psychologically real route humans employ.

Mirror-neuron based ways of coming to know that one falls under a concept or notion that is not anchored in the subject can be seen in a certain way as liberating us. They liberate us, in the task of coming to know that we fall under concepts or notions not anchored in the subject, from having to apply methods of coming to know that are essentially third personal.

Perhaps surprisingly, not all the social and psychological interactions a subject may have with other subjects, not even relatively simple ones, require the subject to exercise the capacity involved in perspectival self-consciousness. This point applies to some of the original cases of joint attention. We can consider two kinds of case.

Take first the case in which you—we can imagine you are in the position of a child—succeed in attending to an object because your caregiver is looking at it. This requires you to look where your caregiver is looking. You can see whether your caregiver is looking at you, or elsewhere, or at some particular object, by looking at your caregiver's eyes and head. None of this involves your applying to yourself some concept not anchored in the subject, in the way you would have to if you were required to think of the way in which you feature in your caregiver's perspective on the world during this interaction.

The case does not even need to involve self-ascription on your part of an experience or perception to yourself. You do need to think, of your caregiver 'She's looking at *that*'. The *that* here involves your use of a perceptual-demonstrative way in which an object or event is given. It does not involve ascribing an experience to yourself. (If the contents here are at a nonconceptual level, there may even be the possibility of having the ability to enjoy representations that attribute seeing a particular object to your caregiver without having the ability to attribute, non-conceptually, seeings to yourself.) But in any case, even if you do have the capacity to self-ascribe perceptual states, you do not need to exercise it to engage successfully in this first kind of joint attention.[11]

---

representations came to exist. I am expressing agreement here with the constitutive element of Ramachandran's view.

[11] Contrast this with some of J. Bermúdez's descriptions of these cases (1998: 258–64). This is a minor disagreement compared with a large measure of agreement with the other

A second sort of joint attention occurs when you want the caregiver to come to perceive and attend to a particular object, one that you currently perceive, and are thereby thinking of demonstratively as *that so-and-so*. If you are able to distinguish between the case in which your caregiver is attending to that object and the case in which she is not, and are able to bring it about that the former case occurs, then you will have brought about an instance of this second kind of joint attention. You may need, in the course of bringing this about, to be able to form representations with such contents as *She's not yet looking there, at that; she needs to look further in that direction, at that box*. None of this, either, seems to involve an exercise of the capacity involved in perspectival self-consciousness.[12]

The social interactions that do draw on a subject's capacity for perspectival self-consciousness are those that in one way or another involve the subject's being aware that she falls under some concept or notion that is not anchored in the subject. It may in simple cases merely be that the subject's own appreciation of her possession of the property picked out by the concept or notion affects how she conducts the social interaction. In other cases, the subject may need to know that her partner in the interaction appreciates that she falls under the notion or concept. In this case, the possession of bouncing ways of representing actions can of course be a massive facilitator of successful interaction, particularly when it involves the communication of moods and attitudes by facial expressions. Having a certain facial expression is, par excellence, a property we humans represent in a bouncing way. Knowing that one has a certain facial expression is a form of perspectival self-consciousness without which our social lives would be radically different, and poorer.

---

major theses of Bermúdez's book, in particular his very welcome insistence on the existence of nonconceptual forms of first person content.

[12] Nor does it seem to need to involve the capacity to self-ascribe perceptions, as opposed to employing perceptually based representations of objects. Contrast Bermúdez: 'The explanatory requirement to assume that the infant is aware of himself as a perceiver is even clearer in the second form of joint visual attention' (1998: 258).

IX

Reflective Self-Consciousness

Reflective self-consciousness is the second of the three varieties of self-consciousness whose nature and relations I will be considering. 'Reflective' is a term of art here, though on the treatment I offer, the use of the term will respect the image of reflection. The reflecting state of the subject is something whose properties, like that of a reflection, are explained by the nature of what is being reflected, something that exists independently of being reflected. Reflective self-consciousness as I understand it here is very different from the perspectival self-consciousness considered in the previous chapter. But it still falls under the general umbrella characterization of being a state that goes beyond the minimal capacity for first person thought, even in the realm of psychological self-ascriptions. Our first task is to characterize reflective self-consciousness, after which we can turn to its significance.

1. Characterizing Reflective Self-Consciousness

A first step in characterizing reflective self-consciousness is to remind ourselves of the concept used in Chapter II, that of a state or event being subject-reflexive. A subject-reflexive state or event is one whose content, *de jure* and primitively, refers to the subject who experiences or enjoys that particular state or event. All of the following mental states or events are subject-reflexive in this sense: having a perception in which there is a door to the left of you; enjoying an action-awareness that you are opening the door; remembering being in Athens. As I said, this notion of a subject-reflexive state or event is essentially a generic notion of a state or event with *de se* content. It is a notion applicable both to some of the states and events of subjects requiring only minimal first person conceptual consciousness, such as knowing one is in front of a desk, and is also applicable to those with more sophisticated states of self-consciousness. In the other direction, downwards, I argued earlier that this notion of subject-reflexivity can also apply to events and states with nonconceptual content.

Using the notion of subject-reflexivity, we can say: reflective self-consciousness is *de se* awareness of being in a *de se* state, or of enjoying an event with *de se* content. It is also part of the characterization that the *de se* awareness of being in a *de se* state or enjoying a *de se* event is, in a sense to be explained, based upon the *de se* state or event. So, corresponding to our examples above, everyday examples of reflective self-consciousness in the intended sense include: your ordinary awareness that you are perceiving something as to your left; your awareness that you are consciously opening the door; and your awareness that you remember being in Athens.

Simply being in pain or feeling elated are not exercises of reflective self-consciousness by this test, for they do not themselves involve any *de se* truth-assessable content, let alone awareness on the part of the subject that he is in such a state or event. A subject-reflexive state has to have a content, and thus a correctness condition, concerning the subject, *de jure*, primitively, and non-descriptively. Being in pain is not something assessable as correct or incorrect. A subject with some representation of ownership will experience certain pains as his own. He will also experience them as located in apparent parts of a body that he also experiences as his own. But neither of these points involves pains being assessable as true or false. In this respect pains differ from perceptual experiences. The same applies to an experience of elation in the case in which the elation has no object.

When a subject judges that he is in pain, in rational response to his own conscious pain, that is a rational responsiveness that does have some significant features in common with cases of reflective self-consciousness as I have been characterizing it. The rational responsiveness equally makes appropriate the image of reflecting a state or event, one which exists independently of its being reflected in higher-level awareness or thought. But such rational responsiveness to one's own pain is not itself a case of reflective self-consciousness, because in judging you are in pain, you do not meet the condition of representing yourself as being in a state, or enjoying an event, with a first person content. You merely use the first person in attributing the pain to yourself. You do not represent yourself as being in a state with a first person content assessable as true or false.

Similarly, perceiving that there's a door in front of one is equally not an exercise of reflective self-consciousness. Someone who enjoys such a perception must indeed be capable of some form of first person representation, since the content is of the form *that's a door in front of me*. But perceiving the spatial world that way is not the same as being aware that one is in a *de se* state or enjoying an event with a *de se* content. Reflective self-consciousness involves awareness of mental states and events. Taking the contents of perceptual experience at face value, even contents with a first person constituent, is not by itself an exercise of reflective self-consciousness.

By contrast, in the self-reflective cases in which you are aware that you see that you have a door on your left, or in which you are aware that you are consciously opening the door, and so forth, you represent yourself as being in a state, or enjoying an event, with a first person content. You do not merely employ the first person notion; you also, in your higher-order state of awareness, refer to the first person notion; and you refer to it as the first person notion. This is perhaps the most primitive form of thinking of yourself as someone who employs first person notions, as opposed merely to using first person notions and exploiting that fact in your thought and representations. It is this that makes reflective self-consciousness a distinctive form of self-consciousness, of theoretical interest to those concerned with the first person and the possibilities it creates for conscious subjects.

For those interested in formal matters and the hierarchy of senses (everyone else can skip this paragraph): we can make clear the need on the part of the subject to employ some concept that refers to the first person, and not merely to use the first person, by considering how to formalize the transitions normally involved in attaining states of reflective self-consciousness. Suppose a thinker x is on a hill, a hill which unsurprisingly we take to be y. Our thinker makes a transition from

an event of his seeing that he is on this hill

to

a judgement that he is seeing that he is on this hill.

In formalizing this transition, I use '{...}' to indicate a nonconceptual content, and as before, I use '<A>' for the sense of the expression A. This transition can then be formally characterized as one from

an event in which: sees-that $(x, \{self\}_x{}^\wedge\{is\ on\}^\wedge\{this\ hill\}_y)$

to

judges $(x, <seeing\text{-}that>^\wedge[self]_x{}^\wedge(<\{self\}_x>^\wedge<\{is\ on\}>^\wedge<\{this\ hill\}_y>))$.

It is in the term $<\{self\}_x>$, which specifies how our subject x is thinking of the first person content of his seeing, that we have something displaying not just use of, but reference to, the first person notion. A mental state containing the nonconceptual content $\{self\}_x$ refers to the subject x in the first person way. A mental state containing the content $<\{self\}_x>$ refers to the first person notion as used by x, and refers to it as the first person notion. Enthusiasts for the philosophical logic of intentional content, who are presumably those who are still reading, will note the quantification into senses here. These senses are object-dependent.

To return to non-technical matters: this characterization of reflective self-consciousness is meant to identify a conceptually and philosophically significant notion that falls under the characterization of being a state that involves awareness of oneself, as oneself, in its content. It is not designed to be historically faithful to the usage of all those who have, in one way or another, used the notion of reflective self-consciousness. Indeed, it diverges in extension from some prominent historical usages, including that of Sartre. Reflective self-consciousness as understood by Sartre in *La Transcendance de l'Ego* and in his 1947 lecture 'Conscience de soi et connaissance de soi' includes awareness expressed in the judgement 'I'm in pain'.[1] As I noted, in awareness that one is in pain, the awareness is of a state of consciousness that does not have (or does not necessarily have) the subject-reflexive character required by the present definition. The awareness may merely be of the pain. We might, stipulatively, call the wider notion Sartre is using 'reflective subject-consciousness', as opposed to reflective self-consciousness. Sartrean reflective subject-consciousness is a notion in good standing. It is just not the one on which I am focusing here. Reflective subject-consciousness

---

[1] Both the monograph and the lecture are reprinted in Sartre (2003).

does not, in my view, involve any reference, in the subject's mental states, to the first person notion or concept, as opposed, as always, to merely using the notion or concept.

The condition for reflective self-consciousness is not to be understood in such a way that the reflectively self-conscious subject is required himself to possess the concept of subject-reflexivity, or even of *de se* content, or of content in general. Subject-reflexivity is a modestly theoretical concept that we as theorists use to pick out a certain class of states and events. The reflectively self-conscious subject just represents a state or event as being of the general type it is (a seeing, and so forth, with a certain specific content). The subject also thinks of the contents themselves in certain canonical ways. But to do all this, the subject does not himself need to exercise the philosophical concept of reflective self-consciousness, nor to exercise or possess the concepts in terms of which it is defined. He needs only to enjoy states that fall under that concept.

Reflective self-consciousness requires that the subject-reflexive awareness of being in a certain subject-reflexive state be attained in a certain way. Take a case of reflective self-consciousness involving awareness that one is enjoying a visual experience of a certain kind concerning oneself. This awareness must be rationally produced by the visual experience itself, operating as the subject's reason for self-applying the notion of experience (more particularly, of an experience with a certain content). We can conceive of a future in which someone can come to know, circuitously and no doubt redundantly, that he is having an experience of a given kind by seeing a real-time scan of a functioning brain, knowing the brain is his own, and having psychophysical knowledge that scans of a certain sort underlie experiences with a certain content. Coming to know inferentially in this way that one has an experience of a certain sort would be employing a way of coming to know that would equally be a means of coming to know of someone else that they have an experience of a certain kind. The example would not be a case of reflective self-consciousness in the sense intended.

2. Metaphysics and Epistemology of Reflective Self-Consciousness

What is the explanation of a thinker's entitlement to make a rational self-ascription of, say, a perception on the basis of the perceptual event itself?

The explanation is in part that the perceptual event is the thinker's own. This last fact about ownership is at the level of the metaphysics of perception and subjects, rather than anything to do with the representation, whether conceptual or nonconceptual, of perception. A perceptual experience enjoyed by the subject himself makes rational the self-ascription of an experience of a certain type, and when all goes well, the occurrence of the perception leads not just to judgement but to knowledge. The transition is of course not inference from a premise about perception. The perception itself is the subject's reason for the self-ascription. It must also be part of the explanation of the rationality of the transition that it is either constitutive of the concept of perceptual experience, or a consequence of what is constitutive, that the occurrence of a certain type of experience makes rational to its subject a self-ascription of an experience of that type. I will not be concentrating on that component of the rationality here, on which there is more in *Truly Understood*, Chapter 6.

This approach ensures Shoemakerian immunity to error through misidentification of ascriptions so made. The rational transition is from the conscious event itself, and not from some premise identifying someone or other as the owner of the conscious event. The only case in which such a self-ascription can be made rationally on the basis of a conscious mental event is that in which the conscious mental event is the subject's own. So not only does the self-ascription not rest upon any identity 'I am *a*', for some *a* which is antecedently known to enjoy the conscious event. Self-ascriptions made in this way also cannot be mistaken in respect of who it is that is known to enjoy the conscious event.

This simple approach to the relation between the metaphysics and the epistemology of these self-ascriptions contrasts sharply with three others.

First, it contrasts with treatments that aim to offer a philosophical elucidation of ownership of an experience or other conscious state or event in terms of the possibility of some kind of self-ascription of that experience, state or event. Campbell (1986) discusses accounts of the latter kind. Under those rival approaches, it cannot be a legitimate explanation of the rationality and potentially knowledge-yielding nature of the transition from a conscious state to its self-ascription to say that in the nature of the case, the procedure applies only to the subject's own conscious states and events. That cannot be explanatory on the rival view, because to say that a state or event is the subject's own is simply to say that the subject can, in some specified way, self-ascribe it. What makes the self-ascription rational and potentially knowledge on the rival view would perhaps have to be a matter of appropriately contextual self-verification (the context being essential to, explaining, the verification). Suitable contextually self-verifying self-ascriptions, when not based on empirical information, are plausibly cases of knowledge on any reasonable epistemology. So the rival views would have a way of answering the epistemological question of why these self-ascriptions are knowledge. Nevertheless, the account of ownership embraced by these rival views seems wrong. A subject can have experiences, but not be capable of self-ascribing them, simply because the subject does not have any notion of experience. We are here back in the territory considered earlier, in Chapter VII, Section 2, when we discussed Strawson's position on ownership in *The Bounds of Sense*, and gave reasons for preferring the ownership-first view to an ascription-first view.

Second, the simple model I have offered contrasts in several respects with perceptual models of the knowledge attained in reflective self-consciousness. One actual holder of the perceptual model of reflective consciousness is David Armstrong (1984). Kant's talk of inner sense certainly tempts one also to attribute the view to him in some passages. There are several possible versions of the perceptual model, as Shoemaker emphasizes in his First Royce Lecture (1996: 203ff.). One obvious respect of contrast between perceptual models and the simple view outlined here lies in the fact that one does not have a further perception of one's perceptions, an experience of them that is distinct from the first-level perceptions themselves (see again *Truly Understood* Chapter 6).

There are various ways of rejecting perceptual models of reflective self-consciousness. To reject the perceptual model does not involve any commitment to the much stronger idea, found in Shoemaker, that mental states and events have no nature independent of our ability to know about them in certain ways (1996: 224–5 and 240ff.). As against Shoemaker's position, I would continue to say about the model of reflective self-consciousness that I have offered here the same as I said in Chapter 7 of *Truly Understood*. Shoemaker argues that for a wide range of mental phenomena, what he calls 'self-blindness' is impossible. For a creature to be self-blind with respect to some mental phenomenon is for it to lack introspective access to it in its own case, even though the creature is able to conceive of that phenomenon (Shoemaker 1996: 226).

Shoemaker develops a position that not only rejects a perceptual model of reflective self-consciousness. He goes further, and rejects the idea that states for which self-blindness is impossible are such that their existence and nature is independent of their being known in certain ways (he rejects what he calls 'the independence condition' for such states). I will not repeat my critique of Shoemaker's views on this issue, but instead refer readers to the relevant pages of *Truly Understood* (268–75). In contrast to Shoemaker, I hold that knowledge of one's own perceptions, including cases of knowledge covered by our characterization of reflective self-consciousness, involves a rational sensitivity to the occurrence of those conscious perceptual events and states themselves. This position is entirely consistent with those events and states having a nature that makes possible and explains, rather than constitutively involves, awareness of those perceptual events and states. The accessibility of first-order conscious mental events and states to rational judgements by their owner is, on the present treatment, a consequence of their nature as subjective conscious events. The accessibility to the subject's own judgement is not something to be written into an account of the original nature, as a constitutive condition. So the position does not involve denying Shoemaker's independence condition.

The third, more extended, contrast I wish to draw is with the position Sartre developed in his 1937 work *The Transcendence of the Ego*.[2] Sartre's position is summarized in the following quotations:

(a) 'the Ego is an object apprehended but also an object *constituted* by reflective knowledge' (2004: 34);

(b) 'this pole [the Ego—CP] appears only in the world of reflection' (2004: 21);

(c) 'unreflected consciousness must be considered as autonomous' (19); 'It is thus . . . on this level [of reflection—CP] that egotistic life is placed, and on the unreflected level that is placed impersonal life' (2004: 20);

(d) 'the Ego is an object that appears only to reflection, and which thereby is radically cut off from the World' (2004: 36).

Sartre gives various arguments for his position. Here is a selection (I cannot claim completeness):

---

[2] The English translations used here are those of A. Brown in Sartre (2004).

(e)   'In fact, the Ego never appears except when we are not looking at it. The reflective gaze has to fix itself on the *Erlebnis*, insofar as it emanates from the state. Then, behind the state, at the horizon, the Ego appears. So it is never seen except "out of the corner of one's eye". The moment I turn my gaze on it and wish to reach it without going via the *Erlebnis* and the state, it vanishes. The reason is this: in seeking to grasp the Ego for itself and as the direct object of my consciousness, I fall back on to the unreflected level, and the Ego disappears with the reflective act' (2004: 39–40).

(f)   Sartre also has a thesis about constitution: 'what is *really* first is consciousnesses, through which are constituted states, then, through these, the Ego' (2004: 34).

(g)   'It is useless, for instance, if we consider a melody, to suppose there is some X which acts as a support for the different notes. The unity stems in this case from the absolute indissolubility of elements which cannot be conceived of as separate, except by abstraction. The subject of the predicate will here be the concrete totality, and the predicate will be a quality abstractly separated from the totality and gaining its full meaning only when it is linked back to the totality.

For these very reasons, I refuse to see in the Ego a sort of X pole acting as the support for psychical phenomena. [. . .] The Ego is nothing other than the concrete totality of states and actions that it unifies . . . ' (2004: 29–30).

(h)   Sartre is well aware that there are apparently many true propositions involving the first person on the unreflected level. He holds that this appearance can be explained away consistently with his view that the ego does not appear at the unreflective level. His explanation involves the idea of 'Body as illusory fulfillment of the *I*-concept' (2004: table, p. 41).

Despite my evident commitment to disagreeing with his principal theses, it seems to me that there are some real insights in Sartre's points. The quotation (e) in particular about the impossibility of finding the ego on the unreflective level is naturally read as putting Hume's famous point about his inability to find himself into the language of a French writer in the 1930s. But as with Hume, I would make the same point as I did back in Chapter III. What is right in Sartre's point is that the ego, as he would put it, cannot be, as I would put it, an object of original, non-derivative attention. It does not follow that the ego or subject does not exist; it does not follow that it does not contribute to the individuation of particular mental events; and it does not follow that it has no role to play in an initial characterization of what it is for an event or state to be conscious. From the absence of a certain kind of phenomenology, we cannot soundly draw any conclusions about the ontology of subjects.

Sartre's positive view of the unreflective level sounds like a moderate reductionist view of the ego or subject, of the sort endorsed by Derek Parfit (1987). Suppose we accept, for reasons of the metaphysics of consciousness and subjects, that when (for instance) there is an event of perception, there must be an unreduced subject who is perceiving. Then if reflective thought about the perception is to attribute it correctly, it must attribute it to the same subject as exists already on the unreflective level, *pace* Sartre. If this metaphysical thesis is correct, there is no room for saying that the subject or ego is metaphysically involved only at the reflective level. In fact, on the positive simple account I have been giving, the ownership by the subject, at the unreflective level, plays an important part in explaining the entitlement, on the part of a subject of a particular experience, to self-ascribe an experience of its relevant kind.

From the standpoint of the metaphysical arguments for an ontology of subjects, Sartre's parallel with melodies, which need no support for the notes that compose the melody, is unconvincing. Any given subject of experience could have had different experiences and other conscious states and events over time. Even the subject's earliest experiences could have been different. By contrast, a melody, considered as a type, could not go differently.

Of a particular actual token event of playing the melody, it may indeed be true that it could have continued differently. But we can make no sense of the token event being a starting of that melody yet also being different in type right from the start. By stark contrast, our concept of the subject of a series of conscious events just is not that of a sequence or sum of conscious events starting with some initial event that is essential to the sequence or sum. It really is, rather, of the subject who has them; and for that particular subject, no particular sequence or initial segment of conscious events or states is required for its existence.

What of Sartre's claim that all uses of the first person in characterizing the unreflective level can be replaced by reference to the body? One can see what he means: at least in the case in which I am embodied, for it to be true that I am in London is for my body to be in London. But taken as an entirely general proposal, this creaks at many points as an attempt at elimination of the first person in characterizing the unreflective level. The first person is still there in the designation '*my* body'; the phenomenology of ownership is a first person phenomenology. Sartre's proposal also does not cover cases in which I have a perceptual point of view in the world but no body with which I can act or feel. Visual experience alone, with no experience of a body, nor even consciousness of a body-schema, can represent something as coming towards one (nonconceptual *de se* content). Sartre's proposal similarly does not do well with ascriptions of action. 'I am raising my arm' does not mean 'This body is raising this arm'. Under the required subject-free reading, the latter would be true when the arm's rising is a reflex, while the former would be false. The phenomenology of bodily action awareness is also first personal. The awareness has a content of the form 'I am doing such-and-such'. For action-types that are not purely bodily, such as assertion, 'I am asserting that p' does not mean 'This body is asserting that p'; and so forth. So I disagree with Sartre's claim that 'the body and bodily images can consummate the total degradation of the concrete *I* of reflection to the "*I*-concept" by functioning for the *I*-concept as its illusory fulfillment' (2004: 90); though it would certainly be pleasant to formulate the thesis with which I have been disagreeing so stylishly.

3. First Person Theories of Understanding, and Empirical Phenomena

Does reflective self-consciousness play any special part in the understanding, or grasp, of psychological concepts? Let us call any thesis that gives a special place to the first person concept in a constitutive account of grasp of a psychological concept a *first person understanding thesis* ('FPUT') for that concept. Similarly, any thesis that gives a special place to the first person concept in a constitutive account of grasp of all psychological concepts of a given kind we can call a first person understanding thesis for concepts of that kind. Theses of either kind that give a special place to exercises of reflective self-consciousness will be first person understanding theses, FPUTs. It will be helpful here to consider FPUTs more generally.

For any given psychological concept, one can conceive of several possible first person understanding theses. Of course the form to be taken by any particular FPUT depends on the correct general form of theories of concepts in general. If one is a pure conceptual role theorist, the first person understanding theses one will endorse will look very different from those who think that referential relations and contributions to truth conditions play a role in understanding. Though one can certainly formulate FPUTs in the framework of pure conceptual role semantics, I will consider here those that involve some grasp of referential relations in one way or another. Within that class of treatments, one common abstract form that may taken by many FPUTs of a given psychological concept ϕ is this:

for the thinker to grasp the content *I'm ϕ now* is for the thinker to meet such-and-such condition C; while to grasp what it is for an arbitrary thing x to fall under the concept ϕ at an arbitrary time t is for the thinker to have some specified kind of appreciation that x must at t stand in a certain relation to the condition C that he meets in his grasp of *I'm ϕ now*.

One of the positions on the understanding of sensation language so strongly attacked by the later Wittgenstein is just such an FPUT. The position he attacks meets the displayed description when the condition C is taken as, roughly: appreciates the correctness of judging *I'm ϕ now* in rational response to the occurrence in the thinker of a sensation of a certain kind. The position Wittgenstein attacks also holds that grasp of what it is for an arbitrary subject to have a sensation of the kind in question at a given time is for the thinker to have tacit knowledge that the subject has to be in the same subjective state as the one to which the thinker is rationally sensitive to in his own self-ascriptions of the sensation concept. Whether any language whose concepts are grasped in this way must also be a private language is, prima facie, not immediately settled (and maybe not indirectly settled either) by this characterization. That such a FPUT can be correct without a commitment to privacy in the sense to which Wittgenstein objected was part of my argument in Chapter 5 of *Truly Understood*.

A FPUT need not be restricted to using a notion of sameness of subjective conscious state in bridging from grasp of the first person case to understanding of the other person case. Bridges that serve the purpose may be built from other materials too. A thinker's grasp of what it is for someone else to have a belief with a certain propositional conceptual content p, for instance, might be argued to involve some kind of tacit knowledge that the other's belief is subject to the same norms for acceptance or rejection, in the content of the other person's attitudes, as is his own belief that p. Or an entirely different kind of bridge could be built from sameness of some kind of specified functional role. We can thus formulate various different sorts of FPUTs for a wide range of psychological concepts: for particular kinds of propositional attitudes, and for propositional attitudes in general; for particular kinds of perceptual states, and for perception in general; for particular emotions, and for emotion in general; for particular kinds of action, and for action in general; and so forth.

We need to distinguish sharply both in intension and in extension between first person understanding and first person knowledge. To say that there is a distinctive kind of first person knowledge that one is φ is not to imply that a first person theory of understanding is correct for the concept φ. There is, for normal humans, a distinctive way of coming to know that their legs are straight, rather than bent at the knee. This way, based on proprioception, is in normal circumstances a way for each person to come to know that his or her legs are crossed, and is not, in normal circumstances, a way of coming to know that anyone else's legs are crossed. This fact does not support a first person theory of understanding for the concept x's legs are crossed. If you have no system of proprioception, you cannot know in that distinctive way that your legs are crossed, but you can certainly have full grasp of the concept x's legs are crossed. You can on occasion see that your own or others' legs are crossed, and so forth.

In the reverse direction, however, it is plausible that if a FPUT is true for a given concept φ, then there will be a distinctive first person way of coming to know that one is φ. The first person theory of understanding for φ will mention a condition appreciation of which is sufficient for understanding, and indeed coming to know, that one is φ. So in any case in which a thinker appreciates that that condition is fulfilled, that will provide a way of coming to know he is φ. That is particularly important when considering proposed empirical objections to FPUTs for particular concepts, or for kinds of concepts. For it implies, by contraposition, that if there is no distinctive first person way of coming to know that one is φ, then a first person theory of understanding for φ is also false.

First person theories can contribute both to the explanation of philosophical data, and sit better than other philosophical theories with some plausible actual explanations of empirical phenomena. FPUTs for such concepts as *x is in pain* and *is having a visual experience of such-and-such kind* can explain how it is that someone can, apparently, understand what it is for someone else to be in pain consistently with having no idea how the subject suffering the pain will act. They can also explain how we can make sense of the possibility of someone who grasps what it is for someone else to have a visual experience of a certain kind, but who is quite unsure whether visual experiences, or some other state, explain the subject's actions. These philosophical points have been discussed elsewhere, and I will not repeat them here (Peacocke 2008: Chapters 5 and 6). It is the relevance of FPUTs to the explanation of empirical phenomena that I will consider here.

Several phenomena recently identified and investigated sit most easily with FPUTs for concepts of seeing and of action. In one experiment of Andrew Meltzoff and Rechele Brooks, 18-month olds were given experience with a trick blindfold that looks opaque, but through which they could in fact see (Brooks and Meltzoff 2008). Children at this age show evidence that they understand that adults cannot see through normal blindfolds. They followed the direction of gaze of a blindfolded person significantly less than they followed the gaze one who is not blindfolded. Some 18-month olds were given experience with the trick blindfold. After such experience, these 18-month olds followed the direction of gaze of blindfolded adults significantly more than control subjects. The most natural interpretation of these results, endorsed by Meltzoff and Brooks, is that children use their own experience in forming conclusions about what others see in various circumstances. From the point of view of a FPUT for the concept of seeing, the 18-month old in this example, when seeing through the seemingly-opaque blindfold, simply self-ascribes seeings on the basis of his own experience of seeing. Such an 18-month old then attributes visual experiences to others he sees wearing the same type of seemingly-opaque blindfold because that is what he experienced under the same conditions. But what might a theorist of the concept of seeing who rejects first person theories of understanding say about this case?

A common strategy amongst those who reject such first person theories is to adopt a theory-theory account of the concept. The concept of seeing, on such a treatment, is the concept of a state that plays a certain role, characteristically a role in the explanation of action in the most simple cases. Provided the role in question does not give any special place to the first person, such theory-theory accounts are not FPUTs.

There are two problems in reconciling such non-FPUTs with the empirical facts.

The first problem can be illustrated by the situation of the children in the Meltzoff and Brooks experiment who wear the trick blindfold. The theory-theory treatment of seeing implies that, prior to experiencing the trick blindfolds, the children think of seeing as the mental state that allows adults, suitably oriented, without barriers, in the right background conditions, to act on objects, learn about them, and so forth, when their eyes are properly oriented towards those objects. Now this raises a question about the children who experience the trick blindfolds for the first time. When fitted with them for the first time, ought they not according to the theory-theory to judge that they are not seeing, since they stand in relations that they have learned to prevent seeing? Yet it would be bizarre and irrational for someone to judge, when wearing the trick blindfold, that he is not seeing. Adults would not so judge, and the experiment shows that not only do the 18-months olds not so judge either, but that they also use the information that they are seeing to draw conclusions about others in their situation too. This is all entirely to be expected under the sort of first person theory of understanding for concepts of conscious states and events I have been endorsing. It is not clear to me that the proponent of the theory-theory treatment of grasp of the concept has a plausible way to respond to this point.

Perhaps the theory-theorist of the concept might reply that the subject wearing the trick blindfold for the first time could reason thus: 'Despite wearing this blindfold, I know about the objects in front of me, so I am in the state that normally plays such-and-such role; hence this blindfold should not be treated as an obstacle that prevents seeing'. A problem with this reply is that not just any way of knowing about the objects in front of one is sufficient to ground an ascription of seeing. Knowledge of the objects in front of one based on earlier perception and knowledge that they will not have moved or changed would not suffice for a correct ascription of seeing how they are now. To reach a correct ascription of seeing to himself, the subject wearing the trick blindfold for the first time must be responding specifically to his own seeings. This is what a theory-

theory of the concept of seeing will find difficult to explain. The correct, and actual, response to the experience when wearing the trick blindfold for the first time seems to involve thinking of seeings in something other than a theory-theory way.

The second, better-known, problem is that much everyday folk 'theory' about seeing is in fact false. We know that seeings do not control concurrent bodily actions, even though almost everyone without knowledge of experimental results would be inclined to say that they do. Concurrent bodily actions are controlled by the completely unconscious, evolutionarily older representational states produced in the dorsal system.[3] To summarize what has become a familiar cluster of points: what makes our concept *seeings* refer to seeings is not any theory we have about them, but in part the special relation we each have to our own seeings, or to our knowledge of what it is like to see (Peacocke 2010a).

Broadly parallel points apply to empirical phenomena involving the ascription of action to others. Amanda Woodward and her colleagues have shown that infants as young as 3 months, using 'sticky' (Velcro-covered) mittens to apprehend toys, will identify a movement of another person's hand as an action with a goal only if they themselves can produce an action of that kind (Woodward et al. 2009: esp. 206ff.). Simply seeing the others do it, without doing it oneself, is not enough for classification of the movement as an action. Much the simplest and most plausible overarching description of the route employed by these infants to the ascription of this kind of action to others is that the infant makes this series of steps subpersonally:

This [performs sticky-mitten apprehension himself, with first person action awareness] is an action

That movement there resembles this action in such-and-such respects

---

So: that movement is an action too.

The structure of such this transition would be in accord with a first person theory of understanding for action-concepts. Empirically one needs more information to distinguish the case in which the first representation, 'This is an action', is a response to the subject's action

---

[3] Goodale and Milner (2004); and Milner and Goodale (2006).

awareness in his own case from several other cases: that in which it is a response to something that causes that awareness; that in which it is a response to some kind of efferent copy produced in performance of the action; and that in which it is a response to the proprioceptive experience of apprehending with the sticky-mitten. But the presence of this abstract structure, starting with the first person case and bridging out to the third person case, is something that can be refined over time in various ways, both in its own structure and in respect of what it responds to. The structure is much better suited to an at least partially first person theory of understanding of action than to a theory-theory treatment of the understanding of action, which gives no special place to the first person in its account of the understanding of action notions.

Reflection on the preceding examples of perception and action should sharpen an appreciation of the distinction between theories of knowledge and belief acquisition on the one hand, and theories of understanding on the other. Andrew Meltzoff's well known 'Like me' hypothesis (2007) reads as an account of how infants and children come to acquire psychological beliefs and knowledge about other people. Susan Carey notes that such an account of the application of the concepts to others does not explain the origins of the child's possession of the psychological concept in the first place, particularly in its first person applications (2009: 188–190). Equally, I would add, the 'Like me' hypothesis does not give an account of what it is to possess the psychological concept in question. In its description of first person use of a psychological concept by the child, the 'Like me' account simply presupposes that the child already possesses the concept. Both the question of origins, and the constitutive question of what it is to possess the concept, have to be addressed. First person theories of understanding, as opposed to theories of belief- and knowledge-acquisition, for certain kinds of action and perception, do aim to address the constitutive question.[4]

With this very brief review of what is involved in first person theories of understanding in hand, we can consider Alison Gopnik's argument in an influential paper twenty years ago that empirical evidence tells against first person knowledge of intentional states, and tells instead in favour of

---

[4] We also have the conception of action-types we could not perform ourselves, and perception-types we could enjoy ourselves. They are conceived as falling under some much more general type as those that we can, respectively, perform or enjoy.

a theory-theory view of concepts of mental states (1993). Her position is particularly pertinent at this point, because, as part of the title of her paper indicates, 'The illusion of first-person knowledge of intentionality', she argued that there is no special first person knowledge of a subject's intentional states. Since we have already made a case that first person theories of understanding do imply the availability of special first person knowledge of intentional states, it follows by contraposition that if there is no such special knowledge, FPTUs are false.

I think it is fair to say the prospects for FPTUs look rather different now than at the time of Gopnik's original paper. First, as we have just seen, some empirical evidence, as in the example of the trick blindfolds in the case of perception, and the sticky mittens in the case of action, seems to sit well with first person theories of grasp of mental notions and concepts. Second, it has become clearer in the twenty years since the publication of Gopnik's paper that there are other sources of evidence that children younger than 36 months enjoy representations of false beliefs in others. Some mistakes in answering questions about how some other agent with a false belief will act are not sufficient to establish that the speaker does not represent the other's beliefs as false. There may be pressures against producing an utterance that involves even an embedded proposition the thinker knows to be false, even though the thinker knows the subject in question to have a false belief; and so forth. These issues have been very well discussed in the literature, and I will not rehearse them here.[5]

The third, more philosophical, point I want to emphasize is the bearing of the above discussion of first person theories of understanding on a point both Gopnik and several of her commentators in the original *Behavioral and Brain Sciences* discussion took for granted. Gopnik summarized her view thus: 'In each of our studies, children's reports of their own immediately past psychological states are consistent with their accounts of the psychological states of others. When they can report and understand the psychological states of others, in the cases of pretense, perception, and imagination, they report having had those psychological states themselves. When they cannot report and understand the

---

[5] Onishi and Baillargeon (2005); Song et al. (2008); Baillargeon et al. (2010). A full discussion of the many issues here, though of great interest in themselves, would distract from our original concern with reflective self-consciousness.

psychological states of others, in the cases of false belief, and source, they report that they have not had those states themselves' (1993: 9). One of her commentators, Simon Baron-Cohen, wrote 'Gopnik's treatment of the link between first- and third-person knowledge of intentionality is persuasive: The developmental evidence she amasses for the notion that the two mature simultaneously, and thus in all likelihood reflect the acquisition of a new theory of mind (own and other's) is impressive' (Baron-Cohen 1993: 29). So we have here the claim that it is positive evidence in favour of theory-theory treatments if children make correct first person ascriptions when and only when they make correct third person ascriptions.

It seems to me, however, that if in fact children make correct first person ascriptions when and only when they make correct third person ascriptions, that would be entirely consistent with a first person theory of understanding for the psychological notion or concept involved in the ascription. A subject whose grasp of a psychological concept is given by a first person theory may or may not be good at working out when the condition for correctness for a third person ascription of the property in question is in fact met in any particular case with which he is presented. The correctness condition takes the form of an identity condition: that some feature of the other's state be identical with some feature of the subject's when the first person ascription is correct (as we noted, it may be sameness of subjective type, it may be sameness of norms governing the judged content, and so forth). This correctness condition is a constitutive condition, not an evidential condition.

Now two thinkers may grasp the same condition, but differ in respect of how good they are at coming to know, by reasoning of one kind or another, when that constitutive condition is met. For a thinker who is good at such reasoning, it may well be true that in a range of circumstances, his first person ascriptions involving a given psychological concept are correct if and only if his third person ascriptions are correct. This biconditional is therefore consistent with a first person theory of grasp of the psychological concept. The truth of the biconditional, if it is true, is not evidence against a first person theory of understanding. Whether the biconditional holds varies with the subject's capacity for assessing whether the condition for a correct third person ascription is fulfilled. That variation is entirely consistent with the presence of a specifically first person clause in the understanding condition for the concept being applied. It is consistent, in particular, with reflective self-consciousness playing a special part in the grasp of a range of psychological concepts.

4. Reflective and Perspectival Self-Consciousness: Their Significance for Inquiry

I now turn to consider some of the relations between perspectival self-consciousness, as described and discussed in the preceding chapter, and reflective self-consciousness. Perspectival self-consciousness and reflective self-consciousness can be seen as meeting the different needs of two sorts of inquiry a thinker may make about the basic case in which he comes to accept a content *I'm* φ, where φ is a concept anchored in the subject, in the sense of the preceding chapter.

One sort of inquiry the thinker may make about himself is: what other properties and relations do I have besides φ? What sort of thing in the world am I? Answering these questions, questions about the reference of the first person, requires the thinker to attain at least perspectival self-consciousness. If he succeeds in such enquiries, he will end up knowing of other concepts that he falls under them, where these concepts are not anchored in the subject, and whose application has no special constitutive relation to what makes something his body.

Another sort of inquiry a thinker may have about his acceptance of such a content *I'm* φ is: is it reasonable to accept it? How is it that I have come to accept it? Since reason-giving states and events are very often conscious states and events with *de se* contents, scrutiny and assessment of one's own reasons requires reflective self-consciousness.

I remarked earlier that a subject can be perspectivally self-conscious without having the capacity to think of his own mental states at all. By contrast, reflective self-consciousness certainly does require that capacity. So perspectival self-consciousness does not imply reflective self-consciousness. I suspect that in principle reflective self-consciousness can exist without perspectival self-consciousness, though arguing that involves commitments on some heavy-duty theses about what the ability to represent one's own mental states involves. Without wading into those issues at this point, I observe that it seems less contentious that there are various kinds of enquiries which, in the nature of the case, require the cooperation of both reflective and perspectival self-consciousness. I mention two kinds.

The first kind concerns, broadly, a subject's understanding, explanation, and correction of his particular conception of his situation in the world and his relation to it.

A full understanding of why one perceives the world as one does will involve a comparison of one's own case with how others perceive the world, when they are situated in a certain way in the world. One wide range of representations of how others are situated in the world will involve the subject's appreciation that the others fall under certain concepts not anchored in the subject. For the subject to gain any understanding of his own situation from this appreciation of the situation of others, he needs to appreciate that he too falls under those same concepts not anchored in the subject—and that is part of what is involved in perspectival self-consciousness. This appreciation then puts him in the position to consider possible errors to which he may be prone, having appreciated that others are vulnerable to them. And in the part of the assessment that involves consideration of his own mental states, either for explanation or for correction, the subject has to exercise his capacity for reflective self-consciousness.

Each kind of consciousness is indispensable in such a project. Without the perspectival self-consciousness, the subject would lack the ability to see the relevance of others' situation to his own. Without reflective self-consciousness, the subject would not have reflective knowledge of the states and events whose explanation and possible correction is in question.

Since understanding and explanation of one's own cognitive situation is part of what Bernard Williams (1978) calls the absolute conception, it is a corollary of this point that both perspectival self-consciousness and reflective self-consciousness are necessary components of any elaboration and application of the absolute conception.

A second kind of case in which perspectival and reflective self-consciousness cooperate involves a class of cases in which one comes to know that another person has a certain conscious state—be it a sensation, a perceptual experience, an emotion, a conscious thought—because one knows that one has it oneself in circumstances of the same type. This kind of case is obviously particularly relevant to the application of the techniques of attribution emphasized in simulationist approaches to the mental. In a range of cases within this general class of attributions, one can make the attribution to the other only if one appreciates that the other is in the same circumstances as oneself. This will involve attribution to oneself of properties that one attributes to the other, in the third person case (bodily properties, in the case of the attribution of sensations and some perceptual experiences). So here one needs reflective self-consciousness to be at the starting point of ascribing the conscious states to oneself; and one needs perspectival self-consciousness to grasp that oneself and the other are in the same kind of situation, which in turn makes the psychological ascription of the conscious state-type to the other reasonable.

The same point applies, independently of any general commitment to simulationism, to any concept of a mental state or event, where the nature of the concept gives a privileged place to first-person application. For such a concept, knowledgeable application to others involves both perspectival and reflective self-consciousness.

5. Reflective Self-Consciousness and the Conception of Many Minds

I suggest that the direction of philosophical or constitutive explanation of understanding runs from reflective self-consciousness to a mastery of the conception of many subjects of consciousness. Each of us has a general notion of a subject of consciousness that involves the idea that such a subject is something of the same general (Aristotelian) kind as he himself instantiates. Each of us has to work out what is involved in being of that kind, of what relations one has to have to things, events and states to be of that kind. Exercising reflective self-consciousness is a crucial part of working out what is involved in being of that general kind, a subject of consciousness. So on this view, notions and concepts of conscious states and events are not the only ones a thinker grasps from his own case, are not the only ones in which the first person plays a special role. The same is true of the general concept of being a subject of consciousness, grasp of which also, though in a different way, involves a special relation to exercise of the first person.

On this approach, the general concept of being a subject of consciousness is a further example of what I called relation-based understanding (Peacocke 2010a). What makes thought thought about subjects is that they are conceived of as having a certain relation to the thing one thinks about in the first person way. As in other cases of relation-based thought, this means that we can make sense of the idea that someone else is still using the same concept, provided it is constrained by that relation, even though this other person has radically mistaken beliefs about what subjects are like. I think that Descartes and we are still thinking about subjects of consciousness, and thinking about them as subjects, even though he and we radically disagree about whether they have to be material, whether they are immortal, and so forth.

This treatment contradicts any thesis that implies that the first person can be used in thought only if the thinker already has a conception of many minds. So there is a substantial commitment here to the existence of sound arguments against those theses. But I would like to close this section and chapter by emphasizing how what I am offering is, in its nature, an approach under which being a subject of consciousness makes available, to many different thinkers, what is nevertheless a uniform conception of multiple subjects. At the level of thought, the idea of multiple points of view is founded on the idea of an individual point of view. The other points of view are conceived of as things of the same kind as one's own. This is indeed an element of subjectivity in the idea of multiple subjects of consciousness. But there is also a uniformity across all thinkers' conception of multiple subjects of consciousness. The crucial point is that there is a level of description, corresponding to the level of description of indexical types in the theory of indexical thought, at which it is the *same* kind of subjectivity for each thinker. Each thinker x conceives of other points of view as things of the same type as he ($[self_x]$ in the theory of indexical senses) enjoys.[6] In this conception that each has, the type of first-person thought—the first person or [self] type— is uniform. It is also uniformly conceived as the type it is.[7] So there is a common character in the subjectivity. When we abstract from the particular thinker who is doing the thinking, the kind of concept being employed in first person thought is the same across different individual thinkers. The position is not one of a kind of solipsism of thought.

---

[6] '$[self_x]$' is the notation of 'Demonstrative Thought and Psychological Explanation' (Peacocke 1981). It is the instance of the first person type of sense that is available for use in thought by x. See Peacocke (1981) for further discussion.

[7] For the enthusiasts for the theory of senses: the [self] type is itself conceived under its canonical mode of presentation. See Peacocke (2008: Chapter 8).

X

Interpersonal Self-Consciousness

The perspectival and the reflective varieties of self-consciousness that were the concerns of the preceding chapters are not the only varieties of self-consciousness, and they are not the only varieties that go beyond the minimal ability to use the first person in thought and other mental states. There is a third variety of self-consciousness, one which in its nature involves relations between two subjects of consciousness. This third variety is interpersonal self-consciousness. Interpersonal self-consciousness is a particular form of awareness that one features, oneself, in another person's consciousness.

Interpersonal self-consciousness is, in one or another of its many subvarieties, a ubiquitous feature of human life and its many social interactions. Awareness that one features, oneself, in another person's consciousness is present in ordinary face-to-face conversation with another person; in e-mail exchanges; in the nonverbal interaction with another driver as one looks at him to resolve who is to cross the intersection first; and in nonlinguistic interactions between a mother and a young child. As with the other varieties of self-consciousness, interpersonal self-consciousness raises a number of constitutive, psychological, and epistemological issues.

I aim here to characterize more sharply a particular kind of interpersonal self-consciousness, which for reasons to be given later I will call ascriptive interpersonal self-consciousness. This particular kind of interpersonal self-consciousness is inextricably and constitutively involved in a range of psychological, social, and linguistic phenomena. I will address some of the theoretical issues surrounding interpersonal self-consciousness. These issues include the way in which knowledge that involves interpersonal self-consciousness can be attained; the role of interpersonal self-consciousness in perception and in various theories of understanding; its relation to the other varieties of self-consciousness; and the status of some of the philosophical theses about interpersonal self-consciousness found in the literature (some of which have already surfaced earlier in this book, in Chapter VIII, Section 3). Though I will not be discussing the history of philosophy here, interpersonal self-consciousness is also a foundational notion for the now centuries-long discussion of recognition of one subject by another in German philosophy. It is equally a pivotal notion for a tradition in sociology dealing with the self as represented by others, in writers from G. H. Mead (1934) to Erving Goffman (1959).

Interpersonal self-consciousness is much closer to what is meant by 'self-consciousness' in everyday conversation than are some of the other notions discussed by philosophers past and present under the heading of self-consciousness, reflective and perspectival self-consciousness included. Some of the significance of interpersonal self-consciousness is the significance of that everyday notion. But before we can argue for that or anything else about the notion, our first task must be to say more precisely what interpersonal self-consciousness is.

1. Illustration and Delineation

A soldier is on patrol in Afghanistan. He is a member of a group, walking at night, in single file along a mountain path. The group proceeds as quietly as possible, to avoid detection by the enemy. Our soldier suddenly hears a click, just a few feet away. He freezes. It is the click made by a rifle being switched from the safe position into one ready to fire.

Our soldier freezes because he is instantly aware that he is the object of someone else's consciousness. Given all the circumstances, he is aware that the person in whose consciousness he features will think of him as a soldier, hence a person, someone capable of what we, though not necessarily he, will call first person intentional states. Both we, and the person holding the rifle that made the audible click, will distinguish between the case in which he merely perceives an object on the path, and perceives a person. So will the person perceived. What the soldier on the path wants to avoid is the case in which he is represented in the other's consciousness as a person.

More generally, there are at least three broadly different ways in which it can be true that one is aware that one features, oneself, in another's consciousness. The three ways are distinguished by the degree of richness of the conception of oneself that one is attributing to the other person. One may be aware that the other person is representing oneself merely as an entity in the other's environment, without the other person even recognizing that one is a conscious subject. The rifle-holder in our example may not have distinguished you from some movement in the foliage next to the mountain path. In a second kind of case, you may be aware that the other is representing you as a subject of mental states, but not one capable of first person propositional attitudes. In a case of the third kind, you are aware that you feature in the other person's consciousness as a self-representing subject, as a person capable of first person mental states about yourself. These are cases of consciousness of yourself being represented by another person as a self-representing subject. It is concern about being an instance of this case that makes our soldier freeze. The case is not confined to the dramas of conflict. The case is instantiated myriad times in our ordinary conversational and non-linguistic interactions with one another. This is the kind of interpersonal self-consciousness, awareness that one features as a self-representing creature in another's consciousness, that I aim to investigate here.

It is a defining feature of this species of interpersonal self-consciousness that the first person notion or concept plays a double role in its instances. The subject who is interpersonally self-conscious with respect to another is aware of himself as represented in a certain way in the other's consciousness. This awareness about himself as so represented has a first person content. It is awareness with a content of the form 'That other person is conscious of *me* in such-and-such a way'. But the relevant 'such-and-such way' also involves the first person too. The content 'conscious of *me* in such-and-such a way' is not merely consciousness of me as a mere material object. The particular way in which our subject thinks of the other as representing him is one that involves the other ascribing the capacity to enjoy states with first person contents to our subject. This ascription on the part of the other involves reference to the first person notion or concept. The interpersonally self-conscious subject enjoys an awareness that the other is referring mentally to the first person notion or concept, and is ascribing the capacity to use it to the subject himself. Because of this distinctive second role of the first person in such cases, I call this species of interpersonal self-consciousness *ascriptive* interpersonal self-consciousness. Ascriptive interpersonal self-consciousness is awareness that you are being represented by another person as a self-representing subject.

The description of the mental states involved in ascriptive interpersonal self-consciousness trips off the tongue in ordinary English. In fact the way in which these states involve the first person concept involves considerable complexity in the theory of intentional content. Suppose that you are ascriptively interpersonally self-conscious with respect to me. Then you are aware that I am not merely employing, I am also referring to the first person concept in my attribution of mental states to you. I am attributing to you use of the first person concept. So—already simplifying somewhat—I am referring to the first person concept (actually under its canonical concept), and thinking that you are employing it.[1] So I am employing a concept of a concept. Since you are aware that I am doing this—you are aware that I am employing that concept of a concept—we are now at a third level in the Fregean hierarchy of concepts (senses). You are thinking about the concept of a first person concept that I am employing. In doing so, you are using a concept (actually once again, the canonical concept) of a concept of a concept. For those interested in such matters, I include a formal treatment of the case, using neo-Fregean apparatus, in Appendix (A) at the end of this chapter.

The example of the soldier may be vivid, but it differs from more ordinary cases of ascriptive interpersonal self-consciousness in several respects. In everyday cases, such interpersonal self-consciousness is symmetrical: each person is interpersonally self-conscious with respect to the other. In the everyday cases, each person perceives the other. Each person's interpersonal self-consciousness involves the other person as given in perception, rather than in some mixed descriptive-demonstrative such as 'the person whose rifle made that click'.

Certain examples of ascriptive interpersonal self-consciousness can arise simply from mutual perception when it attains a certain degree of embedding. It can be helpful for various purposes to develop a description of these common examples, and I will do that briefly now. The description to be developed is a description of an attained state of interpersonal self-consciousness, rather than a description of how the

---

[1] The simplification consists in the fact that I am referring to the first person type; what you are employing in your thought is an instance of that type. More on this later.

state might be attained. We will come to the 'how' question in a later section.

So, let us take a case in which two subjects see each other. The example is not the only instance of this perceptual subspecies—it could not be so, because, once again, the blind can also certainly enjoy states of interpersonal self-consciousness. But the visual case is easier (at least for the sighted) to think about in relation to degrees of embedding. We have then two subjects x and y, and each sees the other:

(1) x sees y
(2) y sees x.

It may aid in thinking about the case to imagine yourself as x, and some other subject as y, and I will sometimes expound features of the case using such an identification.

Conditions (1) and (2) are jointly so weak that they are consistent with each thinking the other does not see him. At the level of conditions (1) and (2), we have no embedding of seeings in other seeings.

To reach the level of the First Embedding of mental states, we add to the description of the case that

(3) x sees that y sees him
(4) y sees that x sees him.

If you are x, then when (3) is true, you might express this fact by saying of y, 'He sees me'.

The First Embedding conditions (3) and (4) are, however, entirely consistent with each of x (you) and y (the other) featuring merely as an object in the other's awareness. You and the other may each think that he is being seen only as a material object, and not as a conscious subject.

At the level of the Second Embedding of mental states, we then add to the description of the case that

(5) x is aware that (4)
(6) y is aware that (3).

When (5) and (6) hold, you and the other must each feature as a subject in the other's consciousness, under the presumption that seeings can be attributed only to subjects. When (5) holds, and you are x, you are aware that the other sees that you see him. What you are aware of is a state of affairs in which the other sees something to be the case that involves your being a subject (an involvement of which you can presume the other has some kind of appreciation).

The fact that these Second Embedding conditions hold does not yet guarantee ascriptive interpersonal self-consciousness in the sense identified above. The Second Embedding conditions ensure that you are aware that the other sees that you see him. What you are aware of is that the other enjoys a seeing with the content something like (7), as thought by the other person:

(7)   That person sees me

where, since this is thought by the other, that last 'me' refers to the other. Here you are indeed ascribing states with first person contents to the other; but you are not thereby representing him as doing the same vis-à-vis you. That is, you are not yet attributing to the other person a mental state which involves ascription to *you* of the use of the first person notion or concept.

Similarly, at this level of Second Embedding, what the other is aware of is that you enjoy a seeing with a content something like (8), as thought by you:

(8)   He sees me.

The other is here ascribing states with first person content to you; but he is not yet attributing to you a mental state which involves ascription to *him* of use of the first person notion or concept.

We do not reach the perceptual subspecies of ascriptive interpersonal self-consciousness until the Third Embedding conditions are fulfilled. The Third Embedding conditions are probably most easily grasped when framed in terms of 'you' and 'the other'. When the Third Embedding conditions hold, each person is aware of the other's awareness as described in the Second Embedding conditions. A simple, and near-enough accurate, way to formulate an instance of this Third Embedding, without involving barely graspable iterations of 'sees', is (9):

(9)   You are aware the other is aware you're in a state in which you'd sincerely say 'He sees me'.

This is near-enough accurate, because it should also be added that the sincere saying 'He sees me' must be thought of by the other as suitably based on the subject's own visual experience, rather than knowledge obtained from inference or testimony. Now in (9), what you are aware of is something that involves the other's appreciation that you are employing the first person notion or concept. The other's attribution to you of grasp of the first person features in your own awareness. So here we do have a genuine case of ascriptive interpersonal self-consciousness. Good manners require relegation of the formalization of the situation to Appendix (B).

Distinctions drawn at these various levels of embedding can contribute differentially to the explanation of action. Take first the distinction between no embedding and First Embedding. When a spy sees that you see him, he will put away or hide his telescope to avoid detection of his activity. No such action is explained merely by the fact that you see him, or that he sees you. What about the additional explanatory power of the Second Embedding relative to the First? You see that he sees you; but this is consistent with his not knowing that you do. So actions of his that can, in context, be explained only by such knowledge will be explained with the Second Embedding conditions being fulfilled, but will not be explained by First Embedding conditions. An example: when he knows that you see that he sees you, he can take something you've visibly done as an indication that you intend to communicate something, (say) that you will attend a certain event. If he didn't know that you see that he sees him, he wouldn't have reason to do that; and so forth.

Someone may protest that the alleged distinction between the Second and Third Embedding is of no significance for the present topic, on the ground that anything that is a conscious and seeing subject must have the capacity for some kind of first person representation, must be capable of mental states with first person contents, whether conceptual or non-conceptual. I dispute the cited ground. It seems to me that we can conceive of conscious subjects who represent objects, events, and their properties and relations, what is in fact their environment, without use of the first person. Such subjects employ a *here* and a *now*, but not an *I*. These are the subjects at what I called 'Degree 0' of self-representation in their conception of the objective world back in Chapter II, Section 3. If you disagree about the possibility of such cases, that does not matter for the purposes of the present chapter. It means only that the conditions for ascriptive interpersonal self-consciousness can be met sooner in the hierarchy of embeddings than on the opposed view.

The ascriptive interpersonal self-consciousness on which I have been focusing is manifestly only one of many notions of interpersonal self-consciousness that we can identify once we have a hierarchy of attitudes and of concepts of concepts. Its importance is psychological, in at least two connected respects. First, in appreciating that another is aware of oneself as a possessor of first person attitudes, one is appreciating that the other is aware of oneself as one really is, with the capacity for self-representation one really has. This is a kind of recognition. Second, this kind of recognition is enormously important to us in our personal, social, and political relations, and in our emotional lives too. This recognition is a precondition of close personal relations, and it has analogues in social and political relations. The point is already present in William James, who took interpersonal self-consciousness as a sub-variety of self-consciousness in his chapter 'Consciousness of Self' in *The Principles of Psychology* (1918). He wrote, 'A man's Social Self is the recognition which he gets from his mates' (p. 293); and 'No more fiendish punishment could be devised, were such a thing physically possible, than that one should be turned loose in society and remain absolutely unnoticed by all the members thereof' (p. 293). Solitary confinement is regarded with fear by even the hardest of prisoners (Abbott 1981).

2. Some Roles of Interpersonal Self-Consciousness

Interpersonal self-consciousness is inextricably implicated in a range of social and psychological phenomena. Here are five examples.

(i) Joint Action

In any situations of joint action beyond the more primitive cases, and certainly in any ordinary situation of joint action of two humans, each participant will be interpersonally self-conscious with respect to the others. Suppose you and I are engaged in some joint action. This will involve my awareness that you know about my first person knowledge and beliefs. This awareness of your knowledge of me affects the way I act in carrying out our joint project. The same applies to you vis-à-vis me. You will on occasion draw on your awareness of my knowledge about your first person knowledge and belief about yourself. We would make mistakes in joint action if there were no such awareness. Maybe we are dancing together. Knowing that you will not dance well if we try to make moves we are not both confident we can make, I will not lead you into a move that I know you believe you can't reliably make.

The interpersonal self-consciousness required in successful joint action has a social dimension that is, prima facie, quite different from two of the other varieties of self-consciousness I mentioned at the outset. One of those was reflective self-consciousness, awareness of one's own *de se* mental states (as one's own), awareness attained in a distinctive way. Reflective self-consciousness by itself is of no help in joint action unless the other also has some knowledge of those states, which is what ascriptive interpersonal self-consciousness involves. The same applies to perspectival self-consciousness. Perspectival self-consciousness does involve some kind of conception of oneself as an object in the world of the same kind as other objects. But just as in the case of awareness of one's own *de se* mental states, this perspectival self-consciousness will be of no help in joint action unless it is also the object of another's knowledge of oneself.

It may be that there is a philosophical case to be made that there is some connection between one or another apparently non-social notion of self-consciousness and interpersonal self-consciousness. The point at the moment is just that the case would need to be made. Perspectival self-consciousness and reflective consciousness of one's own mental states are not apparently themselves social notions.

(ii) Linguistic Communication

Linguistic communication is a special case of joint action and joint awareness. This is so whether communication is face-to-face or in any other medium. In any such communication, at the starting point, there may be more or less knowledge of your interlocutor's history and circumstances. But as communicative exchanges proceed, an occasion-specific background is built up of what has been said and possibly accepted, what denied or disputed, what knowledge has been revealed (and what has not). This accumulating occasion-specific background helps to determine the nature of the joint attention in such a conversation. Attitudes that involve interpersonal self-consciousness will be essential in specifying the nature of this accumulating background. You may for instance be aware that your interlocutor knows that you represented yourself as knowing so-and-so, for instance. This affects the joint perception of the conversation, and how it proceeds. Human conversation would be utterly different if it did not involve multiple instances of such interpersonal self-consciousness. It would hardly be recognizable as normal human conversation at all.

It is also the case that specification of success in a linguistic exchange, an aim that is essential to the nature of linguistic communication, already involves interpersonal self-consciousness. When you say that p, and I understand you, in central cases I am aware that you know that I am aware you have asserted that p to me. This awareness of mine is an instance of ascriptive interpersonal self-consciousness.

(iii) Understanding the Second Person

The second person pronoun is a word whose successful use involves ascriptive interpersonal self-consciousness. Suppose you say to me, 'You are F'. Your intention in the primary, central case is that I should thereby come to know that I am F. I understand your utterance only if I come to know thereby that you are saying that I am F. As many writers have noted, it is does not suffice for understanding a second person utterance that I know that you intend, of whoever is your addressee, that that person come to know that he is F. I understand your utterance only if I come to know that I am your addressee, and that what you are saying is that I am F. In a case of your successful communication with me in which you use the second person, I as audience know that you, the speaker, are aware that I know that you are saying that I am F. This is, in more than one way, an instance of ascriptive interpersonal self-consciousness on my part. One source of the interpersonal self-consciousness here is the very first person content that I know you are saying to me. A successful practice of using the second person is possible only for creatures who are interpersonally self-conscious with respect to one another.

This description of what is involved in using and understanding the second person does not invoke a special second person concept or way of thinking. It uses only third person and first person singular concepts, and concepts of those concepts (and further concepts thereof, up the Fregean hierarchy). So as not to distract attention from the description of the range of cases in which interpersonal self-consciousness is involved, I defer consideration of whether there is a second person concept, not explicable in terms of the first or third person concepts, to Section 3.

(iv) 'Self-Conscious' in ordinary usage

Here are four quotations selected by the editors of the *Oxford English Dictionary* (Second Edition): from Carlyle, in *The French Revolution*: 'Self-conscious, conscious of a world looking on'; from J. Hawthorne, *Fortune's Fool*: 'He was singularly free from self-consciousness; and she was so exquisitely self-conscious as completely to conceal it'; from Orwell's *Road to Wigan Pier*: 'Self-conscious Socialists dutifully addressing one another as "Comrade"'; and from J. Irving, *158-Pound Marriage*, 'She had never been self-conscious about what she wore'.[2] Lucy O'Brien (2012) has discussed very well the ordinary notion of self-consciousness expressed in these sentences. The ordinary notion of being or feeling self-conscious involves ascriptive interpersonal self-consciousness in the sense I have been trying to delineate. Feeling self-conscious involves awareness that there is a certain standard others think your actions should meet, a standard they think you should know, and which you are concerned to meet (or they think you should be). That is an awareness that others are attributing to you certain first person attitudes: knowledge that such-and-such standards are the ones you should be meeting. Ascriptive interpersonal self-consciousness is a precisification and generalization of a notion involved in our everyday applications of a notion of being, or feeling, self-conscious.

(v) Relationships of mutual concern

In a relationship of mutual concern, one person may do something for another because the first realizes that the second has a certain attitude, including an emotion, with a first person content. The second person may realize that this is the reason the first person is doing it. This realization involves an exercise of interpersonal self-consciousness. The first person may also value this realization on the part of the second person. Relations based on anything from mere recognition of common humanity with a neighbor, to friendship and up to and including deeper relationships, may thus essentially involve exercises of interpersonal self-consciousness. Such capacities for interpersonal self-consciousness, and for their recognition, can also of course be abused by the cruel person.

---

[2] All quotations from the *Oxford English Dictionary Online*, <http://oed.com>, accessed 17 April 2013, under sense 2 of 'self-conscious'.

3. Is There an Irreducible Second Person Concept?

It is, or ought to be, uncontroversial that there is a use of 'you' in thought, and that it can occur in thinking that is not expressed out loud in language, and is not intended as part of any communicative act. I may see someone driving dangerously, and think 'If you go on driving like that, you will be involved in an accident'. One of the philosophical questions in this area is not whether there is such a use of 'you' in thought, but whether it, or anything else, requires us to acknowledge the existence of a second person concept that is distinct both from third person concepts and first person concepts, and concepts explained in terms of such concepts. It certainly seems that in the example just given, the use of 'you' in thinking involves imagining addressing the driver in question as 'you', an expression we have explained in (ii) as not involving an irreducible second person concept. The driver thus imagined as the addressee is thought of as *that driver*, a perceptually based mode of presentation.

The thesis that there is no distinctive second person concept is equivalent to the proposition that any occurrence of 'you' in thought can equally be explained in terms of other concepts that do not involve an irreducible second person concept. I myself am in agreement with Richard Heck, when he writes, 'there is no such thing as a second-person belief' (2002: 12).[3]

A thinker may use 'you' in thought without realizing that he is referring to himself. Take John Perry's example in which he is pushing a trolley in a supermarket, seeing someone in a mirror at an angle above pushing a trolley from which a stream of sugar is pouring on to the floor (Perry 1979). Perry may think 'You are making a terrible mess'. He might even shout out loud 'You in the grocery aisle, you're making a terrible mess', without realizing he himself is in the grocery aisle. But Perry does

---

[3] Heck also says that the claim is obvious, and writes, 'I don't really know how to argue for this claim'. Presumably what has to be argued for is the eliminability claim in the text above, a claim that can be made increasingly plausible as explanation of uses of 'you' in terms of other concepts come to seem generalizable across examples. Sebastian Rödl, in his book *Self-Consciousness* (2007: 187), fairly complains against Heck's remark that 'you' can be analysed as 'That person to whom I am speaking'. But the soundness of that complaint does not establish an ineliminability thesis.

not think 'I am making a terrible mess'. If the notions of concept and mode of presentation are to be constrained by their role in cognition in the most basic way, this shows that the concept 'you' employed by Perry on this occasion and the first person as employed by Perry are distinct. This conclusion seems to me to be in conflict with the thesis of the penultimate sentence of Sebastian Rödl's book, which states that 'Second person thought is first person thought' (2007: 197).

Rödl raises a series of objections which would apply against what I have said about understanding the second person pronoun. In discussing McDowell, Rödl writes,

> ... the capacity to know that thoughts stand in a certain relation depends on the capacity to share them. Understanding you, who are addressing me with 'You...', McDowell proposes, I know that your thought stands in a certain relation to a thought I think and which I would express by 'I...'. But how do I represent your thought in knowing this? If I do not think your thought, how then does it figure in my thinking? Figure there it must, if I am to know that are you thinking it. (p.196)

Rödl concludes the paragraph from which the preceding quotations are taken with the claim that 'I possess the notion of a thought that bears the relevant relation to my thought [a thought I express by "I..."—CP] only if I understand you; my understanding you is the source of my possessing that notion, not the other way around'. (p.196)

So let us consider a case in which a is the utterer of 'You are F', and b is the hearer who understands this utterance, which is in fact addressed to him. In a central case, a intends b to gain the information that b would express in a sincere utterance of 'I am F'. On one neo-Fregean treatment of indexicals, what would be so expressed by b in that sincere utterance is the Thought

$$[\text{self}]_b{}^\wedge<\text{is F}>$$

where $<\ldots>$ denotes the sense of $\ldots$, and where [self] is the first person type indexed with the object b. For more on this apparatus and its deployment, see Peacocke 1981. In a second person utterance, the utterer does mean the hearer to convey first person information to the hearer, and means the hearer to appreciate that. Rödl's question can then be raised about how b represents a's intention, and knowledge, about what information a is providing to b in this second person utterance. But

Rödl's question does have a straightforward answer on a neo-Fregean treatment of indexical content. The utterer *a* refers to the first person type of mode of presentation, and intends, of the instance of it that *b* is capable of employing in thought (viz. [self]$_b$), that his hearer come to know the Thought that consists of it combined with the concept <is F> in predicational combination. So I, like any neo-Fregean who proceeds in this way, reject Rödl's principle that 'the capacity to know that thoughts stand in a certain relation depends on the capacity to share them'. You can know that my first person Thought is of the same first person type as your first person thoughts without having attitudes to the very same Thought.

In this respect, first person Thoughts and present tense Thoughts should be treated on a par. You and I can know now that Napoleon at noon on 1 January 1810 thought (let us suppose he wrote it in his private diary) 'Now would be a good time to invade England'. We know that Napoleon's Thought was of the present tense type. Only those thinking at noon on 1 January 1810 can think of that time in the present tense way, can think of it using a mode of presentation of the [now] type, as neo-Fregeans would say. But nothing here prevents us now, in 2013, from knowing what Thought it was that Napoleon expressed in his diary in 1810. It was a Thought of the present tense type, as thought at noon on 1 January 1810, in predicational combination with the sense <would be a good time to invade England>. This is full knowledge of which Thought it was that Napoleon was thinking.

Rödl himself thinks the temporal parallel cuts the other way, saying that '"Today..." said yesterday and "Yesterday..." said today express the same act of thinking' (p.196). The token acts of a thinking occurring today and a thinking occurring yesterday are distinct, since they occur at different times. Rödl's claim is presumably that they have the same Fregean content (so we could say that that the utterances in question express the same act-type). I am not disputing that there is some special relation between the Thoughts expressed by 'now' as uttered yesterday and 'yesterday' as uttered today. The latter thought is how the earlier one must be updated in one's memory if information is to be stored in a form that preserves correctness (and a fortiori knowledge). But that does not make them identical Thoughts. I will not proceed with a full-dress critique of the claim that they are identical, but will confine myself to two critical observations.

First, if the claimed identity holds, what are we to make of these three Thoughts:

'Five minutes ago it was raining' thought now
'300 seconds ago it was raining' thought now
'It is raining' thought five minutes (equals 300 seconds) ago?

If the claimed identity holds, then the first and second Thoughts specified here are identical with the third. Yet someone could rationally judge the first without thereby judging the second, if she did not know how many seconds there are in a minute (or how many seconds there are in five minutes, for that matter). The third Thought cannot be identical with each Thought in a pair whose members are distinct from one another.

The other observation is that identity of sense in Frege is answerable to facts about cognitive significance at a given time. There certainly will be constraints on what it is rational to accept as time passes. But those constraints can be formulated in terms of Thoughts that stand in a certain relation to one another, a relation that need not be identity.[4]

4. Philosophical and Psychological Issues

How do we actually attain the awareness of others' attitudes about us that is involved in interpersonal self-consciousness? An answer to this question must provide a means that is, on occasion, capable of yielding knowledge. Interpersonal self-consciousness is naturally characterized in terms of awareness-that, a state that is both factive and knowledge-entailing. We do often enjoy such awareness.

One subclass of instances of interpersonal self-consciousness is provided by cases of full joint attention. Suppose I am seated next to a table; you and I are in the same room; each of us is in the other's visual field, and so is the table. In an entirely normal case meeting these conditions, there is joint awareness between us that we are in such a situation. Simply for speed and smoothness of exposition, in describing this state of affairs, we can use Jon Barwise's elegant formulation in terms of situations S,

---

[4] These are not the only points I would want to make about Rödl's final chapter 'The Second Person'. Since I have been critical on his treatment of 'you', let me also emphasize that there is much interesting and important material in the earlier chapters of his book.

where (in a slight variant) I will write 'S: A' for 'A holds in situation S' (Barwise 1988, 1989). Then on Barwise's treatment, the case just described is one in which there is a situation S meeting these conditions:

S: I am seated next to a table
S: I am aware of S
S: You are aware of S.

This is a self-involving situation in Barwise's treatment. It may be possible to obtain the benefits of self-involvement in a different way, by speaking of states of joint awareness that make reference to themselves. Those interesting issues are not pivotal to the present topic.[5] What matters here is that, as Barwise emphasized, situations such as S generate the distinctive features of joint awareness and of common or mutual knowledge.[6] Computational mechanisms that operate on specifications of the situation of which I and you are aware in this example will generate the familiar embeddings. When there is such a situation S, the following can be computed from the above specification of the situation:

I am aware I am seated next to a table
You are aware I am seated next to a table
I know that you are aware that I am seated next to a table
You know that I am aware that I am seated next to a table
I know that you know that I am aware that I am seated next to a table

The fifth line here is an attribution of interpersonal self-consciousness, if the knowledge it attributes is conscious knowledge. It attributes to me knowledge that you are attributing to me an awareness with a first person content, that I am seated next to a table.

So that is one route to interpersonal self-consciousness. It is a kind of route that is instantiated many times over, every day, in our interactions with others, in respect of those parts of the worlds that we jointly perceive and with respect to which we are engaged in joint attention. The content 'I am seated next to a table' could have been replaced with contents concerning my perceptible relations to anything else in the jointly perceived environment, or concerning my jointly perceived properties.

---

[5] For further discussion, see the Appendix to Peacocke (2005).
[6] For the classic characterizations of common or mutual knowledge, see Lewis (1969); and Schiffer (1972).

The example of iterated seeing and awareness that we considered earlier as an illustration of interpersonal self-consciousness is a special case of joint attention, the case that is sometimes called 'contact attention'. That was the special case of joint attention in which, again using Barwise's apparatus, we have a situation S such that:

S: I see you
S: You see me
S: I am aware of S
S: You are aware of S.

In general, joint awareness may or may not have, as its most embedded content, a content that is first personal, or a content that is about seeing or perception. In visually based contact attention, the most embedded content has both of these features.

Joint awareness cannot however be the only source of interpersonal self-consciousness. There are cases of interpersonal self-consciousness in which you are aware of my knowledge and beliefs about myself that go far beyond anything that can be discerned from the currently jointly attended world, or from memories thereof. Because of your knowledge of my values, my history, my prejudices, my past encounters, our past interaction, I may be aware that you represent me as having attitudes about myself that relate to anything on this list. These attitudes of mine need not be available in joint awareness alone. Perhaps joint awareness is a basic kind of case of interpersonal self-consciousness that makes possible all the others. All the same, we still have to give some account of how we attain those instances of interpersonal self-consciousness that are not given in joint attention.

A very different source of interpersonal self-consciousness is second order simulation. A second-order simulation is one in which you simulate someone else's simulation. Second-order simulation can yield the awareness involved in interpersonal self-consciousness. To attain interpersonal self-consciousness, it suffices for you to attain a state of awareness of, for example, this form:

(10)   You are aware: he believes you think you're F.

How can you reach an awareness with the content following the semicolon in (10)?

You can reach it in three steps:

Step 1:   You ascribe beliefs to him on the basis of simulation, and ask: what would you believe about yourself if you were in his situation vis-à-vis you?

Step 2:   He knows my situation, my history, perceives my actions and their results; in that situation, if he also had the background attitudes ascribable to me on the basis of my actions, he would think that he is F.

Step 3:   So by simulation, he believes that I think I'm F.

Second order simulation is here a mechanism for ascension through higher levels of embedding of mental states with content.

Interpersonal self-consciousness attained by this second order simulation need not be reached by conscious personal level inference. A subpersonal, content-involving computation can proceed through Steps 1 through 3. Correspondingly, the awareness attained need not be a judgement made by a sequence of conscious rational steps. It may not be a personal level mental action at all. It can simply be an awareness that simply occurs to the thinker.

The need to work out, consciously and often with difficulty, what attributions to make to others, and what actions to perform, is something distinguishing those occupying some point on the autistic spectrum from those who are not autistic. The more autistic subjects have neither states of interpersonal joint awareness, nor subpersonal rapid simulation of other's mental states and likely actions. They have to reach some of the attributions we ordinarily obtain in cases by interpersonal self-consciousness by slow, conscious reasoning they often find painfully difficult. Here is a passage from Temple Grandin's description of her own autistic condition (2006):

When I have to deal with family relationships, when people are responding to each other with emotion rather than intellect, I need to have long discussions with friends who can serve as translators. I need help in understanding social behavior that is driven by complex feelings rather than logic.

Hans Asperger stated that normal children acquire social skills without being consciously aware because they learn by instinct. In people with autism, 'Social adaptation has to proceed via intellect.' Jim, the twenty-seven year old autistic graduate student I have mentioned in previous chapters, made a similar observation. He stated that people with autism lack the basic instincts that make communication a natural process. Autistic children have to learn social skills systematically, the same way they learn their school lessons. Jim Sinclair summed it up when he said, 'Social interactions involve things that most people know without having to learn about them.' He himself had to ask many detailed questions about experiences other people were having to figure out how to respond appropriately. He describes how he had to work out a 'separate translation code' for every new person. (pp.155–6)

In the nature of the case, the ability to simulate another's situation is involved twice over in second order simulation. So if autistic subjects have difficulty with simulation, interpersonal self-consciousness will be especially hard for them to attain when it requires second order simulation.

So, both joint attention and second order simulation can lead to states of interpersonal self-consciousness. Prima face, neither joint awareness nor second order simulation can be assimilated as a special case of the other. On the one hand, joint awareness does not seem to involve simulation of any kind at all. The iterations of knowledge or potential awareness do not involve considering what one would think or experience if one were in some other situation. The iterations flow from the actual structures and awareness, independently of any such consideration by the participants, and equally independently of running any belief-forming mechanisms off-line. On the other hand, in cases of second order simulation, the mechanisms that lift us to iterated attitudes seem to have nothing to do with any of the various distinctive properties that have been proposed as crucial to full overt joint awareness. There does not seem to be any essential involvement of self-involving situations, nor of states or events of awareness that make indexical reference to themselves, in successful second order simulation. Joint awareness and second order simulation seem to be psychologically independent ways of attaining interpersonal self-consciousness.

For second order simulation to be successful, it is important that it be available to the other person that one of your actions is, say, a reaching to a cup in order to drink. Without such information, he could not so successfully simulate you. He could not so successfully use information about your past and current actions to attribute background attitudes to you. It follows that the existence of perspective-independent notions of particular actions, notions that can enter both the content of intentions and the content of another's perception of those actions as discussed in the literature on mirror neurons, plays an important role in facilitating interpersonal self-consciousness.

Perhaps we can in principle conceive of the instantiation of interpersonal self-consciousness without such perspective-independent notions, but we could not attain it so easily or smoothly. Without the perspective-independent notions, there would have to be an additional layer of computational complexity, at which subpersonal mechanisms in a subject somehow compute basic intentional characterizations of actions from the physically described movements of another agent, drawing on who knows what further information. By contributing to the identification of another's goals, the perspective-independent notions contribute to the attribution of attitudes to another, and to facilitating interpersonal self-consciousness.

Vittorio Gallese has written of 'a new conceptual tool: the shared manifold of intersubjectivity' (2005: 111). Gallese's shared manifold consists of specifications of events using perspective-independent notions that feature both in intention and in perception, specifications that I would put in the form 'e is a ϕ-ing', where ϕ is one of these perspective-independent notions. The ϕ-ing might be a drinking from a cup, or reaching for a particular object. Gallese writes, 'in humans, and even more so in monkeys, the shared space coexists with but does not determine self-awareness and self-identity. The shared intentional space underpinned by the mirror matching mechanism is not meant to distinguish the agent from the observer'; 'Rather, the shared space instantiated by the mirror neurons blends the interacting individuals within a shared implicit semantic content' (p.111). Gallese's thesis is that we recognize that other human beings are similar to us by means of this shared manifold, and that it makes possible 'intersubjective communication, social imitation, and mind reading' (p.115). In effect I have just been supporting Gallese's position, for the special case of interpersonal self-consciousness, and in particular when it is attained by second order simulation.

The approach I have been offering also suggests, however, that Gallese's shared manifold is just the first of a hierarchy of shared manifolds. The hierarchy is generated from Gallese's base manifold by the operation of applying a simulation mechanism to a given level, to attain attributions of mental states not represented at that lower level. The resulting attributions form a new level, to which simulation operations can be applied again, to generate another new level; and so forth. I suspect that the idea of a shared manifold of intersubjectivity has application at these higher levels too. As far as I can see, this extension is entirely within the spirit of Gallese's approach. The extension has his shared manifold at its foundation, its basic level on which all other levels are built.

In a well-known paper 'Five Kinds of Self-Knowledge', Ulrich Neisser (1988) advances various claims that bear on the foundations of interpersonal self-consciousness. He introduces the notion of 'the interpersonal self', which is 'the self as engaged in immediate unreflective social interaction with another person' (p.41). Neisser's view is that this interpersonal self 'can be directly perceived on the basis of objectively existing information' (p.41). What is perceived in another is 'activity' (p.41). In Neisser's presentation of his points, this is offered as an extension of a Gibsonian conception to the intersubjective realm. I have already noted that the mental states involved in interpersonal self-consciousness need not be reached by conscious personal level inference. I think the classical and convincing arguments of Fodor and Pylyshyn (1981) against the Gibsonian conception of information pickup as explaining perception of the physical world apply straightforwardly to interpersonal perception too. The arguments against the Gibsonian conception are entirely general, and not restricted only to some specific domain. The only argument offered by Neisser for 'direct perception' in his sense are studies about infant/mother interaction, and the distress suffered by infants when mothers' interaction with their infants is not synchronized in the normal way.[7] This is not evidence for the Gibsonian conception, since the phenomenon is consistent with the infants' perceptions of their mothers' actions being a consequence of subpersonal computations. The computational structures underlying a computational process may of course be innate. But let us set aside that old, and (in my view) settled issue. For Neisser also propounds some more interesting claims that are independent of his Gibsonian allegiance, and that raise issues about the bases of interpersonal self-consciousness.

First, Neisser offers a characterization of intersubjectivity: 'If the nature/direction/timing/intensity of one person's actions mesh appropriately with the nature/direction/timing/intensity of the other's, they have jointly

---

[7] Neisser (1988: 43) cites Murray and Trevarthen (1985).

created an instance of what is often called *intersubjectivity*.' (p.41). There can, however, be meshing of such actions without intersubjectivity. Suppose there is what I take to be an inanimate robot, in motion nearby to me. I may delight in copying its movements, perhaps to make lines of parallel motion in the sand. My actions mesh with its movements, and they could do so in respect of their nature/direction/timing/intensity. Now perhaps it is not really a robot controlled by some very simply pre-programmed movements, but actually is a genuine agent. Its movements are, unbeknownst to me, genuine actions. Then Neisser's sufficient condition for intersubjectivity is fulfilled: each of our actions does mesh with the other's. But this is not plausibly a case of intersubjectivity, on any intuitive understanding of that notion. Intersubjectivity must at a minimum involve the recognition by each party to the interaction of the status of the other as agent, and as acting on the particular occasion in question. In interactions that are manifestations of intersubjectivity, each participant draws, no doubt tacitly, on some conception of the other's movements as flowing from the emotions, purposes, inclinations, desires, or needs of a continuing subject who is also the agent of the actions on the particular occasion in question. Indeed, the very notion of the 'appropriateness' of a response, present in Neisser's sufficient condition, cannot plausibly be elucidated except in terms of what seems appropriate to a subject of a certain kind, a member of a certain species with certain emotions, purposes, inclinations, desires, and needs.

When, by contrast with the thing mistakenly taken for a robot, an adult perceives an infant's smile as a smile, and smiles back and waves, and the infant responds, we do have intersubjectivity. There is intersubjectivity here because there is action perceived as action, there is an adjusted response to this action, a response itself perceived as action; and so forth. The example is an instance of what Philippe Rochat describes as 'the irresistible drive *to be with others, to maintain social closeness, and to control social intimacy*' (2009: 2). The adult's interaction with the infant is also continued because of each party's pleasure at the other's pleasure in the interaction. These more primitive examples of intersubjectivity contain the materials from which are built the more sophisticated cases of interpersonal self-consciousness (and which are not always such fun).

Autistic subjects are said not to gain positive affect from rapid interaction with other persons, in the way non-autistic subjects so often do. It seems to me this lack of positive affect should be treated as consequential upon the lack of certain representational capacities. The autistic subject suffers the lack of positive affect in such interactions because of an absence of subpersonal mechanisms with rich representational contents concerning the mental states of his co-participant, including mental states with contents that involve the kinds of embeddings making reference to the first person that we mentioned earlier. When, however, the affect is present as in normal subjects, the pleasure taken in the fact of the other's pleasure in the interaction is something that can iterate up the hierarchy. Such pleasure can itself involve instances of interpersonal self-consciousness. One can be aware, and take pleasure in the fact, that the other is taking pleasure in the fact that one has certain attitudes and occurrent emotions with first person contents. Some cases will fit Barwise's self-involving form. We can speak of there being a situation S such that:

S: you and the other interact in such-and-such fashion
S: you take pleasure in the existence of S
S: the other takes pleasure in the existence of S.

Neisser goes on to write of 'the self that is established in these interactions' (p.43). If that means something ontological, something at the level of reference—that there is a self that does not exist independently of such social interactions—that seems hard to defend. It seems that one and the same subject who does not at an earlier time have the capacity for intersubjective interactions may later gain that capacity. That does not bring a new subject into existence. It rather enriches the capacities of a continuing subject who was there already. Perhaps this talk of selves is merely a façon de parler, and the apparent introduction of an ontology should not be taken too seriously.

There is, however, a closely related thesis that does not need to be formulated in metaphysical or ontological terms, a thesis endorsed by Neisser in the same passage as that just quoted, and which can be understood as concerning only modes of representation, rather than what is represented. Neisser writes that Gibson's 'principle that all perceiving involves co-perception of environment and self applies also to the *social* environment and to the *interpersonal* self...Just as the ecological self is specified by the orientation and flow of optical texture, so the interpersonal self is specified by the orientation and flow of the other individual's expressive gestures' (p.43). Even in the case of perception of the spatial, physical environment, there can be subjects who enjoy such perceptions without using first person contents that place themselves in the world. These are the subjects I described in Chapter II, who enjoy perceptual states with demonstrative perceptual contents concerning some of the objects and events around them, who use a *here* and a *now* but who do not use any form (even nonconceptual) of the first person. In the terminology of that chapter, they are the subjects with Degree 0 of involvement of any self-representation in their conception of the objective world. Even when such a subject makes a transition to representing itself as having a location in the spatial world, the notion of self-representation it then employs does not, I would argue, have to be explained in terms of spatial location. It can be explained in terms simply of a notion or concept that, de jure, refers to the subject in whose mental state it is featuring. To say, what is true, that in mature human perception, spatial content concerns both the environment and the subject, is not to say or imply that: first person representation has to be explained in part in terms of the spatial content of experience; nor is it to say or imply that being a subject is to be elucidated in terms of such spatial experience.

I suggest that structurally similar points apply to the subject who is interpersonally self-conscious, and to the first person way in which such a subject thinks about himself, even when engaged in intersubjective interactions. The first person notion, which I emphasized is both used and thought about in the characterization of ascriptive interpersonal self-consciousness, is the *same* first person notion that enters the content of non-social perception. So I am in disagreement with Neisser's thesis, even if it is construed merely as one about concepts or notions, rather than as one about their referents. No new first person notion or concept is involved in a transition to the intersubjectivity involved in interpersonal self-consciousness. Some strange consequences would follow if a new concept or notion were involved. A subject who later acquires a sufficiently rich conception of those with whom he interacts to be interpersonally self-conscious may remember his earlier encounters with objects and events, prior to his acquiring this richer conception. It seems wholly natural to say that these earlier memories have a first person content, 'I was building a snowman' for instance. Would there be some fallacy in this subject's saying to someone, on the basis of these memories, now that he is interpersonally self-conscious, 'I once built a snowman'? It is hard to see that this is anything but correct and reasonable. It does not rest on any identity inference involving two different species of first person concepts or notions. It is not as if this subject had to distinguish between two different kinds of belief and knowledge, with two different kinds of first person concept involved in each. There is only one first person concept that he employs, both before and after his acquisition of richer psychological and interpersonal conceptions. The newly acquired conceptions are richer conceptions of his relations to other subjects, and not literally newly acquired first person concepts.

These remarks do not apply only to Neisser, whose talk of various kinds of self is an instance of a tradition extending both backwards and forwards from him, in both developmental psychology and in sociology. These remarks apply equally to talk elsewhere in that tradition of 'the social self', 'the presented self', 'the self represented by others', and the like. In all these cases, I would say that the important claims made using such vocabulary should be regarded not as involving a new kind of entity, nor a new kind of first person concept, but rather as claims concerning how just one subject thinks of himself (ordinary first person), or perceives himself (ordinary first person), as represented by others. No additional ontology or first person concept or notion is required for the description and explanation of the phenomena.

One could of course stipulatively introduce an ontology of intentional objects, interpersonal selves that have no nature beyond what is given in the content of the interpersonal attitudes of a particular subject. Introducing or articulating such an ontology cannot settle substantive philosophical issues about whether the same subject who did not previously enjoy interpersonal self-consciousness now does so. Nor can it settle whether such a subject is using the same first person notion or concept as is deployed outside intersubjective interactions.

5. Self-Consciousness: The Relations of the Interpersonal to Other Varieties

What is the relation of interpersonal self-consciousness to perspectival self-consciousness and to reflective self-consciousness? Does it presuppose either or both of them?

Let us start with the question of whether the interpersonal variety of self-consciousness presupposes the perspectival. Though there are certain kinds of perspectival self-consciousness associated with the mirror-neuron representation of actions, it does not seem that anything beyond that is involved in simple instances of interpersonal self-consciousness. Consider an example. I can tell that you are looking at me, and I can reach an awareness that you know that I know that I am standing on your foot. This does not seem to require that I adopt a third person perspective on myself. It seems only to involve the attribution to you of knowledge of spatial properties I perceive myself to have. This perception seems to involve only a first person perspective.

I visually perceive my foot as on top of yours. You also perceive it as standing in that relation to your foot. The way in which my foot is given in perception to me (both visually and proprioceptively) is very different from the way in which it is given to you (both in vision and in touch). But I neither need to know, nor do I at any level have to represent, the way in which you experience these two objects. My foot and yours are such that I know of them that you know I know the first to be on top of the second. If I reach this knowledge via the mechanisms of joint awareness, although there will be ways in which these objects are given to you, those ways do not need to enter the processes involved in joint awareness. The existence of ways in which you perceive these objects, and their systematic variation with the ways I perceive them, is something on which this interpersonal self-consciousness relies. But interpersonal self-consciousness does not, and does not need to, represent the systematic variation: reliance of a computational process on something is to be distinguished from representing it. I end up in a state of knowing that you perceive of one object that it stands in a certain relation to another object without engaging in computations about the ways in which those objects are given to you. No doubt some subjects could engage in such computations, but humans do not need to in cases like these.

This relative independence of interpersonal self-consciousness from perspectival self-consciousness contributes to an explanation of how it can be the case that for a subject, the social world, and how he is represented by others in that social world, including his attitudes about himself, can be real and possibly vivid for him, even if he has a rather limited range of knowledge of those of his properties that he could only know about in a third person way. Appreciation of oneself as represented in the mental states of others, and as having attitudes, can be present in a subject even if the subject lacks the rather modest ability to gain knowledge about himself in such third person ways as looking in a mirror, or observing the shape of his shadow. The ability to represent 'they are looking at me', and 'they are doing such-and-such in relation to me', do not imply the ability to gain knowledge about oneself from a third person perspective on oneself.

There is a different relation that holds between interpersonal self-consciousness and perspectival self-consciousness. When a subject is capable of the interpersonal self-conscious states involved in linguistic communication (or indeed in non-linguistic communication), such communication can convey to the subject information that he would otherwise be able to attain, if at all, only by an exercise of perspectival self-consciousness. Facts about yourself that you could know only in a third person way, that is, in a way that would equally in normal circumstances could equally give you information about someone other than yourself—such as inferring that there is a paint on your back because you have leaned against a newly painted wall—will be available from helpful interlocutors, without your having to engage in those ways of coming to know. Information that the other person has about you is, in the nature of the case, obtained in a third person way. In such a case, you are the person given in a third person way in the other's perspective on the world.

What of the other question, of whether interpersonal self-consciousness presupposes reflective self-consciousness? Consider first the case in which the means by which a state of interpersonal self-consciousness is attained is the operation of the second order simulation described earlier. In simple cases, this does not require any exercise of reflective self-consciousness.[8] Suppose it is your interpersonal self-consciousness that is in question. Then the second step of that simulation involves assessment of whether the other, given his knowledge of your situation, would judge that if he were your situation, he (the other) would think himself to be so-and-so. This must involve your making an assessment of what he would judge, given certain perceptions and background information (and possibly misinformation). That in turn seems to involve your

---

[8] My thanks to Michael Martin for setting me straight on this.

making a first person assessment of what you would judge, given certain perceptual states and background information (and misinformation). But although I have just described the operation of this procedure in terms of what you would judge given certain perceptual states, it seems clear that you would not even need a concept or a notion of perception to go through this procedure yourself. For you need only to think of what you would judge in circumstances described as objective states of affairs in which there are things and events of such-and-such objective kinds standing in so-and-so relations to you. Your ability to think of these things, events and relations may be dependent, constitutively, on your capacity to perceive them in various ways. But it does not follow that to think of them in these objective ways, you must also be capable of thinking about those experiences. (If that were so, a subject could not have observational concepts without also having concepts of perceptual states; but in fact a subject could do so.) You think of the objects, events and the rest under concepts made available by your capacity to perceive. That is to be distinguished from thinking about perceptions. So interpersonal self-consciousness attained by second-order simulation does not need to involve exercises of reflective self-consciousness.

There may, however, be arguments by a different route that interpersonal self-consciousness involves reflective self-consciousness. We noted that a case can be made that interpersonal self-consciousness attained by mechanisms of joint attention may in one way or another be more basic than interpersonal self-consciousness attained by second-order simulation. Joint attention characteristically involves awareness of each participant of the other participants' perceptual states, and it is plausible that there is a first person component, involving the ability to self-ascribe, in grasp of any notion or concept of perception. If all that is true, then at least for humans like us, there will be no interpersonal self-consciousness without the self-ascriptive abilities involved in reflective self-consciousness.

6. Concluding Remarks

The literature on the philosophy of mind abounds with theses that either directly or indirectly involve interpersonal self-consciousness. Those theses include the idea that the concept of a subject other than oneself who also employs the first person concept needs to be explained in terms of second person thought.[9] They include also theses in somewhat different traditions, such as Sartre's claim that 'for me the Other is first the being for whom I am an object; that is, the being *through whom* I gain my objectness. If I am to be able to conceive of even one of my properties in the objective mode, then the Other is already given' (1992: 361, in the section entitled 'The Look'). Though I am sceptical of many such theses, the bearing of this Chapter upon them, if it is correct, is that they should be assessed against the account of interpersonal self-consciousness with the features I have outlined here.

Theses about interpersonal self-consciousness are by no means exhausted by concerns about the metaphysics of the subject, or the nature of the intentional content involved in first person mental states, or the epistemology of self and others. Interpersonal self-consciousness is also foundational in our emotional lives and in what we value. Martin Buber (1958: 17) writes 'I become through my relation to the *Thou*; as I become *I*, I say *Thou*. All real living is meeting'. One can find much in his points, even if one doubts them when such sentences are taken as theses in the metaphysics of the conscious subject, or as theses in the theory of intentional content. Buber's claims can instead be taken as points about what matters to us, about some of our values and our emotional lives. We must also draw on an account of interpersonal self-consciousness in that territory that is still somewhat neglected in the tradition to which this book belongs.

Appendix A

Suppose we have a case in which you are interpersonally self-conscious with respect to me, CP. In such an example, you are aware that CP attributes to you a first person Thought, say that you are F. The first person Thought you would have to be thinking for this attribution to be correct is one you could express by saying 'I'm F'. How do we regiment this Thought in neo-Fregean terms? Let $<...>$ be the sense of...; let [self] be the first person type of sense. For each thinker x, $[self]_x$ is the instance of the first person type usable only by x to think of x. $\wedge$ is predicational combination in the realm of senses. The looseness in these

---

[9] Thus Rödl, *Self-Consciousness*, p.187: 'thought about another self-conscious subject is a thought whose linguistic expression requires use of a second-person pronoun'. In Rödl's terminology, a self-conscious subject is simply a subject capable of first person thought. Rödl uses the terminology mentioned at the start of Chapter VIII, on p. 189, this volume.

characterizations can easily be amended by anyone who takes notice of it. This is the terminology and apparatus of Peacocke (1981). In this neo-Fregean notation that aims to respect the distinctive status of indexical and demonstrative senses, we would regiment your thinking that you are F thus:

(a) Think (you, $[self]_{you}{}^{\wedge}<is\ F>$).

When you are interpersonally self-conscious with respect to me, CP, you are aware that I (CP) am attributing a thinking of the Thought specified in (a) to you. For this to be true, it has to be that:

(b) Thinks (CP, $<Thinks>^{\wedge}[that\ person]^{\wedge}[[self]_{that\ person}{}^{\wedge}<<is\ F>>)$,

where 'that person' expresses the way you are given to me. So (b) regiments 'CP thinks you think you are F'. Here we have the double embedding shown by the double square brackets, the canonical sense of the instance of the first person sense-type, $[self]_{that\ person}$, that is employed by you. (The subscripted indexing place here is transparent. Since you are that person, $[self]_{that\ person}$ and $[self]_{you}$ are one and the same singular sense, though presented differently since their indices are presented differently.)

Finally, since this is a case of interpersonal self-consciousness, you are aware that (b) holds. Let 'this person' express the way I (CP) am given to you. Then we have a triple embedding in the regimentation of your awareness that (b) holds:

(c) Aware-that (you, $<Thinks>^{\wedge}[this\ person]^{\wedge}$
$<<Thinks>>^{\wedge}[[self]_{that\ person}]^{\wedge}[[[self]_{that\ person}]]]^{\wedge}<<<is\ F>>>)$.

Enthusiasts for this sort of issue will realize that I have made several oversimplifications here, in formulations that are already complex enough to make the present point. One point a stricter formulation should make explicit, that is not properly provided for here, is a certain degree of transparency. From your being aware that I think that you think that you yourself are F, it does follow that: you are aware of someone x (viz. yourself) of whom you are aware that I think of that person x that he thinks himself to be F. Another point to be taken into account in a stricter formulation is that you may not know, or have any beliefs, about how you are given to me, and nor do you need to do so in order for interpersonal self-consciousness to be present. You need only to have the existentially quantified awareness that there is some way in which you are given to me. Similarly, I need only to think that there is some way in which I am given to you; I need not know what that is, either. What matters for the present point is only the triple embedding in (c). That is essential to the formal representation of the fact that in interpersonal self-consciousness, you are aware of me as treating you as self-representing.

Appendix B

We characterized Third Level embedding as, intuitively, cases in which (9) holds:

(9) You are aware the other is aware you're in a state in which you'd sincerely say 'He sees me'.

When (9) holds, what you are aware of is a state of affairs in which the other has an awareness with a content:

(i) That person sees that I see him.

How should this be regimented in neo-Fregean terms? We can regiment the content expressed by (i) in neo-Fregean terms thus, as thought by the other person: for some mode of presentation m, the mode of presentation m under which that person sees me,

(ii) Sees-that (that person, <see>$^\wedge m^\wedge$[self]$_{\text{that person}}$).

When you are aware that (ii) is the content of the other's awareness, the condition for ascriptive interpersonal self-consciousness is met. That is so because the content (ii), which specifies the content of the other's awareness, of which you are aware, is one that attributes to you use of the first person. This is a more formal way of explicating how Third Level embedding conditions imply ascriptive interpersonal self-consciousness.

XI

Open Conclusion: The Place of Metaphysics

Much of this book has been concerned with the epistemic, with the conceptual, and with the content of some distinctive mental states, rather than with metaphysics. But it is striking at how many points in this material we have needed to appeal to the metaphysics of a subject matter to explain adequately epistemic, conceptual, and mental phenomena. Here are four examples.

(1) In the early chapters, I argued that the conceptual first person has to be understood philosophically in part by its relation to the nonconceptual *de se*, which in turn is to be explained by its relations to a subject, a subject that can exist without representing itself in first person terms at all (the Degree 0 case of Chapter II).

(2) We needed to appeal to the metaphysics of the ownership of conscious events and states by a subject of consciousness in explaining the status as knowledge of the self-ascriptions made in reflective self-consciousness (Chapter VII, Section 2, Chapter IX, Section 2).

(3) We needed to appeal to the metaphysics of what makes one body rather than another a particular subject's body in explaining why certain perceptual judgements were merely basic uses of the first person, rather than being exercises of perspectival self-consciousness (Chapter VIII, Section 2). This metaphysical claim was also employed in explanation of the boundaries of immunity to error through misidentification (Chapter V, Section 1).

(4) We aimed to characterize what is distinctive of perspectival self-consciousness by using the notion of a concept being anchored in the subject. It is plausible that certain concepts are anchored in the

subject only because of the metaphysics the property that is picked out by the concept. It is in the nature of the property in question that it involves a relation to a subject of mental states (also Chapter VIII, Section 2).

If these points are correct, then in this area at least, the metaphysics of subjecthood and consciousness is prior, in the order of philosophical explanation, to the theory of concepts, to the theory of intentional content, and to any theory of linguistic meaning that draws on the theory of concepts and intentional content. Such an explanatory priority of metaphysics is in head-on conflict with a famous thesis of Michael Dummett's, to the effect that metaphysical disputes are really disputes in the theory of meaning, or at least the theory of thought, and can be resolved only by a construction of a theory of meaning or thought (1991: 14ff.). If, at least in the case of the first person, both conceptual and nonconceptual content can be philosophically elucidated only by reference to a metaphysics of subjects and their states and events, then the theory of thought, far from underlying a metaphysics, presupposes one.

This then opens a series of highly general questions. Is there an explanatory priority of metaphysics over the theory of content in other areas too? Or only in some, and if so, which ones? And if only in some, what is the principle of the distinction? So we face the general issue of the relation between the metaphysics of a domain and the theory of intentional contents about that domain. There will be no end of all our exploring until we understand that relation.

References

Abbott, J. (1981), *In the Belly of the Beast: Letters from Prison* (New York: Random House).

Adams, R. (1974), 'Theories of Actuality', *Noûs* 8: 211–31.

Ameriks, K. (2000), *Kant's Theory of Mind: An Analysis of the Paralogisms of Pure Reason* (Oxford: Oxford University Press, second edition).

Anderson, J. (1967), *Principles of Relativity Physics* (New York: Academic Press).

Anscombe, G.E.M. (1975), 'The First Person', in *Mind and Language: The Wolfson College Lectures 1974*, ed. S. Guttenplan (Oxford: Oxford University Press).

Armstrong, D. (1984), 'Consciousness and Causality', in *Consciousness and Causality*, ed. D. Armstrong and N. Malcolm (Oxford: Blackwell).

Baillargeon, R., Scott, R., and He, Z. (2010), 'False-belief Understanding in Infants', *Trends in Cognitive Sciences* 14: 110–18.

Baron-Cohen, S. (1993), 'The Concept of Intentionality: Invented or Innate?', *Behavioral and Brain Sciences* 16: 29–30.

Barwise, J. (1988), 'Three Views of Common Knowledge', in *Proceedings of the Second Conference on Theoretical Aspects of Reasoning about Knowledge*, ed. M. Vardi (Los Altos, CA: Morgan Kaufmann).

Barwise, J. (1989), *The Situation in Logic, CSLI Lecture Notes 17* (Stanford, CA: CSLI).

Bayne, T. (2004), 'Self-Consciousness and the Unity of Consciousness', *The Monist* 87: 219–36.

Bayne, T. (2010), *The Unity of Consciousness* (Oxford: Oxford University Press).

Bayne, T. and Chalmers, D. (2003), 'What is the Unity of Consciousness?' in *The Unity of Consciousness: Binding, Integration and Dissociation*, ed. A. Cleeremans (Oxford: Oxford University Press).

Bermúdez, J. L. (1998), *The Paradox of Self-Consciousness* (Cambridge, MA: MIT Press).

Block, N. (2007), *Consciousness, Function, and Representation: Collected Papers, Volume 1* (Cambridge, MA: MIT Press).

Botvinick, M. and Cohen, J. (1998), 'Rubber Hands "Feel" Touch that Eyes See', *Nature* 391: 756.

Brandom, R. (1994), *Making It Explicit: Reasoning, Representing, and Discursive Commitment* (Cambridge, MA: Harvard University Press).

Brooks, R. and Meltzoff, A. (2008), 'Self-experience as a Mechanism for Learning about Others: A Training Study in Social Cognition', *Developmental Psychology* 44: 1257–65.

Buber, M. (1958), *I and Thou*, tr. Ronald Gregor Smith (London: Continuum Press).

Burge, T. (1988), 'Reason and the First Person', in *Knowing Our Own Minds*, ed. C. Wright, B. Smith, and C. Macdonald (Oxford: Oxford University Press).

Burge, T. (1993), 'Content Preservation', *Philosophical Review* 102: 457–88.

Burge, T. (2003). 'Perceptual Entitlement', *Philosophy and Phenomenological Research* 67: 503–48.

Burge, T. (2010), *Origins of Objectivity* (Oxford: Oxford University Press).

Campbell, J. (1986), 'Critical Notice of Peacocke (1983)', *Philosophical Quarterly* 36: 278–91.

Campbell, J. (1994), *Past, Space, and Self* (Cambridge MA: MIT Press).

Campbell, J. (2012), 'Lichtenberg and the *Cogito*', *Proceedings of the Aristotelian Society* 112: 361–78.

Carey, S. (2009), *The Origin of Concepts* (New York: Oxford University Press).

Carpenter, E. (1975), 'The Tribal Terror of Self-Awareness', in *Principles of Visual Anthropology*, ed. P. Hockings (The Hague: Mouton).

Chalmers, D. (2010), *The Character of Consciousness* (New York: Oxford University Press).

Colapinto, J. (2009), Profile of V. S. Ramachandran 'Brain Games', *New Yorker* 85: May 11, 76–87.

Coliva, A. (2012), ed., *The Self and Self-Knowledge* (Oxford: Oxford University Press).

Davidson, D. (2001), 'The Individuation of Events', in his *Essays on Actions and Events* (Oxford: Oxford University Press).

de Vignemont, F. (2007), 'Habeas Corpus: The Sense of Ownership of One's Own Body', *Mind & Language* 22: 427–49.

Dennett, D. (1978), 'Where Am I', in his *Brainstorms* (Montgomery, VT: Bradford Books).

Dennett, D. (1993), *Consciousness Explained* (London: Penguin).

Descartes, R. (1984), *The Philosophical Writings of Descartes*, Volume 2, ed. J. Cottingham, R. Stoothof, and D. Murdoch (Cambridge: Cambridge University Press).

Descartes, R. (1985), *The Philosophical Writings of Descartes*, Volume 1, ed. J. Cottingham, R, Stoothof, and D. Murdoch (Cambridge: Cambridge University Press).

Dummett, M. (1981), *The Interpretation of Frege's Philosophy* (London: Duckworth).

Dummett, M. (1991), *The Logical Basis of Metaphysics* (Cambridge, MA: Harvard University Press).

Evans, G. (1982), *The Varieties of Reference* (Oxford: Oxford University Press).

Fine, K. (1995), 'The Logic of Essence', *Journal of Philosophical Logic* 24: 241–73.

Fine, K. (2005), 'Tense and Reality', in his *Modality and Tense: Philosophical Papers* (Oxford: Oxford University Press).

Fodor, J. and Pylyshyn, Z. (1981), 'How Direct is Visual Perception? Some Reflections on Gibson's "Ecological Approach"', *Cognition* 9: 139–96.

Frege, G. (1967), *Kleine Schriften*, ed. I. Angelelli (Hildesheim: Olms).

Frege, G. (1977), *Logical Investigations*, tr. P. Geach and R. Stoothof (Oxford: Blackwell).

Gallese, V. (2005), '"Being Like Me": Self-Other Identity, Mirror Neurons, and Empathy', in *Perspectives on Imitation, Vol. 1: From Neuroscience to Social Science*, ed. S. Hurley and N. Chater (Cambridge, MA: MIT Press).

Gallup, G. Jr (1970), 'Chimpanzees: Self-recognition', *Science* 167: 86–7.

Gallup, G. Jr (1979), *Self-recognition in Chimpanzees and Man: A Developmental and Comparative Perspective* (New York: Plenum Press).

Gibson, J. J. (1986), *The Ecological Approach to Visual Perception* (Hillsdale, NJ: Erlbaum).

Goffman, E. (1959), *The Presentation of Self in Everyday Life* (New York: Doubleday).

Goodale, M. and Milner, D. A. (2004), *Sight Unseen: An Exploration of Conscious and Unconscious Vision* (Oxford: Oxford University Press).

Gopnik, A. (1993), 'How We Know our Minds: The Illusion of First-person Knowledge of Intentionality', *Behavioral and Brain Sciences* 16: 1–14.

Grandin, T. (2006), *Thinking in Pictures: My Life with Autism* (New York: Random House).

Grice, H. P. (1969), 'Vacuous Names', in *Words and Objections: Essays on the Philosophy of W. V. Quine*, ed. D. Davidson and J. Hintikka (Dordrecht: Reidel).

Harman, G. (1999a), 'Meaning and Semantics', in his *Reasoning, Meaning, and Mind* (Oxford: Oxford University Press).

Harman, G. (1999b), '(Nonsolipsistic) Conceptual Role Semantics', in his *Reasoning, Meaning, and Mind* (Oxford: Oxford University Press).

Heck, R. (2002), 'Do Demonstratives Have Senses?', *Philosopher's Imprint* 2: 1–33.

Hurley, S. (1994), 'Unity and Objectivity' in *Objectivity, Simulation and the Unity of Consciousness: Current Issues in the Philosophy of Mind (Proceedings of the British Academy Volume 83)*, ed. C. Peacocke (Oxford: Oxford University Press).

Hurley, S. (1998), *Consciousness in Action* (Cambridge, MA: Harvard University Press)

Iacoboni, M. (2008), *Mirroring People: The New Science of How We Connect with Others* (New York: Farrar, Strauss and Giroux).

James, W. (1918), *The Principles of Psychology* (New York: Holt).

Jeshion, R. (2002), 'Acquaintanceless De Re Belief', in *Meaning and Truth: Investigations in Philosophical Semantics*, ed. Joseph Campbell, M. O'Rourke, and D. Shier (New York: Seven Bridges Press).

Kahneman, D., Treisman, A., and Gibbs, B.J. (1992), 'The Reviewing of Object Files: Object-specific Integration of Information', *Cognitive Psychology* 24: 175–219.

Kant, I. (1998), *Critique of Pure Reason*, tr. and ed. P. Guyer and A. Wood (Cambridge: Cambridge University Press).

Kant, I. (2002), *Theoretical Philosophy after 1781*, ed. H. Allison and P. Heath (Cambridge: Cambridge University Press).

Kierkegaard, S. (1980), *The Sickness unto Death*, tr. E. Hong and H. Hong (Princeton: Princeton University Press).

Kripke, S. (1980), *Naming and Necessity* (Oxford: Blackwell).

Kripke, S. (2011a), 'The First Person', in his *Philosophical Troubles*, Volume 1 (New York: Oxford University Press).

Kripke, S. (2011b), 'Frege's Theory of Sense and Reference: Some Exegetical Notes', in his *Philosophical Troubles Volume 1* (New York: Oxford University Press).

Lambert, K. and van Fraassen, B. (1972), *Derivation and Counterexample: An Introduction to Philosophical Logic* (Encino and Belmont, CA: Dickenson).

Lewis, D. (1979), 'Attitudes De Dicto and De Se', *Philosophical Review* 88: 513–43.

Lichtenberg, G. (1971), *Schriften und Briefe*, Vol. II, ed. W. Promies (Munich: Carl Hanser).

Lockwood, M. (1971), 'Identity and Reference', in *Identity and Individuation*, ed. M Munitz (New York: NYU Press).

Lockwood, M. (1989), *Mind, Brain and the Quantum: The Compound 'I'* (Oxford: Blackwell).

Longuenesse, B. (2008), 'Kant's "I think" versus Descartes' "I Am a Thing That Thinks"', in *Kant and the Early Moderns*, ed. D. Garber and B. Longuenesse (Princeton: Princeton University Press).

Mach, E. (1914), *The Analysis of Sensations*, tr. C. Williams and S. Waterlow (Chicago and London: Open Court).

Martin, M. (1995), 'Bodily Awareness: A Sense of Ownership', in *The Body and the Self*, ed. J. Bermúdez, A. Marcel and N. Eilan (Cambridge MA: MIT Press).

McDowell, J. (1984), 'De Re Senses', *The Philosophical Quarterly* 34: 283–94.

McDowell, J. (1994), *Mind and World* (Cambridge, MA: Harvard University Press).

McDowell, J. (1998), 'In Defense of Modesty', in his *Meaning, Knowledge and Reality* (Cambridge, MA: Harvard University Press).

Mead, G. H. (1934), *Mind, Self, and Society* (Chicago: Chicago University Press).

Meltzoff, A. (2007), 'The "Like Me" Framework for Recognizing and Becoming an Intentional Agent', *Acta Psychologica* 124: 26–43.

Milner, D. A. and Goodale, M. (2006), *The Visual Brain in Action* (Oxford: Oxford University Press, second edition).

Moore, G. E. (1993), 'The Refutation of Idealism', in *G. E. Moore: Selected Writings*, ed. T. Baldwin (London: Routledge).

Murray, L. and Trevarthen, C. (1985), 'Emotional Regulation of Interactions Between Two-month-olds and their Mothers', in *Social Perception in Infants*, ed. T. Field and N. Fox (Norwood, NJ: Ablex).

Nagel, T. (1971), 'Brain Bisection and the Unity of Consciousness', *Synthese* 22: 396–14.

Nagel, T. (1974), 'What Is It Like to be a Bat?', *Philosophical Review* 83: 435–50.

Neisser, U. (1988), 'Five Kinds of Self-Knowledge', *Philosophical Psychology* 1: 35–59.

Nietzsche, F. (2000), *Basic Writings of Nietzsche*, tr. W. Kaufmann (New York: Random House).

O'Brien, L. (2012), 'The Ordinary Concept of Self-Consciousness', in *Consciousness and the Self: New Essays*, ed. J. Liu and J. Perry (Cambridge: Cambridge University Press).

Onishi, K. and Baillargeon, R. (2005), 'Do 15-month-old Infants Understand False Beliefs?', *Science* 308, 8 April: 255–8.

Parfit, D. (1987), *Reasons and Persons* (Oxford: Oxford University Press).

Parsons, T. (1974), 'A Prolegomenon to Meinongian Semantics', *Journal of Philosophy* 71: 561–80.

Peacocke, C. (1978), 'Necessity and Truth Theories', *Journal of Philosophical Logic* 7: 473–500.

Peacocke, C. (1981), 'Demonstrative Thought and Psychological Explanation', *Synthese* 49: 187–217.

Peacocke, C. (1983), *Sense and Content: Experience, Thought and their Relations* (Oxford: Oxford University Press).

Peacocke, C. (1985), 'Imagination, Experience, and Possibility' in *Essays on Berkeley*, ed. J. Foster and H. Robinson (Oxford: Oxford University Press).

Peacocke, C. (1988), 'The Limits of Intelligibility: A Post-Verificationist Proposal', *Philosophical Review* 97: 463–96.

Peacocke, C. (1992), *A Study of Concepts* (Cambridge, MA: MIT Press).

Peacocke, C. (1993), 'How Are A Priori Truths Possible?', *European Journal of Philosophy* 1: 175–99.

Peacocke, C. (1999), *Being Known* (Oxford: Oxford University Press).

Peacocke, C. (2000), 'Explaining the A Priori: The Programme of Moderate Rationalism', in *New Essays on the A Priori*, ed. P. Boghossian and C. Peacocke (Oxford: Oxford University Press).

Peacocke, C. (2001), 'Does Perception Have a Nonconceptual Content?', *The Journal of Philosophy* 98: 239–64.

Peacocke, C. (2002), 'Principles for Possibilia', *Noûs* 36: 486–508.

Peacocke, C. (2004), *The Realm of Reason* (Oxford: Oxford University Press).

Peacocke, C. (2005), 'Joint Attention: Its Nature, Reflexivity, and Relation to Common Knowledge', in *Joint Attention: Communication and Other Minds*, ed. N. Eilan, C. Hoerl, T. McCormack, and J. Roessler (Oxford: Oxford University Press).

Peacocke, C. (2008), *Truly Understood* (Oxford: Oxford University Press).

Peacocke, C. (2010a), 'Relation-Based Thought, Objectivity and Disagreement', in a Special Issue on Concepts, ed. E. Lalumera, *Dialectica* 64: 35–56.

Peacocke, C. (2010b), 'Self-Consciousness', *Revue de métaphysique et de morale* October–December (issue 4): 521–51 (entitled *Le Moi/The Self/Le Soi*, ed. B. Longuenesse).

Peacocke, C. (2012a), 'Explaining *De Se* Phenomena', in *Immunity to Error through Misidentification: New Essays*, ed. S. Prosser and F. Recanati (Cambridge: Cambridge University Press).

Peacocke, C. (2012b), 'Descartes Defended', *Proceedings of the Aristotelian Society, Joint Session* 86: 109–25.

Peacocke, C. (2012c), 'First Person Illusions: Are They Descartes', or Kant's?', *Philosophical Perspectives: Philosophy of Mind* 26: 247–75.

Peacocke, C. (2015), 'Perception and the First Person', in the *Oxford Handbook of the Philosophy of Perception*, ed. M. Matthen (Oxford: Oxford University Press).

Perry, J. (1979), 'The Problem of the Essential Indexical', *Noûs* 13: 3–21.

Perry, J. (2002a), 'The Self, Self-Knowledge, and Self-Notions', in his *Identity, Personal Identity and the Self* (Indianapolis: Hackett).

Perry, J. (2002b), 'The Sense of Identity', in his *Identity, Personal Identity, and the Self* (Indianapolis: Hackett, 2002).

Prior, A. (2003a), *Papers on Time and Tense: New Edition*, ed. P. Hasle, P. Øhrstrøm, T. Braüner, and J. Copeland (Oxford: Oxford University Press).

Prior, A. (2003b), 'Egocentric Logic', in his *Papers on Time and Tense: New Edition* ed. P. Hasle, P. Øhrstrøm, T. Braüner, and J. Copeland (Oxford: Oxford University Press).

Proops, I. (2010), 'Kant's First Paralogism', *Philosophical Review* 119: 449–95.

Pylyshyn, Z. (2007), *Things and Places: How the Mind Connects with the World* (Cambridge, MA: MIT Press).

Ramachandran, V. (2004), *A Brief Tour of Human Consciousness* (New York, NY: Pearson).

Recanati, F. (2012), *Mental Files* (Oxford: Oxford University Press).

Reid, T. (1785), *Essays on the Intellectual Powers of Man* (Edinburgh: Bell).

Reiss, D. (2011), *The Dolphin in the Mirror: Exploring Dolphin Minds and Saving Dolphin Lives* (New York: Houghton Mifflin Harcourt).

Reiss, D. and Marino, L. (2001), 'Mirror Self-recognition in the Bottlenose Dolphin: A Case of Cognitive Convergence', *Proceedings of the National Academy of Sciences* 98: 5937–42.

Rochat, P. (2009), *Others in Mind: Social Origins of Self-Consciousness* (New York: Cambridge University Press).

Rödl, S. (2007), *Self-Consciousness* (Cambridge, MA: Harvard University Press).

Russell, B. (1966), 'On the Nature of Acquaintance', in *Logic and Knowledge: Essays 1901–50* ed. R. C. Marsh (London: Allen and Unwin).

Salmon, N. (2005), 'Impossible Worlds', repr. in his collection *Metaphysics, Mathematics, and Meaning: Philosophical Papers*, Volume 1 (Oxford: Oxford University Press).

Sartre, J.-P. (1943), *L'être et le néant* (Paris: Gallimard).

Sartre, J.-P. (1956), *Being and Nothingness*, tr. H. Barnes (New York: Philosophical Library).

Sartre, J.-P. (2003), *La transcendance de l'ego et autres textes phénoménologiques*, ed. V. de Coorebyter (Paris: Vrin).

Sartre, J.-P. (2004), *The Transcendence of the Ego*, tr. A. Brown with an Introduction by S. Richmond (London and New York: Routledge).

Searle, J. (2001), *Rationality in Action* (Cambridge, MA: MIT Press).

Shepard, R. and Chipman, S. (1970), 'Second-Order Isomorphism of Internal Representations: Shapes of States', *Cognitive Psychology* 1: 1–17.

Shoemaker, S. (1968), 'Self-Reference and Self-Awareness', *Journal of Philosophy* 65: 555–67.

Shoemaker, S. (1984), 'Embodiment and Behavior', in his *Identity, Cause, and Mind: Philosophical Essays* (Cambridge: Cambridge University Press).

Shoemaker, S. (1996), *The First Person Perspective and Other Essays* (Cambridge: Cambridge University Press).

Sklar, L. (1976), *Space, Time and Spacetime* (Berkeley and Los Angeles: University of California Press).

Snowdon, P. (1996), 'Persons and Personal Identity', in *Essays for David Wiggins: Identity, Truth and Value*, ed. S. Lovibond and S. Williams (Oxford: Blackwell).

Snowdon, P. (2010), 'On the What-It-Is-Like-Ness of Experience', *The Southern Journal of Philosophy* 48: 8–27.

Song, H., Onishi, K., Baillargeon, R., and Fisher, C. (2008), 'Can an Agent's False Belief be Corrected by an Appropriate Communication? Psychological Reasoning in 18-month-old Infants', *Cognition* 109: 295–315.

Stalnaker, R. (2003), 'Possible Worlds', revised and repr. in his collection *Ways a World Might Be* (Oxford: Oxford University Press).

Stalnaker, R. (2008), *Our Knowledge of the Internal World* (Oxford: Oxford University Press).

Strawson, P. (1959), *Individuals* (London: Methuen).

Strawson, P. (1966), *The Bounds of Sense: An Essay on Kant's 'Critique of Pure Reason'* (London: Methuen).

Strawson, P. (1974), *Subject and Predicate in Logic and Grammar* (London: Methuen).

Swarns, R. (2009), 'First Chores? You Bet', in *The New York Times*, February 21, 2009.

van Inwagen, P. (1990), *Material Beings* (Ithaca, NY: Cornell University Press).

Vlach, F. (1973), *'Now' and 'Then': A Formal Study in the Logic of Tense Anaphora* (UCLA Dissertation).

William, B. (1978), *Descartes: The Project of Pure Enquiry* (Harmondsworth: Penguin).

Williams, B. (1973), 'Imagination and the Self', in his *Problems of the Self* (Cambridge: Cambridge University Press).

Wilson, M. (1978), *Descartes* (London: Routledge and Kegan Paul).

Wittgenstein, L. (1958), *The Blue and Brown Books* (New York: Harper).

Wittgenstein, L. (1961), *Notebooks 1914–1916*, tr. G. E. M. Anscombe (New York: Harper and Row).

Wittgenstein, L. (2001), *Tractatus Logico-Philosophicus*, tr. D. Pears and B. McGuinness (London: Routledge).

Woodward, A., Sommerville, J., Gerson, S., Henderson, A., and Buresh, J. (2009), 'The Emergence of Intention Attribution in Infancy', *Psychology of Learning and Motivation* 51: 187–222.

Index

Abbott, J. 243
absolute conception (B. Williams) 233
absolute location 59
acquaintance 84–5, 99–105
  constitutive mode of 102–5
action awareness 6–7
Adams, R. 135
agents 60
Ameriks, K. 155n
Andler, D. ix
animalism 76–7
Anscombe, E. 11, 104, 118–19, 150–2,
  206n
ascription-first views of a subject's
  having an experience 181–3,
  218–19
attention, original and derivative 45–9
  to something given in a certain
    way 46–7
  no such thing as original attention to
    something given in purely first
    personal way 47–57
  impossibility of attention to
    consciousness as object of
    attention 54–7
  intellectual 56
  possible objects of attention 52–7
Armstrong, D. 219
Augustine 3, 80
autism 253, 257–8
Autonomy Thesis 33

Baillargeon, R. 230n
Baron-Cohen, S. 231
Barwise, J. 250–2
Bayne, T. 8, 62, 64, 73–5, 77n, 93
Berker. S. ix
Bermúdez, J. 2, 211n, 212n
Block, N. xi, 40
body 31, 38–9, 42, 47, 66, 69, 72, 95,
  103, 176–87, 184–5, 199–201,
  222–3, 267
  my body/I equivalences 199–201
Boghossian, P. ix

Botvinick, M. 51
bouncing ways of representing
  actions 209–11, 212
Boyle, M. xi
brain 39, 130, 185
  bisection 77, 185
Brandom, R. 23
Bridges, J. ix
Brooks, R. 226–7
Brown, A. 220n
Buber, M. 264
Burge, T. ix, 9n, 141n, 148
Butterfield, J. x

Campbell, J. ix, x, 155, 218
Carey, S. 229
Carlyle, T. 246
Carpenter, E. 194
Carroll, L. 198
(CC) principle about co-
  consciousness 61–4, 150
centered worlds 123–6
  and content of experience 124–5
  as present in virtue of some further
    condition holding 125–6
  characterizing entitlements 126
certainty 147–8
Chalmers, D. xi, 60n, 62, 64
Chen, C. xi
chimpanzees 192
Chipman, S. 19
Cogito (Descartes) Chapter VI,
  Chapter VII
  canonical form of 128–9
  and truth-preservation 129–46
  entitlement 146–53, 164, 167
  'second Cogito' 149–50
  Cohen, J. 51
Colapinto, J. 210n
Coliva, A. ix
common knowledge 251
concept anchored in the subject 194–203
  and perspectival self-
    consciousness 195–203, 232

concept anchored in the subject (*cont.*)
the absolute conception 233
concepts, *see* conceptual content
conceptual content 6–7, 15, 37–9, 81–6
as individuated by fundamental
reference rule 81–6
conceptual role treatments of 89–90,
146, 195
knowledge 200
see also explanations of cognitive and
psychological phenomena
conscious events 40–3, 57–64
basic form of attribution 53
correctness conditions 7

Davidson, D. 42
de jure reference by the first
person 9–11, 48, 192
de se content 10–14, 20, 25–9, 49, 51, 52,
54, 74–5, 80, 86–9, 91, 121–3,
155–6, 196–7, 213–14, 244
de Vignemont, F. 121n
degree of self-representation 30–9,
188–9
degree 0 30–5, 66, 74–5, 125, 152,
242, 259, 267
degree 1 32–7, 89, 125
degree 2 37–9, 125
Dennett, D. 69–73, 95, 119, 185
Dolphins 190
Doppelgängers 208–9
Dummett, M. 155, 268
Descartes, R. 2, 3, 4, 38, 42, 58, 59, 65,
78, 79, 101–2, 105, Chapter VI
Dretske, F. xi

Ego (Sartre) 220–1
'Egocentric' (Prior) 137–8
embodiment, *see* body
epistemic-pragmatic relations
(Perry) 92–3
epistemology 1
Evans, G. 9n, 11, 18, 23, 34n, 83, 91, 96,
107, 152n, 189
explanations of cognitive and
psychological phenomena 80,
110, 146
as related to nature of concepts
involved 80, 106
illustrated by the a priori 110

metasemantic explanations 110,
115–16
explanatory priority 2, 267–8
expressive power of mental states 32

facial expression 212
false belief task 230
Farkas, K. ix
Fichte, J. 35n, 205
Fine, K. 41n, 137–8
Finkelstein, D. ix
FINSTS (Pylyshyn) 17–20
first person 1, 6 passim
distinct from descriptive-
demonstrative notions 8
first person concept 6, 8, 11, 23, 37–9
first person and attention 47–57
need for account of reference 71–2, 75
individuation of conceptual by
relations to nonconceptual Ch
IV; as individuated by thinker-
rule 83–6
as genuinely indexical 90–2, 103
rational links involving 94–6, 111–13
relation to sensation and
perception 97–9
whether involves
acquaintance 99–105
distinct from any perceptual
demonstrative 102, 160–2
and constitutive acquaintance 102–5
alleged dispensability of the
concept 113–26
and imagination 122–3
and centered worlds 123–6
minimal use 189, 213, 236
and spatial predications 198–200
identifying reference as same at
different times 151–2
using versus referring to 207, 215–16
relation between ascriptions and third
person 230–2
first person type [self] 83, 235
as playing a double role in
interpersonal self-
consciousness 238–9
relation to the second person 245
same in ascriptive self-consciousness
and in non-social
perception 259

priority of metaphysics in many
    phenomena involving 267–8
'first-personal realism' (Fine) 137–8
first person understanding thesis
    ('FPUT') 223–32
    relation to distinctive first person
        knowledge 225
Fisher, C. 230n
Fodor, J. 256
free logic 131
Frege, G. 3, 41, 51, 56n, 81, 99–100, 103
fundamental reference rules 81–6, 195

Gallese, V. 255–6
Gallois, A. ix
Gallup, G. 190
Geach, P. 41n, 56n
German idealism 3
Gibbs, B. 15
Gibson, J. 36, 256, 258
Goffman, E. 237
Goodale, M. 90n, 228n
Goodman, R. ix
Gopnik, A. 229–32
Grandin, T. 253–4
Grice, P. 14
guaranteed reference 150–2
Gupta, A. ix

Harman, G. 89
Hawthorne, John ix, x
Hawthorne, Julian 246
Heal, J. x
Heck, R. 247, 247n
Hegel, G. 190
here 33–4, 90
Heine, H. 208
hierarchy of senses and concepts
    (Frege) 215–16, 239
Hume, D. 2, 3, 41, 44–57, 205, 221
Hurley, S. 2, 61

I (conceptual first person), see first
    person
i (nonconceptual first person) 10–14,
    22, 25, 36, 48, Chapter IV
Iacoboni, M. 209n
identity, awareness of over time 16–17,
    157, 173–5
    inferences involving
        Chapter V, 191–3,

illusions of identity 69
imagination 122–3
immunity to error through
    misidentification 106–13
    deficiency in modal characterization
        of 109
    Strawson's explanation 176–7
    and mirror test 192
inadequate-grounds interpretation (of
    First Paralogism) 163–4
    and perspectival self-
        consciousness 200–2
    and reflective self-consciousness 218
    role of metaphysics in explanation
        of 267
indexicality, genuine 90–4
inserted thought 129
integrating apparatus 15, 20–2, 44,
    65–8, 91, 156
integrating contents of states 14–15, 44
intention 23
interdependence of conscious events and
    conscious subjects 40–4, 70,
    130–1;
    extreme and moderate views
        thereof 43–4
    consequences thereof 57–68, 130–1
interpersonal self-consciousness 188,
    Chapter X
    theoretical issues involving 236–7
    and sociology 237
    and everyday notion of self-
        consciousness 237
    examples 237–8
    ascriptive 238–9
    joint attention as means of
        attaining 250–2
    second order simulation as means of
        attaining 252–6
    and autism 253–5
    and Neisser on the 'interpersonal
        self' 256–60
    relation to perspectival self-
        consciousness 261–2
    relation to reflective self-
        consciousness 262–3
    and emotional life 243, 264
    formal characterization of in neo-
        Fregean apparatus 264–5
intuition (Kant) 157, 159–62, 164,
    167–8

Jacobi, T. xi
James, W. 243
Jeshion, R. 15
Johnston, M. xi
joint action 243–4
joint attention 244, 250–2
  with infant 211–12
  and interpersonal self-
    consciousness 250–2
  independent of second order
    simulation 254

Kahneman, D. 15
Kant, I. ix, x, 3, 4, 21–2, 35, 38, 60,
  67–8, 74, 132, Chapter VII, 190,
  205, 219
keeping track of an object 16–9
Kierkegaard, S. 190, 208–9
Kitcher, Patricia ix
knowledge-providing relationships 86,
  91, 96, 114–15
Kripke, S. x, 9, 65, 84–5, 99–105

Lambert, K. 131
Lear, J. vii, ix, x, 25n
Levine, J. ix
Lewis, D. 100, 136, 251n
Lichtenberg, G. 130, 132–9, 168
  'Lichtenberg's revenge' 133–9
'Like me' hypothesis (Meltzoff) 229
linguistic communication 244
  success in and interpersonal self-
    consciousness 245
local holism of *here, now, I* 33–4
Locke, J. 1, 77–9
Lockwood, M. 15, 61
logic 29
'logical subject' (Kant) 157–9, 172–3
Longuenesse, B. ix, x, 155n, 168–72

Mach, E. 9
Madden, R. 77n
Marino, L. 190
Martin, M. xi, 121n, 262n
Masrour, F. xi
Matrix, The 71, 102, 119–20
McDowell, J. 9n, 82n, 174–5, 175n, 248
McGuinness, B. 50n
Mead, G. 237
Meinong, A. 71
memory 6–7

mental files complementary and radical
  views of 24
  explanatory task of 25–9
metaphysics 1, 2, 41
  its principles to be distinguished
    from what is in the perspective
    of consciousness 140–1
  explanatory priority of 267–8
metasemantic explanations of immunity
  to error 110–3
Meltzoff, A. 226–9
Milner, D. 90n, 228n
mirror-motivated criterion 192–4, 197
mirror-neuron phenomena 209–11, 255
mirror test 190–4
missing properties interpretation (of
  First Paralogism) 164,
  166–8
misunderstood-concept interpretation
  (of First Paralogism) 163–6
Modality 133–8
Momtchiloff, P. xii
Moore, G. 52–3
multiple personality disorder 73
mutual concern 246
mutual knowledge 251
mutual perception 239–42
  embeddings of mental states in 240–2
  explanatory significance of
    embeddings in 242

Nagel, T. 1, 40, 77n, 102
Neisser, U. 256–60
  on intersubjectivity 256–8
  apparently ontological theses on
    selves 258–60
  on the 'interpersonal self' 256–60
Newton, I. 59, 68
Nida-Rümelin, M. xi
Nietzsche, F. 60
no-ownership views 2, 43, 57–61, 64,
  144–6
nonconceptual content
  and first person, 2, 6–7, 9–11, 21–2,
    30–5, 48–9, 78, 81–2, Chapter IV
  and linguistic expression of states with
    nonconceptual content 88
  and description of states with
    nonconceptual content 88–9
notions (nonconceptual ways of being
  given) 12, 196

now, *see* present tense mode of
      presentation

Obama, B. 190
O'Brien, L. 208n
object file 15–17, 26
observational concepts 144
Onishi, K. 230n
ordinary notion of self-
      consciousness 246
Orwell, G. 246
other minds, conception of 203–12
ownership, phenomenology of 8, 51,
      72, 121
ownership of experiences by a subject,
      metaphysics of 178–87, 218, 267
ownership-first views of a subject's
      having an experience 181–3

Parfit, D. 57–61, 68n, 144–6, 222
Parsons, C. xi
Parsons, T. 71
Peacocke, C. 9n, 19, 24, 31, 49n, 68,
      81–2, 89, 95, 110, 122, 134, 135,
      138, 139, 141, 141n, 142, 143,
      147n, 155, 175, 198n, 200, 206n,
      207n, 219, 224, 226, 228, 234,
      235n, 248, 251n
Pears, D. 50n
Perception 6–7, 16–7, 23
   thesis that the subject cannot be
      perceived 44–57
perceptual demonstratives 9, 83, 84,
      102, 211–12
Perry, J. x, 46, 84, 92–5, 114–26, 247–8
perspectival self-consciousness
      Chapter VIII
   social generalizations of 203
   as meeting certain needs of the
      thinker 232
   in cooperation with reflective self-
      consciousness 232–4
   and the absolute conception
      (B. Williams) 233
   and third person ascriptions of
      conscious events 234
   relation to interpersonal self-
      consciousness 261–2
philosophy of mind 1
Pippin, R. vii, ix
possible worlds 133–8

present tense mode of presentation 13,
      49, 83, 85, 101, 163, 249
Prior, A. 13n, 137–8
Proops, I. 155n, 161–2
Proust, J. ix
Pylyshyn, Z. 16–17, 256

Ramachandran, V. 34, 210, 210n
rational judgements and the first
      person 94–6, 111–13, 200, 202,
      214, 217–18
'rational psychology' (Kant) 154,
      157–62, 172–3
Recanati, F. vii, ix, x, 15, 24, 93, 115
reflective self-consciousness 84,
      Chapter IX
   as *de se* awareness of being in a *de se*
      state 214
   as distinct from Sartre's concept with
      the same name 216
   perceptual models of 219–20
   as meeting certain needs of the
      thinker 232
   in cooperation with perspectival self-
      consciousness 232–4
   and the absolute conception
      (B. Williams) 233
   and third person ascriptions of
      conscious events 234
   and conception of many minds 234–5
   and joint action 244
   and second order simulation 262–3
relation-based thought 141–2, 234–5
reorientation account of perspectival
      self-consciousness 196–212
Reid, T. 153
Reiss, D. 190
remembering being *F* 13
Rey, G. ix, x
R-informative ways of knowing
      (Perry) 114
Rochat, P. xi, 257
Rödl, S. 85–6, 96–9, 189, 248–50, 264n
Rosen, G. xi
rubber hand illusion 51
Russell, B. 45, 99

Salmon, N. 135
Sartre, J.-P. 34–5, 42, 142, 190, 204–7,
      216, 220–3, 264
scenario content 19

Schiffer, S. 251n
Schopenhauer, A. vii, 51
Searle, J. 38
Sebanz, N. xi
second person 245–50
    and understanding of 'you' 245
    relation to the first person 245
    alleged irreducibility of 247–50
self-blindness (Shoemaker) 219–20
self-conceptions 70–1
self-consciousness
    varieties of, 188–90
    terminological issues 189
    see also interpersonal; perspectival
        self-consciousness; reflective self-
        consciousness
self-files 15–30, 37, 72, 156
    and relation to interdependence of
        subjects and conscious
        events, 67
    what makes something a self-file and
        labelling 117–20
self-representation, see de se; first person
selves 38
sensitivity to an identity 18–19
shared manifold (Gallese) 255–6
    as base of a hierarchy 255–6
Shepard, R. 19
Shoemaker, S. 3, 107–8, 192, 199, 200,
    219–20
simulation, second order 252–6
    as sometimes subpersonal 253
    and autism 253–5
    and mirror neuron phenomena 255
Snowdon, P. ix, xi, 40, 69, 76–7
Soldati, G. xi
Song, H. 230n
Stalnaker, R. 123–6, 135
sticky mittens (Woodward) 228–9, 230
Stoothof, R. 41n, 56n
Strawson, P. 2, 3, 15, 104, 149,
    175–87, 190
subject files, see self-files
subject of consciousness 2, 3, 20, 40–4,
    58–61
    conception of subject as not in the
        world 50–1
    diaphanous character in first person
        content 52–3
    fission of 61
    material realization of 42, 65–6, 152

identity dependent upon identity of
    integrating apparatus 65–8
as centres of narrative gravity 69–73
as merely intentional objects
    71–5, 260
as Bayne's virtual objects 74–5
Locke's conception of same
    consciousness as grounding
    identity of subject 79
conception of another 143–4
conception of as immaterial and
    indivisible 152–3
and spatio-temporal routes through
    the world 178–87
subjects and memory 187
blind 194, 197–8
conception of oneself as a
    subject 206–7
subject-constitutive hypothesis 10–11
subjectless characterizations of mental
    events 132–46
subject-reflexivity 12–14, 20, 22, 23,
    38–9, 88–9, 213–14, 217
subpersonal representation 23–4
substance (Kant) 159–62
Swarns, R. 190

thar (invented pseudo-indexical) 90–1
theory of intentional content 2
theory-theory (of psychological
    concepts) 227–9
thinker-rule 83–6, 95, 155
time-reflexivity 13
transitivity of co-consciousness 61–4
Treisman, A. 15
trick blindfolds 227, 230

unity of consciousness 61–4, 74–5, 77,
    157, 167, 173
updating files 16–19

van Fraassen, B. 131
van Inwagen, P. 77n
verificationism 68, 175
Vlach, F. 134

Walker, R. ix
way of coming to know 191, 203, 204
Wedgwood, R. x
what it is like 40–2, 62–4, 77
Wiggins, D. ix

Wikforss, A. ix
Williams, B. 122, 132–46
Williamson, T. ix
Wilson, M. 166

Wittgenstein, L. 3, 48, 50–1, 108,
    205, 224
Woodward, A. 228
Wong, H.-Y. xi

Printed in Great Britain
by Amazon

53842550R00165